In Your Face

LIA MILLS

PENGUIN
IRELAND

PENGUIN IRELAND

Published by the Penguin Group
Penguin Ireland, 25 St Stephen's Green, Dublin 2, Ireland
(a division of Penguin Books Ltd)
Penguin Books Ltd, 80 Strand, London WC2R ORL, England
Penguin Group (USA) Inc., 375 Hudson Street, New York, New York 10014, USA
Penguin Group (Australia), 250 Camberwell Road, Camberwell, Victoria 3124, Australia
(a division of Pearson Australia Group Pty Ltd)
Penguin Group (Canada), 90 Eglinton Avenue East, Suite 700, Toronto, Ontario, Canada M4P 2Y3
(a division of Pearson Penguin Canada Inc.)
Penguin Books India Pvt Ltd, 11 Community Centre, Panchsheel Park, New Delhi – 110 017, India
Penguin Group (NZ), 67 Apollo Drive, Rosedale, North Shore 0632, New Zealand
(a division of Pearson New Zealand Ltd)
Penguin Books (South Africa) (Pty) Ltd, 24 Sturdee Avenue,
Rosebank, Johannesburg 2196, South Africa

Penguin Books Ltd, Registered Offices: 80 Strand, London WC2R ORL, England

www.penguin.com

First published by Penguin Ireland 2007
1

Copyright © Lia Mills, 2007

The moral right of the author has been asserted

Set in 12/14.75 pt PostScript Monotype Bembo
Typeset by Rowland Phototypesetting Ltd, Bury St Edmunds, Suffolk
Printed in Great Britain by Clays Ltd, St Ives plc

A CIP catalogue record for this book is available from the British Library

ISBN: 978-1-844-88156-7

www.greenpenguin.co.uk

Penguin Books is committed to a sustainable future
for our business, our readers and our planet.
The book in your hands is made from paper
certified by the Forest Stewardship Council.

Prologue

Not very long ago I'd have said, without thinking, that I'd give anything to lose a bit of weight. Here I am, now, three stone lighter.

Be careful what you wish for.

This story began when a wisdom tooth crowded the lower right-hand corner of my mouth so that I started to chew my cheek in my sleep. Going to the dentist is not high on my list of fun things to do, so I put up with this for a good long while before going to have the tooth removed, early in 2005. And that, I thought, was that.

Months later my cheek became sore again, with whitish patches which my dentist put down to the same habit of cheek-chewing. The next time I saw him, I asked what I could do about it and he recommended a gel commonly used for mouth ulcers. A further visit was no more helpful than that.

Meanwhile, the sore area spread and changed colour and the second dentist I consulted came to the conclusion that I had a condition known as erosive lichen planus. He began to treat it in various ways, replacing old fillings, prescribing antibiotics and steroid tablets which I had to lodge in my cheek until they dissolved. This was excruciatingly painful, and didn't do much good. The plan was that he would refer me to the Dental Hospital if these methods didn't work.

I went on the internet, as you do, and read that erosive lichen planus can be a pre-cancerous condition. If it persisted one should go to one's GP to get it checked. I asked the dentist about this and he said not at all, and he was glad that I'm not the kind of person who runs to my GP at the first suggestion from the net.

I quite like not being that kind of person too. However, when more time passed and the sore area in my cheek was getting worse instead of better, I did go to my GP. By then I had a swollen gland in my neck as well.

She and I agreed that a referral from the dentist was probably the quickest way to get an appointment with the Dental Hospital, so I collected my letter from the dentist and brought it in.

I carry a notebook and a pen with me wherever I go. I have a habit of recording what I see and hear because writing is how I make sense of life and of the world around me. As the drama of my diagnosis unfolded, I wrote everything down, obsessively. I made notes about things that happened to me and around me, about what I felt, what I saw, what I worried about. The pile of notebooks grew and grew until they seemed to be breeding independently beside my bed, although in reality my husband, Simon, and my daughters, Zita, Emma and Nessa, were charged with bringing me new ones on an almost daily basis.

The notebooks grew into a detailed, sequential account of my experience and how I felt about events as they happened. Some of my entries surprised me when I read back over them. There were many incidents, emotions and details that were so intense I thought I'd never forget them. But I would have forgotten, if I hadn't found them afterwards, written in my own hand, in my own words.

Chapter 1

22 March 2006

The receptionist at the Dental Hospital looks about twelve. She is completely indifferent to me and to the painful open sore in my mouth. She takes my dentist's referral letter and says that someone will contact me with an appointment. I ask her when. 'It could take seven months,' she says, looking not at me but at the person behind me in the queue.

'Seven months? Are you serious?' My cheek throbs in sympathy.

She shrugs. 'Could be. They'll read the letter and decide.' The person behind me is already moving forward. I get out of the way.

It's my sister Jackie's birthday. I want to get her the BBC's *Bleak House* on DVD, so I ignore the pain in my face and head for the shops. When I turn into Wicklow Street I'm confronted by a small army of charity muggers, clipboards and lethal smiles at the ready. The soundtrack for *High Noon*, if I could only remember it, might as well be blaring in my head. A few weeks ago, Nessa, my youngest daughter, had trouble with these people – she was bullied on the street, then harassed on her phone. For a second I actually consider taking a different route to my destination, but then my temper flares. This is my city, and I'm not about to be terrorized out of it by a bunch of young people in gaudy vests. I start to walk up the street. A cute blondey boy does a pratfall in front of me and smiles. I hold my hand up, *stop*, and tell him in a voice that surprises even me by its meanness, 'Don't.'

He tilts his head to one side. His whole body undulates, as if in sympathy. We both know that we'll be chatting for at least half an hour if he manages to engage me at all. 'Don't,' I say again, this time loud enough for his friends to hear. It seems to me that the whole street stops what it's doing to listen, but maybe it's just the American tourists in matching pink parkas who turn to stare. I point at the cherubic boy, air-stabbing. 'Don't even open your mouth to me. I mean it.'

The charity muggers part like the Red Sea to let me pass. Some mealy-mouthed part of me wants to stop and apologize to the boy, but another, wiser, part advises me to keep going and I do.

27 March 2006

I go to my GP and tell her what happened at the Dental Hospital. She shakes her head. 'This can't wait any longer.' She consults a colleague, makes a few phone calls and in the end I'm given an appointment with a maxillo-facial surgeon, Professor Leo Stassen, in St James's Hospital, ten days from now.

I've never heard of a maxillo-facial clinic, even though I used to work as a radiographer, back in the last century.

5 April 2006

Up early with a sense of a journey ahead of me, standing-room only on the DART, the sea a benign blue. Pale-faced school-children huddle on the floor. Three loud boys beside me talk about Maths. One of them, his voice still high-pitched, says that if he had one wish it would be to make exams easy.

'Really?' His friend's voice is deeper, more weighted. 'That's *really* what you'd wish for?' There's a hush in the carriage as we wait for his answer.

At St James's, in the maxillo-facial clinic, I'm shown into a room like a dentist's office. There's only a dental chair to sit on. I'm taken aback when I first see Professor Stassen because he looks exactly like my brother-in-law, David. He has the same broad smile, the same light in his eyes. A good sign.

I explain that this is all a mistake. The swelling in my cheek has gone down and I'm sorry for wasting his time. He says it's better to get these things checked out. He begins to poke around and says at first what other people have said. It looks like a trauma, I've probably been chewing my own cheek. He pokes around a bit more and says, 'Mmm, maybe not.' He decides to do a biopsy straight away. There's some banter to distract me from what happens and the instruments he uses: a horse-sized syringe, a piece of gauze crammed into my mouth to soak up blood, the anaesthetic; then the punch biopsy, which he does with a yoke that looks exactly like a single-hole punch. His hands know what they are doing. After the punch biopsy he uses a scalpel to cut a sliver of tissue from my cheek. He says he's sorry, he knows it hurts.

Another doctor comes in and Professor Stassen says, 'Come and have a feel.'

'Are you not going to introduce us first?' I ask.

They laugh, politely. More people come in and move around, gathering for a look. Professor Stassen puts stitches in my cheek and wads my mouth with extra gauze. Bits of it stick out. I can't speak. There's a taste in my mouth, chemical and bloody. He marks the biopsy request as 'urgent' and tells me to come back next week for the results. He says to bring an overnight bag with me, just in case. The biopsy might be inconclusive, in which case they'll bring me in to do another one under general anaesthetic.

He warns that I'll be in pain for a few days. I ask what I should do about the meeting that I'm supposed to chair tomorrow and he says it's up to me, it depends what kind of person I am. I know the kind of person I want to be: the kind who carries on regardless.

I emerge from the consulting room shocked and sore. The waiting room has filled up, but I can't look at anyone directly. I don't feel like myself any more. I still have a piece of bloody gauze hanging out of my mouth. I'll have to wait a while before I take it out.

I text Jackie, who meets me at the train and takes me for lunch, but I can't eat. We go to a pharmacy and each of us buys separate packets of painkillers. They're all for me but the law allows only one packet per person. It reminds me of buying slimming tablets back in the seventies, when I used to pad myself up with sweaters and coats and do the rounds of various chemists, to avoid suspicion.

A ghastly little old woman skips in front of me to an empty seat in the DART and laughs into my face – she's beaten me to it. There are plenty of other seats, and usually I'd tell myself not to react, that you never know what people have on their minds, but today I feel such rage I could throw her off the train. I nearly forget to get off myself, I'm staring so hard at the sunshine, the sea, schoolkids pulling off their jumpers in the heat, daffodils.

These days seem weighted. I am forty-eight now, the age my father was when he died. The year I turned thirty-three, the age at which my sister Lyn died of breast cancer, I found a lump in my own breast that mysteriously vanished when I turned thirty-four.

6 April 2006

The pain in my cheek throbs and swells, like a musical note; it flowers, a dark bloom with thorns. It's a filter, a veil of colour. When the wave rises and falls, the fall has a sorrowful note to it, where some part of the chorus feels sympathy for the organism, for its frailty.

I keep thinking about the man with the heavy overcoat and the black hat who used to walk along our street with his stiffening, slowing dog. They used to be there at the same time every morning as I drove the girls to school. A few months ago I started to notice that they came later and later in the day, the two of them moving more slowly. Step, pause. Step, pause. Who was keeping whom on track? My breath used to catch, every time, because I wondered if this might be the last time I'd see them. We used to say hello. He'd raise his hat and smile, a very old smile. We talked about the weather. I haven't seen them now for weeks even though the days are lightening.

I went ahead and chaired the readings tonight, in another one of those daft, lovable, secret Dublin buildings – it would have been easy to back out, but I'm glad I didn't. I forgot all about my face while I was listening to other people read from their work and talk. I love it when people I know rise to the challenge of performance at these things. I love the way it feels when it happens for me, too.

7 April 2006

There is a moment on waking when the pain seems to be abating, it might even be gone. The hammerbeat of my heart until I get control of it. I sit up in bed and look out the window, across Dublin Bay. This morning, Howth is a mauve mountain. There's ice on the windows.

My jaw snags on the wire of my stitches, or the sore, or whatever it is it snags on – when's the last time I had an uninhibited, full-stretched yawn? I used to love them.

The flowers from my publisher are still extraordinarily beautiful. Lush and trembly, orange and green, there are bendy shoots from some slaughtered shrub that I can't name. They spiral and twist and now they are sprouting tiny velvety lime-green leaves.

I venture out to a local bookshop to sign some books and buy some new ones to bring with me: Paul Auster, Marilynne Robinson and a new collection of stories by Irish women. Then to Penney's, where I get a bit overwhelmed by the summer profusions, by the ludicrousness of my situation: shopping for things I'll need if I have to go into hospital when everyone else has arms full of bikinis and towels, flipflops dangling from their fingers. Meanwhile the weight in my cheek grows, the heat of the lump and its throb make me feel conspicuous. For some reason, it makes me think of a kidney, hot and toxic. It pulls me down, a tug at the root. It goes up the cheekbone and deep into the jaw now as well, radiates, an acrid little blade, a tongue of flame. Blisters of fizz on the tongue. That little pouch of saliva, silky and heavy.

Still, I head off for Tesco and do the shopping – the place is bedlam. I watch everyone. Whatever fears, worries or wild ambition we harbour, we go through the same motions, the numb dance of fill and empty, of cards and cash, the rituals of greeting and farewell.

I found the first wasp of the year yesterday. Fat and sluggish, more like an autumnal wasp than a spring one. Rain by the bucketful, literally. One of these days we'll have to sort out the broken slate on the roof.

8 April 2006

A rotten night. I've been on the internet again and now I'm sleepless with pain and sudden anxieties, projecting all the possibilities.

These days I sneak long looks at my daughters and at Ryan (my five-year-old grandson) when they aren't paying attention; ring Simon for no reason. He's working over in London. I have an appalled recognition of the work I still want to do, the sheer extent of it, and how far I am from getting there – I'm not even in the room yet. Still gathering notes. Yesterday, on the radio, Seamus Heaney read a poem for John McGahern. Introducing it, he talked about the sadness of loss, but the sense of a work completed. No one could say that for me, not even close.

I was held awake by a swelling globe, dull red and glowing, stretching, thinning. This is new, to be kept awake so long by it, to be anchored near the surface of my restless mind all night. The texture of my cheek changing, thickening.

I don't know how to deal with talking to people, who to tell and why – I don't know what to say. I don't want to moan and bleat for no reason. It's easier to say nothing. So, when a friend, preoccupied with her own, very real, disasters, cancels an arranged meeting and says *I'll be in touch*, I think, well, maybe you won't – but she doesn't know what's on my mind, how could she; her attention is bent elsewhere. How many times have I been the unknowing person in that equation?

When I do tell people, it's interesting to see who's determined to avoid the pit that's opening at my feet, who doesn't notice it at all, and who takes it in. The thing is, we are all really alone. There are those who stretch out their hands to you (and mean it) and others who fold their hands into their own pockets, around what's theirs, and look away.

Now, when I talk about having time to write, I don't mean a week in Annaghmakerrig. A good twenty-five years might do it.

10 April 2006

One of my writing groups, the novelshop, meets this afternoon. There are five of us, friends, all working on novels. We meet regularly to read and critique work-in-progress. I fill them in on where things stand. We talk about our plans for a week-long summer workshop in Carraroe this August. The things I say feel hollow.

A pink moon rises, hangs above the steeple, and launches itself across a cold and starry sky. Raspberry light.

I've decided that I know what's going to happen when I go in for the results – because it's Easter week, they'll say, *Yeah, yeah, it's inconclusive . . . but go away and come back next week to be admitted for tests . . .* or some such thing. I'm afraid that they'll think I'm wasting their time with my minor problem, when there are people with real illnesses who need to be looked after.

11 April 2006

The swelling has subsided a bit, although the crater is still there and the pain is vicious. It woke me up loads of times – what if it all turns out to be psychosomatic? All this fuss about nothing. Re-evaluations of everything – for nothing. No, not nothing, it's good to mull these things over from time to time, to lift up the slimiest of rocks and see what's underneath.

It's all a cod. I'll be back here tomorrow evening, in front of the fire, books to hand. Embarrassed, but relieved. Then I'll have the rest of my life to face.

12 April 2006

The sky is pillowed this morning, like one of those old-fashioned, diamond-patterned mattresses. As I watch, it flushes pink and the clouds break into separate islands. I could sit here and do nothing but stare and listen to the falling notes of birds for ever. All I want is the taste of coffee and the slow stare of the sea, those odd notes burgeoning in the background.

The doctor who calls me in to the consulting room at St James's wasn't there when they did the biopsy. He looks into my mouth and asks me where I had it done. I tell him I've come for the results.

While we wait for the lab to fax my results to a nearby extension, he grills me about writing, an occupation which he seems to find not only pointless, but incomprehensible. There is a problem with the fax machine, but at last we hit it lucky with a different number and the nurse carries in a sheet of paper. The doctor studies this for a while, then starts to make notes in my file. 'Well?' I ask. 'What does it say?'

He says that the consultant will give me the results.

The nurse says that the consultant has left the clinic.

For the first time, this doctor looks uncertain. He gets on the phone, trying to track down a person who will tell me the contents of a document which he holds in his hand, inches away from me.

'Can I see?' I ask.

'What?'

'Let me see.'

He hands over the sheet of paper. My eyes skim through layers of unfamiliar language and symbols to the key phrase near the bottom of the page: 'invasive non-differentiated squamous cell carcinoma'. I read it again to be sure that it says what I think it says. The key word is 'carcinoma': that means cancer. I ask the nurse to call my sister in from the waiting room. I give her the piece of paper, point to the stark, ungrammared phrase. She holds my hand while we wait for whatever comes next. I think we're both remembering Lyn, who died. The doctor, meanwhile, is still on the phone.

It seems I have to be admitted. I ask why – I don't feel sick. He says I need to have more tests. I ask if I could come in from home to have them. He says I'm free to leave if I want to, but I need to get into the system as quickly as possible. Eventually he brings us around to the Admissions Office, where I am to wait for a bed.

When I ring Simon in London with the news, he goes straight into shock. We agree to be completely open about everything. What I'm told, what he hears, what we feel. Right now, I don't feel anything. He hurries off to check out oral cancer on the net. Don't censor whatever you find, I say.

I tell him that I'm fine, and it's true. I don't feel sick at all. He's due to come home tomorrow night, I'll see him then.

I ring my daughters one by one to say that I won't be home for a while, that I have to have more tests. We knew this could happen, I remind them, even though none of us thought it would. I don't say any more because I don't want them to hear such news alone, or on the phone.

About half an hour later Simon rings back to tell me that I have a 50 per cent chance of surviving. I choke down a mouthful of bad soup in the hospital café and curse the net, the distance between us. I've been to the same sites, the figures aren't new to me. But I've had time to read around them, to sift the information. I've decided that those figures don't really relate to me, to my situation.

The figures suggest that the majority of people who get oral cancer are older men, usually heavy smokers and/or drinkers. I'm younger, for a start. I gave up smoking eight years ago. I decide that these things give me a fighting chance.

Surprised by how much I managed to absorb while I was pretending that none of it had anything to do with me, I explain all this to Simon while my soup goes cold. I didn't want it anyway. I'm still waiting for a bed. I think this won't feel real until I get one.

(*Later*) There are five of us in this ward. I'm the youngest by decades. At least two of my neighbours are confused – one believes she has a train to catch and repeatedly tries to climb over the bedrail. She comes close to making it, several times. I have to intervene. She calls out names of people who fail to materialize. 'Keep in touch!' she calls after a nurse who walks out of the ward. In the afternoon, a stooped, bespectacled man comes in, peers at each of us in turn, then leaves. A nurse brings him back in again and points to the train woman, who is, uncharacteristically, asleep. 'That's not her,' the man says. 'Yes it is,' says the nurse. The woman opens her eyes. 'Oh, Jesus,' the man says. 'It is.' He pulls himself together and goes to sit with her.

Later, she begins a new mantra: 'Help me.'

An intern with crinkled blonde hair comes to admit me. She is friendly while she asks her questions, but she has an air of confidence as well. She knows what she's talking about. She's not much older than my daughters. I ask what a 'squamous cell carcinoma' is. She tells me that squamous cells are thin and flat, like fish scales. They 'shed'. She explains that I will have a barrage of tests over the next week to find out the extent of the cancer, what stage it has reached and whether it has spread. Blood tests, X-rays, scans.

I ask about treatment. She says they'll decide on an approach when they've ascertained what stage my cancer is at – the size of the tumour, how many lymph nodes it has infiltrated, if any, and whether it has spread to other parts of the body.

I will see Professor Stassen tomorrow, or the next day. In the meantime there'll be other doctors from the max-fax team who'll come to talk to me. I'm going to meet a lot of new people, she warns. There are several different specialties involved in treating oral cancers. A 'team' of doctors, nurses, dieticians and others will be assigned to my case from each specialty. The different teams usually travel in groups – any number of them can show up at your bed at any given time, depending on who's on duty.

Nessa comes in while the intern is still there. While she goes off to look for a chair I tell the intern that I don't want to tell any of my daughters the definite diagnosis until all three of them are together in one place, where I can see them. The intern says she understands, no one will discuss it, except with me. Then she goes away.

When Nessa comes back I tell her not to worry, that I feel fine, which is true. I say that they need to do more tests to find out what we're dealing with. Which is also true. Sort of. Nessa seems to accept it, anyway. When I ask, she tells me about her day in college, we talk about her flatmates's summer plans. She keeps texting someone, responding to texts, while we play cards.

Then Simon appears. It turns out that he was the one texting her all along. When his flight landed. When he got into the taxi. When he reached the hospital, and how should he get to the ward? It didn't occur to me that he would fly over straight away – he was due to come home tomorrow anyway.

During visiting hours a fat man with big eyebrows and a stained suit comes around selling Padre Pio medals. When I decline the medals he turns to my visitors instead. I wonder if this is his pitch, if he works the hospital on a regular basis or is he just an opportunist, here to visit a relative, putting his time to good use?

There's a drugged-looking fly, very fat, circling my bed. An entire swarm in a single body. I don't like the fact of this fly. I dislike the things it calls to mind.

One of the lifts has an out-of-order sign when I walk Simon and Nessa out to say goodbye. Someone is stuck in the other one. A porter calls in to them that help is on its way.

I can't sleep. I talk to the ward assistant in the small hours of the morning when things are quiet. He tells me that he lives in Phibsborough.

'Then why don't you work in the Mater?' I ask.

'Oh, well,' he says. 'I grew up in Chapelizod.'

That just about sums Dublin hospitals up, for me. How they used to be before the old hospitals like the Meath and the Richmond and the Adelaide were closed; how this one still feels. So local as to be almost tribal.

There's a regular sound like a peacock calling – a high-pitched, falling *caaaw!* I wonder where it comes from. There's no one to ask. Sad ghost? Malfunctioning equipment?

If I close my eyes I can imagine myself in my attic bedroom at home, place the windows on either side of the room, the sea, the moon, the trees.

13 April 2006

Beckett's birthday. He suffered from a painful cyst in his mouth that required surgery when he was older than I am now. This cheers me a little, because he lived so far and so productively beyond it. That great photo is pinned to my noticeboard at home. He's staring at my empty chair. I have tickets to some of the plays in the centenary festival. I've already spoken to the intern about getting out to see them.

There are men peering into the lift shaft as I go down to X-ray. I take the stairs.

In the X-ray department I'm given a plastic folder to carry to Nuclear Medicine. The label on it reads:

LIA MILLS. SQUAMOUS CELL CARCINOMA RIGHT
CHEEK, FOR PRE-OP STAGING.

I'm shocked when I read it. It's too blunt. The plastic folder contains the dense, revealing negatives of X-rays; inner worlds, arcane shapes and smoky shadows. You could mount these on an exhibition wall, give dimensions, name the medium. But this is not art. I feel the weight of my diagnosis now.

The tide of shock recedes and I take my place in the waiting room. I wonder if this is how the knowledge of a diagnosis like mine works, that it comes over you, then retreats while you get your bearings, then returns. An incoming tide doesn't flood in all at once with the force of a burst dam. It sends warning, each successive wave advancing a little further than the last until the tidal lands are flooded. Then the retreat begins. My tide of understanding is on the way in, but it's not fully here yet. High tide comes later.

★

The thought of breaking this news to my daughters terrifies me. My stomach knots and plummets, like one of the hospital lifts, all the way to the basement. Then sinks further. It's one thing to think *I have cancer*, but I'm not sure I can say it out loud. Once I let this news out there'll be no going back.

The girls come in, all of them. Zita has brought Ryan. We sit in the coffee shop, Ryan on my knee. I'm glad of his familiar, solid weight. His brown eyes are steady as he takes in the hospital lobby, the people. Then Simon takes him outside. I have pins and needles everywhere as I watch them go.

I begin to circle around the subject. 'It's still very early . . .'

'Is it cancer?' Nessa interrupts.

'Yes.'

They look at each other, then at me. I can read so much in their faces. Anger, dread, confusion, love. Then we all start to talk at once. They rescue me with questions, the ones I can't answer and those I can. I tell them everything the young intern has told me. We go over what happened when and what might happen next. Reassurances. Plans. It's so easy in the end, a relief to have it confirmed. We're all laughing when Simon and Ryan come back. I feel lighter. All that static discharged.

The woman who wants to catch a train has set up a non-stop cry: 'Will nobody help me?' Now she points at me. 'Shame,' she says. I avoid her eye. 'Who'll you play with when I'm gone?' she taunts.

Another sleepless night and I hatch a plot, a thriller-type scenario originating in the scene where I got my diagnosis. Imagine if there was a personal element in that, a motive like revenge for some wrong of which the character who is the patient is unaware. It has good ingredients – his goal is revenge and hers is survival; the power belongs to him but her motive is stronger; they are in the crucible of a hospital world, surrounded by issues of life and death.

14 April 2006

The morning crawls along and then there's a sudden surge of activity – rounds, tests, samples.

A tall Italian doctor with long hair glides into the ward for rounds. His accent and manners are enticing. The ward freshens up, becomes more feminine while he's there. He flirts unashamedly with the older women that he's here to see. They blush and smile long after he's gone.

'He's lovely,' one says wistfully, looking at the door. 'And look at the state of me.'

Down to Nuclear Medicine for a scan. I'll be injected with contrast. They warn me about the sensation of heat I am likely to experience. How many times in my days as a radiographer did I utter these blithe phrases? 'You'll feel hot . . . it will pass over soon . . . there may be a strange sensation in your bladder.'

I am totally unprepared for the intense bolt of fire through my body, the urgency I feel. So *that's* what patients complained about, all those years ago. I wish I'd been more sympathetic.

A thin, brown-haired woman with a quick tongue is moved in from a different part of the ward. She talks low and fast, like a burglar wanting to get in, wreak havoc and get out again as quick as she can. She prays a lot. She's been here for a while, has views on the characters of various nurses. She asks for the commode, but when a male nurse brings it she says she's changed her mind and doesn't need it. When he has gone, she wrinkles her nose to us. The look she shoots after him is feral. 'Not that one,' she says. And rings her bell again.

A proud-looking African woman comes with the commode after a while. The brown-haired woman screws up her face again but allows the curtains to be drawn around her bed. Next thing we hear: 'I don't need paper.'

'But –'

'I'm dry,' the woman says. 'I'm a clean person. Go away.'

A student nurse laughs when I ask about the peacock-cry. 'That's a good one,' she says.

She tells me that the cry comes from a woman who is calling out for company. An attendant is beside her all the time. They talk to her but, oblivious, she goes on calling.

My first results come back: bone scan, dental X-ray, chest X-ray, lung, liver and kidney function; all normal. No sign of disease. I have to take one step at a time, absorb each fact alone. This is the latest news, and it's good.

They are going to send cameras on a fact-finding mission to my stomach, throat and lungs, check out my tongue on the way, determine the strength and status of the enemy. I'll have a general anaesthetic. The nurses bring a bright blue paper gown for me to change into and then I'm on my way to theatre.

15 April 2006

I'm in a different ward but there are the same problems. A woman across the corridor calls out *Hello?* constantly for people who don't materialize.

I go outside in my pyjamas, pass the smokers, pace along the tiny path in front of the hospital while I ring my friends to tell them where I am. It's cold and breezy but the air is fresh. This is not the kind of phone call that I would like to get. I wish that I could tell them face to face instead. But it's too late for all that.

Cancer. The crab. I know it's inaccurate to link the star sign with the disease, but it describes the way I imagine my tumour perfectly: hard-shelled and ugly, flesh-coloured, swelling and sucking at my cheek. Then those pincer-nips, the vice-like grip clamped to my mouth, dragging me down into that sink-hole of soft gloopy substance, half-water half-sand, created by low tide; the kind of substance where life begins.

There is something about this tumour's being externally visible. People look for the swelling on my cheek, then their eyes jump away. Has my voice already changed? Is this a one-way journey? Even if it is, there's nothing to be done but to keep going. We laugh and play cards, offer each other chocolate.

16 April 2006, Easter Sunday

I'm allowed home for the day. On the way out we take detours around the route of the parade commemorating the Easter Rising. I'm struck again by the crooked charm of the quays and how I love the many sweetnesses of this city. We pass children feeding swans on the canal; low tide at Scotsman's Bay, boats grounded in sludge at Bulloch. The sea throws up diamonds of light in Killiney Bay, which Shaw considered to be the most beautiful in the world.

I'm tired and achy after the anaesthetic. My throat and stomach hurt. The crab nestles in against my teeth, sucks on me. I wish I could rip it out. It looks close to the surface, but it's deeply entwined in blood-and-nerve supply central.

It's bliss to be home, with people dropping in, bringing the flowers I'm not allowed to keep in hospital: they've been banned, supposedly to reduce the spread of infection. My sisters are here. When they leave, I doze while Nessa plays the piano downstairs. Messages tumble into my phone. Kindness and offers of help.

Everyone is eager to tell me stories of survival. What I want to know is, if everyone in the stories survives, who dies?

Time pours away so fast, at home. Every time I look up, another hour has passed.

17 April 2006

The results of Friday's tests were all negative. This news is so good that I begin to wonder if the diagnosis might be wrong. If it is, how could I begin to undo all the sympathy and concern that has been lavished on us?

It feels as if I am on a train that has been shunted off on to a parallel track and now I'm in a siding. Everyday life thunders past on the main line. I can do nothing but wait for the signals to shift before I resume my journey. People ask if I'm angry, but I'm not. Not yet, anyway. Some trouble waits for all of us and this is mine right now. I keep thinking about Annie LaMott's phrase, that we are all in it up to our necks, but what matters is the kind of people we choose to be in the face of that.

Yeats believed that the key to a character is to discover which myth they embody. My myth keeps changing. Enter Ariadne with her simple gift . . . but that story ends badly for everyone. What if she'd kept her thread for herself, found her way out of her own myth, back to everyday life? Sounds good to me.

18 April 2006

Cancer of the mouth – other people have the same reaction as I did. They didn't know it was something you could get. I should have known. You can get cancer anywhere.

The crab is awake, sucking and squeezing. Sharp anchors scrape against my jaw all night. In the morning it is like a boiled sweet lodged in my cheek, as if I could suck on it. But the truth is, my mouth is eating me.

These notebooks have become a problem. I don't want to leave them lying around. What will I do with them? What about my other files, at home?

I'm fasting again. I have to go out to the Blackrock Clinic for a PET scan to determine if the cancer has spread and, if so, how far. Simon comes home early to drive me there.

The nurse who explains the procedure to me tells me that she has a degenerative disease. Months ago she was barely able to lift her arm. Now she looks fit and healthy.

'I'm living proof,' she says. 'Don't give up.'

These scans remind me of old spy films: searchlights and waste ground. Shadows moving into position. The radio-active glucose is carried in a heavy metal box, handled with gloves. The isotope slithers, cold, up my arm. After the injection they dim the lights. I have to lie still for an hour before entering the scanner: no jigging about, no talking. Reading, I'm told, can give false results because during the scan glucose is drawn to places where there is activity in the body and reading draws it to the eyes.

I'm so intrigued by this idea that it keeps me busy for the hour. I wonder what effect thinking might have. What my imagination looks like.

The doctor comes in. She offers me a cool boneless hand.

She asks about the lump in a way that no one else has done. Does it hurt? Can she touch it? I guide her hand. She asks to see it. I show her. She says, thanks, she doesn't often get the chance to look at a tumour directly. I don't suppose many people do.

They strap me to a thin table and feed me into a noisy plastic tunnel with a keen red eye of its own. It revs and clicks while the motor spins, but I am cocooned. Untouchable. People say the scanner is claustrophobic but it doesn't bother me. I close my eyes. Celia's poem, where a CT scan 'snaps poems I have written, poems / I have yet to write,'* keeps me and my involuted imagination company.

Later, back in the ward, I'm waiting for meds. My mouth is on fire, as if acid is flowing through it. Why am I up again and writing? Because I'm tired of whining and feeling sorry for myself under my sheet. The woman across the way is still calling out her sad song of names: *Joe! Joe! Marie! Hello?* I could tell her I know where her ghosts are – they're hiding out and playing in my mouth.

19 April 2006

A nun comes around with Communion. I say I don't want it. The other women in the room all take it. Next thing she starts a general prayer and they join in. My skin goes clammy, my pulse races. Sweat breaks out under my hair.

When she's gone I try to understand my reaction. A lot of people have said that they are praying for me, have sent mass cards. I'm delighted – the more prayers that come my way, the better, as far as I'm concerned. But those people care

---

* Celia de Fréine, 'In the Land of Wince and Whinny', in *Scarecrows at Newtownards*, Scotus Press, 2005.

about me, they have my interests at heart. There is something about these institutional, public invocations that makes my flesh creep. I feel coerced. It's like being back in school, your every move watched and controlled by women who think they know all about you, who will bully you into anything they can get away with. I know my reaction isn't rational, but there's not much reason to be found in anything that's happening at the minute.

I deal with this by writing. I have extended conversations with the page. I've always done this, even when it got me into trouble in the past, when my mother and the nuns thought that writing was transgressive. They used to read my letters and diaries, whatever loose bits of paper they could find. I often wonder why it never stopped me writing.

There is something lonely about what's happening, despite the fuss and the high level of activity and the streams of people that come to discuss this aspect of my care or that. My notebook is my companion. It's the piece of gold sewn into the lining of a coat in hard times, a talisman in the present, a belief in a future.

It's odd, and a little shocking to me, how matter of fact everyone is. That I have cancer is known by everyone, taken for granted, material, obvious. Indicative words like radiotherapy and chemo are thrown around lightly. But I still half expect them to tell me that it's a mistake, that I'm here under false pretences, that I've to pack my bags and leave. Would our health insurance still cover it, I wonder, if the initial diagnosis was wrong?

It's not a mistake. The max-fax team come in, form a solemn group around the end of the bed. The excellent young intern closes the curtains before she gives a verbal summary of my results so far. The disease doesn't seem to have spread beyond the localized area. It's in my cheek, mandible (jaw) area, the submandibular gland and a lymph node in my neck. It's not in the tongue, so far as they can tell at this stage.

Professor Stassen takes over. He doesn't smile when he describes what they plan to do, and that scares me as much as anything. He says they will have to operate, to remove the tumour. During surgery, they will remove quite a bit of jaw, some cheek. The nerves to my tongue might be damaged. My facial nerves will certainly be damaged, affecting my smile. My mouth and neck will need to be bypassed for a while, so I'll have a tracheostomy. I'll also have a skin graft, plastic surgery. Before they do the major operation, they'll insert a feeding line called a 'PEG tube' directly to my stomach because I will need to be fed artificially for a while. I will retain this tube for a period of months, because it's likely that I will need it again during the radiotherapy which will almost inevitably follow.

This is as much as I can absorb of what is said to me.

I'm aware that the atmosphere in the ward has changed. The closing of the curtains around the bed is the most rhetorical of gestures – everyone knows everyone else's business in here. After they've gone, one of the daughters of my friend in the next bed looks in to see if I'm okay. She tells me that her mother has a PEG tube, that I can shower or do anything with it. She warns me about MRSA, advises me to use tea-tree oil at every opportunity. The other women in the ward come over at different times to see if I'm okay. Later that day, my friend's daughter brings me a gift of tea-tree shower gel. Everyone here is kind, a word I haven't really thought about in years.

I ring a friend on her mobile phone to tell her where I am. She answers from her bed . . . she's got broken ribs, after a fall. We commiserate with each other. We agree that I win in the drama stakes.

My friends shock me with their capacity for love. Word is spreading. We can't control it any more. Simon says, 'It's in the wild.'

It's early, but the woman across the way has started to weep and call up her ghosts. Poor M, who hasn't had a single visitor since I've been here, struggles around her bed to answer her phone when it rings.

'Hello?' she says. 'Hello?'

After all that, it's a wrong number.

Some things are already gone. My face has already changed . . . now, when it's too late, it seems like something I could learn to like, will miss.

I worry about Oz, our dog. He has growths in his belly and in the bone of his shoulder. He's having tests as well.

20 April 2006

I'm fasting again today. Yesterday it was for bloods, today it's for the operation to insert the PEG tube in my stomach. While I wait to go down to theatre I think about what's happening.

The results of the PET scan amount to hard news, but good news. This way of looking at it may be formulaic, but it works for me. The tumour is large, but, so far as the tests have shown, the disease doesn't appear to have spread beyond the one node in my neck which is probably affected. When they operate, they will be looking to remove the tumour completely, plus a rim of healthy tissue around it, to make sure they get it all. This rim is known as a 'clear margin'. If they get this margin, we can relax a little. I may need radio-therapy afterwards, to make sure they blast away any hidden cancer cells.

I think about my voice, how much it means to me. How will I cope without it, if I lose part of my tongue, my throat? I think about work – about teaching, and workshops and readings. How I used to dread them, years ago. My gut would start to clench in advance. But they seem precious to me now. Not the fear beforehand, but the rush that comes after-wards, from audience response. The thrill as the atmosphere in a room changes when you begin to speak a story into it.

I imagine I can feel my crab inch towards the corner of my mouth, lay itself lazily along my tongue, drape itself across the roof of my mouth. Stay where you are, you little bugger. Don't grow. Go to sleep.

A friend who works in a hospice sends in a meditation CD. It's a Buddhist poem, a chant. I borrow Nessa's old Discman, held together with an elastic band, to listen to it. It's like plugging in to a different world. It helps to make the waiting easier.

In the afternoon, a nurse comes to say they won't insert the PEG tube today after all, they'll do it tomorrow. He brings me tea and biscuits. I crack a joke about the St James's diet. I'll lose loads of weight, at this rate.

The dietician has been round to weigh me and to go through my diet. She is petite and freckled, friendly. Now she comes back to show me a PEG tube so that I know what to expect. She explains the feeding regime.

The feed is a liquid which contains soy and other ingredi-ents to make up as balanced a diet as possible for people who are at risk of malnutrition. It's delivered directly to the stomach through the PEG tube, which has to be clamped shut when not in use. It also has to be flushed with sterile water at regular intervals so that it doesn't get clogged.

I think about liquidized food, juices and smoothies. I ask about meat, remind her that I don't eat it. She looks thrown for a minute. No, there'll be no meat in it.

She goes and gets a bag and a tube to show me what to expect. She has a way of tilting her head and smiling when she comes towards the bed that makes me glad to see her, no matter what she's carrying.

The feed comes in EasyBags in dayglo shades of green and blue. These can be hung upside down from a drip stand for a steady flow. She says that as I get used to it, I'll learn to tolerate larger amounts at a time, with longer gaps between them, approximating meal times.

The tube looks fatter than I expected.

21 April 2006

I look up from my bed and one of our friends is standing there, with a present from him and his wife. It's one of those beautifully wrapped parcels that I'm reluctant to open. Smart, crinkly paper and acres of gauzy ribbon. When I do open it, there's a strong-minded striped dressing gown inside, made of soft, light cotton. It's perfect. It will be my armour.

Waiting to be taken to theatre for the PEG tube insertion. Am I making a mistake by not looking for more information, making more demands? Not finding out more about each thing before it happens? I don't know. I'm surprised by how passive I am. I feel frozen, as in immobile. Stuck with my hot acid mouth. Every second that passes is an opportunity for the tumour to spread.

I give my belly a dose of moisturizer, running my palms across its unbroken surface for the last time. This will be the first cut.

I won't get to see *Krapp* after all. I've missed all of the plays I had tickets for. I'll be having surgery on the day that I was supposed to see *Godot*. At the theatre only a few weeks ago, I saw a woman in a wheelchair. She wore a black evening dress and was intent on the play. When I saw how thin and grey she looked, I was crass enough to wonder if this might be her last time at the theatre. Now look. Thoughts of mortality have bent my mind to a new shape for months. I must have known, even when I didn't know.

They want me to swallow a tube under sedation. This tube has a light on the end of it, which they will position inside the wall of my stomach. Then they will cut down from the surface towards the light, under local anaesthesia, and feed the PEG tube from the surface to the inside of my stomach. It will be used to feed me after the main operation, when my mouth will need to be kept dry and the tissues of my neck are likely to swell, making swallowing difficult. Later on, I will probably need the tube during radiotherapy, because of soreness in my mouth and throat, difficulty with swallowing. I recite this information to myself, trying to get the hang of it. It's like news about someone else, someone I've heard of but have never met.

The theatre is a well-lit, busy room, full of equipment and of people talking about normal everyday things, like the coming weekend. They move around adjusting dials, checking tubes. The sterile nurse holds up her hands as if she's waiting for someone to wind wool around them. Everyone wears blue or green scrubs and they all seem to wear clogs, even the men. It's a while since I've seen clogs. I wonder where they get them.

A surgeon appears, gowned and scrubbed, and tells me how good Professor Stassen is.

'I'm sorry for you,' he says. 'You've a battle ahead of you. But you're in the best possible hands – he's the best, not just in this hospital, but the best I've ever seen.'

Then he goes away again.

We're waiting for an anaesthetist, a different surgeon. At last everyone is here and we can start. I already have a cannula in my left arm so they can feed various chemicals into my system to sedate me. A blood pressure cuff is tight on my right arm.

Before they begin, the surgeon asks how I would feel about helping out with final-year medical exams on Monday. 'You won't have to do anything,' he says. 'The students will ask you questions, there'll be an examiner there. It's to test them on their clinical and diagnostic skills.'

I want to laugh out loud. I want to ask him how many people say no to any request of his as he reaches for his scalpel. But, in fact, I don't mind doing what he asks. They have to learn somewhere and, God knows, I'm grateful for the expertise they have. So I say yes. Then we get down to business.

They feed a tube through a hard plastic ring between my teeth. It's hard for me to open my mouth wide enough because the crab is clamped to the side of it, squeezing it down. After the ring comes a rubber strap to hold it in place, a scold's bridle. A nurse pushes on my cheek, not realizing that I have a tumour there. I wince away from her hand and they get confused – I can't explain through the gear around my mouth, the fingers of tubing that carry oxygen through my nose, the straps around my face, the hard plastic cylinder I bite on. But we get sorted and they start in earnest.

The tube I have to swallow is fatter and harder than I'd expected. The surgeon pushes, I swallow; he pushes again, I gag and swallow; he pushes – and it's in, hard and fast. They roll me on to my back. I'm retching. They keep talking to me, telling me what's happening, trying to soothe and reassure me. The local anaesthetic stings the skin of my abdomen and deeper, and then I feel pressure and the low deep pain of a cut. It's like being in a vice. I'm lowing like a cow.. Then everything speeds up and they pull out.

Was she given sedation? someone asks. *Not enough,* someone else answers.

There's a documentary on the radio tonight that features an interview with me, about becoming a writer. How things have changed since I did it. Simon brings in a radio but I don't listen to it. I don't think I could bear to hear myself.

22 April 2006

Each shock is new. This post-op state of sudden weakness, pain, vulnerability, need, is a stronger version of what I felt after the biopsy. If this is what I'm like now, what will I be like after the major operation? I'm like a raw recruit who gets wounded during training.

The lovely intern comes round to say goodbye; it's her last day working with my team. I'm sorry she's going, she's made a huge difference to me and not just because she's the only woman doctor on the team.

I have to be wheeled down to X-ray in a chair. We bounce over grey bands of something like rubber that have been laid where segments of the building join. The porter says they are there to counteract the building's expansion and compression from heat and cold.

'They're like speed bumps,' I say, bracing myself for yet

another jolt. I imagine joyriding patients speeding along hospital corridors in their chairs, doing wheelies after midnight. But I feel every bump in the fresh wound in my stomach, even though he slows for each one.

I get nervous in the one working lift, but it's okay. On the way back up we have to join a queue. Perfectly able-bodied visitors to the hospital wait for the lift to take them up one flight of stairs. The porter and I maintain a self-righteous silence, but when we get out on to the floor my ward is on we natter away like old friends, passing judgement as freely as any village elders.

I wish they hadn't put the PEG tube in before the weekend – I don't feel like myself, even when they let me go home for the day. I am more than usually insecure, these days. I lie on the couch most of the afternoon, doze through phone calls and rugby matches – a normal enough weekend afternoon, when you think about it, except for me, inching my way around and wincing. Zita, Eoin and Ryan – we call them the little family – have come to stay, for solidarity. Emma is studying for her finals.

I go upstairs to our attic bedroom with the bag of bandages and sachets of sterile water the nurses gave me when I left the ward. Nessa comes with me. She sits beside me, asks how she can help.

I need to flush the PEG tube with the water to keep it clean. It's a simple enough process, but I'm not used to doing it on my own yet, so I'm awkward. I'm grateful, and astonished, that she's there. I wonder if I could have done the same thing so willingly at her age.

First we have to clamp the tube, so that the contents of my stomach don't gush out when we open the cap. Nessa helps me clean the cap with a swab and stands ready with a syringe full of sterile water while I open it. The cap is not designed to open easily, for which I suppose I should be grateful. We need all four of our hands to manage this sequence. When the cap is open Nessa attaches the syringe to the mouth of the tube and injects the water straight to my stomach. I feel a rush of cold to the back of my throat. Then she detaches the syringe and we close the cap. Afterwards we have to redo the bandage around the wound. Raw as it is, Nessa doesn't even flinch when she sees it. A week ago she'd have squirmed at the sight of a torn fingernail.

The crab is fizzing and spitting today, as with rage – that creepy feeling that it's still trying to do its lethal work, embedding itself wherever it can find purchase. The burn of my tongue against it.

Imagine what it will be like to have half a face.

Back to St James's. Sounds of weeping in the night – they seem to seep through the walls, to billow out from under beds. I'm surrounded by grief and loss.

23 April 2006
It's Census day and I won't be home at midnight, so I can't be included on the form. I've always been the one to fill it out, because Simon has been away, working. This time I won't be counted as one of the family, I'll be registered in the hospital instead. I hate the way that makes me feel.

I'm allowed out again. On the way home we go for a short walk at Sandycove and see a seal swimming towards the Forty Foot. The water in the bay is navy and sparkling. Inside the walls of Bulloch Harbour it turns green. The gorse on the hill is bright as fire. The girls have got me gorgeous flowers.

Orange cannas, sunflowers and a tall one that looks like a yucca, yellow. Tied with orange straw. My very own flares.

One of my oldest friends calls in. We went to the same schools, grew up on adjoining streets. She talks strategy. There are four of us who grew up in houses not much further apart than the circumference of a hockey pitch, if you took the short cut through the old convent as we used to do. They are like sisters to me. They have a plan. We will set up a driving rota for appointments, a food run. They will be here to help out in whatever way they can.

It feels unreal to talk about this. I can't imagine needing any of it.

Another friend from school rings to see how I'm doing. She's an oncologist in Canada now. She offers to fly over and meet the doctors with me if it would help. 'Just say the word,' she says, 'and I'll come.' I'm stunned by this, as I am by every single thing that happens.

We go for a drive. At Shanganagh, I think how we've never gone in to look at the cemetery, although we've meant to do it. We've bantered about whether or not the price of a grave has gone up like every other inch of real estate around here. It would be impossible to joke about it today.

The gorse riots across Wicklow, the birds shrill out mad songs. How quickly we are changed. A month ago we were up here in the ice, got stuck in snow at the side of the road. Today it's lambs and gorse, fast-running water and soft green mounds. That phrase 'what doesn't kill you makes you stronger' spools through my brain as I take in signs of early spring and summer. I plan on getting a whole lot stronger.

We drive past Luggala and stop to look down into the corrie. It sparkles black, ringed with browns and greys, a green with metal in it. Dark. On towards the Sally Gap. It's like being on a brown moon up here. Bare silver trees crouch in the folds and creases of hills. Glencree, then down old roads through older trees and home again. It's ridiculous how much I love that silly road, the ramshackle, meaningless village where we live.

The woman who calls her greetings to dead air sounds like someone else when I get back to the ward. Her voice has sunk several octaves and comes out hoarse and forced as if it has further to travel to get here, with earth and roots still clinging to it. Her incessant call is almost as frequent as breath. But she's determined, no matter what it costs: she's down to one name now: Marie. It might even be her own name, the rock she clings to as she drowns. She coughs and this is new, a deep racking spasm, as if all the air she's breathed is trapped behind closing doors; it sounds like an elemental effort, to bring out her one word. I worry about what this effort costs her. I think I saw her once, sitting up in a wheelchair in a doorway, a tiny woman with a fine-boned, absent, Dublin face, white hair falling straight as curtains, hands quiet in her lap. She was quiet then, slow-moving as in a dream of stillness, of the past.

A woman who is being discharged tomorrow asks if I'm nervous about the operation I face. 'I always get nervous,' she says. 'There's always a risk, isn't there? Even with a small operation.'

That's enough of this conversation for me.

24 April 2006

Jackie's husband, David, had an accident last night. He's injured his spine. They're in A & E in St Michael's Hospital in Dun Laoghaire. David's father went into St Vincent's yesterday for an eye operation. We are spread around three different hospitals now. Poor Jackie.

A very young doctor comes to collect us for the final-year exams. I go down with a woman who had a tumour removed last week and is full of details about her illness. She doesn't ask about mine.

We are brought to another ward, shown into a room that smells of coffee. There's a trolley with pots of coffee and tea, plates of croissants and other goodies. There's an examining table and a regular table with several chairs around it, as if we've interrupted a meeting. There are viewing boxes on the wall, with someone's chest X-ray on display, an enlarged heart. We are led behind a portable curtain and asked to sit back to back. They bring us drinks of water.

I look at the signs warning against MRSA.

'Will the students touch us?' I ask. I'm worried about the fresh wound in my stomach, about my mouth.

'Don't be afraid to ask people to wash their hands; no one will mind if you do,' the young doctor says. Then he leaves us to wait.

The woman behind me goes back to talking about her tumour. She tells me how they found it, three months ago, and then she had to wait all that time for a bed even though she has health insurance. She's indignant. She mentions that her husband is a professional man. I think about how quickly things are moving for me. It seems that I've been lucky. She tells me what her husband had to say about the health service. How they have just found out her tumour was benign. What her husband said about that. Her husband is a professional man, she says again. He likes golf. Her consultant is X.

'Do you know him?'

'No.'

'He's a brilliant man. Brilliant.' She says that she's getting out soon, maybe even today.

Then the first student comes in. He appears around the curtain with a consultant and a woman I've never seen before. The student is pale. I swear to God he's shaking. His long hands tremble on the spindles of his wrists as he gestures towards the tube sticking out from the blue pyjamas that my girls bought for me in Penney's at the weekend. He reminds me of my sisters when they were in medical school, staying up all night slaving over textbooks, fuelled by coffee and nicotine. I remember their pallor and their tension and I know I won't mention the hand-washing issue any time soon.

Prodded by the consultant, the student asks questions that might lead him towards guessing my condition.

'Eh, when did you have this done?'

I'm disappointed for him. It's not a useful question.

'Describe what you see,' the examiner prompts.

'A plastic tube leading from the, er . . .'

I lift the pyjama top, trying to be helpful.

'Just above the navel.' One long finger hovers above the ends of the tube, its twin heads.

'Do you know what this tube is called?' the examiner asks.

Silence.

'What it might be used for?'

'Not for waste . . .' Bit by bit, the student picks up speed.

I realize that I am the trick question in this exam. You'd need to be alert to track a connection between the fresh wound in my stomach and the tumour that rages in my mouth. And I can't help much, I can only answer the questions that he asks. It's like a cross between a courtroom scene and *ER*. His Adam's apple bobs. We all heave a sigh of relief when his ordeal is over and he goes round to deal with the benign-tumour woman. I try not to listen to what they say about her, even though I've heard it all already.

Another, more confident, student comes through and we get into the swing of things. After a while they ask us to leave the room, because it's time for the examiners' coffee break. We leave the comforting, coffee-rich air behind and we're shown to a small, neutral room where two men are already ensconced. One is an outpatient who has a problem with his leg. The other man is older than all of us. He leans to one side in a wheelchair. He has drains and an ileostomy bag, an IV stand. This room is square and cramped. There's one window, no wash-hand basin. Bedsheets have been rigged up on IV stands to separate us into 'cubicles', but the sheets sag and we can see each other across them. We are left there for ages, waiting. Reading the signs about MRSA. A nurse comes in to give the man in the wheelchair his meds, check his bag. She asks if he's okay and he says yes. I'm not sure I believe him.

When the examiners get going, they power through. There are two, sometimes three, students in the room at a time, each one with two examiners. It's a riot in there, of potted medical histories, questions, deductions, brief clinical exams. They consider our respective surgical incisions, tubes, drains and bags; they look in my mouth, feel my swollen glands. They move from one of us to the other: leg, bag, tube, mouth. Near the end, one single student uses one of those snazzy hand-cleaning bottles that some of them wear pinned to the pockets of their white coats as he goes from one of us to the other. I want to say, 'Give that fella an A!'

Then, abruptly, they all bustle out and the room goes very quiet. They seem to have taken all the oxygen with them.

I struggle to open the window. The man with the bad leg helps me.

After a considerable time, it dawns on us that they're not coming back. The leg man goes off to ask if we can leave. Another nurse comes in, looks at the man in the wheelchair and says that she's taking him back to bed whether they've finished with us or not.

It turns out that they have. The benign-tumour woman and I go back to our ward. We've been gone for more than three hours. We've missed lunch. They've saved some battered fish for us, which they reheat in the microwave. It tastes rubbery and foul.

I feel hunger now as an actual pain, a curling spasm near the mouth of the tube.

A healing priest is rumoured to be in one of the side wards. Visitors murmur about this, think it's a good thing to be close to. I'm not so sure – what if all the good energy is deflected in his direction?

Simon and the girls come in to meet the max-fax team. They have reviewed the scans, the pathology, the biochemistry. Now they are going to explain what they've found and what they intend to do.

We meet in a bare room with bad furniture. The five of us take up most of the chairs. The place is crammed by the time the team, who I think of as *my* team, have filed in. One of them has what looks like blood-spatters on his surgical boots. We are all nervous.

They tell us about the extent of the tumour (it's in my cheek and gums, underneath my teeth, and in at least one lymph node); the surgical remedy (removal of part or all of my lower jaw, the inside of my cheek, all of the lymph nodes in my neck); and the after-effects of that (disfigurement; facial nerve damage resulting in a droop to that side, paralysis, scars, the loss of my ability to smile). A plastic surgery team will take a length of bone from somewhere else in my body (most likely the arm), along with a pad of fatty tissue and associated arteries, veins and nerves, which they will use to rebuild the inside of my mouth.

Surgery will probably be followed by radiotherapy. They explain the side- and after-effects of that, the recovery process, how I'll have to learn to talk and swallow. The prognosis, according to conventional statistics, is fairly bleak (40 per cent survival rate at five years), but I'm a young woman, they say, without a trace of irony, and healthy up until now. There is a chance, as with all major surgery, that I won't survive the operation. Things can go wrong, but they wouldn't put me through it if they didn't think I had a fighting chance.

I ask what I can do to prepare myself.

You might want to think about your will, is the response.

The room goes very quiet. I look at each of my girls, then at Simon. He, Zita and Emma are looking at Nessa, to see how she is taking it. The team suggest that I consider my options in terms of medical decisions, in case things do go wrong. They advise me to get a rubber ball and practise squeezing it, to build up the muscles in my arm as far as possible – this will help me recover from the bone graft. When I ask, they say that my arm will recover its function. Work at the keyboard won't be affected.

Then they repeat that if they didn't think I had a chance they wouldn't do this operation, they wouldn't waste their time or mine. They warn me against unmonitored and potentially inaccurate information on the internet. They suppose I'll go there anyway.

In fact I've decided to trust them, but I don't say so. I think I really didn't take it in before now.

40

I want to live.

How melodramatic and clichéd that sounds, but it is the truest thing I can think of, right here and now.

25 April 2006

All the things I've done wrong from the beginning crowd around the bed and tug at the sheets to wake me up. Why did I not pursue this more vigorously? Sooner? Why did I not insist that someone pay attention? There is a terrible instinct to find someone to blame, but I'm the one who put up with a degree of disruption and pain in my mouth that I wouldn't have endured in any other organ, wouldn't have let my kids ignore for a second. None of those things mean anything now. It's a matter of time. We stalk each other, the tumour and I, one eye on the clock.

It's early and most of the ward is still asleep. I go in to our bathroom, where I find a nurse swilling water in a bedpan beside the basin.

She stops. We stare at each other.

'It's not what you think!' She is angry, as if I'm the one who's in the wrong. 'I didn't empty it there.'

Maybe not, but it sure as hell looks as if she's rinsing it from the tap.

I wash my teeth in that basin, rinse my mouth there with the special mouthwash they've given me.

Don't they have sluice rooms any more?

This place is full of hidden enemies – germs, bacteria, micro-organisms, rampant infection. Random encounters that could have catastrophic effects. Thinking back on yesterday's lack of handwashing, I curse myself for not insisting on it. I think the max-fax team would be furious if they knew.

And when I came back from the medical students' exams, one of the nurses flushed my PEG tube for me – did opportunistic bacteria from the morning find a way into my system?

I can't keep thinking about these things, things I can't even see, or I'll go mad. Stop thinking about what might happen. Focus on what you can *do*.

Simon and Nessa buy me two brightly coloured squishy balls. From now on I'll carry them everywhere.

Waiting for a taxi to take me to the Dental Hospital, I text my sister Trudi, who works in Holles Street. She says she'll meet me there.

It feels weird going down to the front door by myself, in street clothes, going out – unprotected. Illicit. I get into a small canary-yellow taxi with a familiar-looking driver. An intellectual in a check jacket. The traffic is brutal and we discuss the relative merits of different routes through the city while we sweat in the bus lane.

I arrive late and stumble in to the building, awkward with the tube. Trudi is waiting and it's great to have her there. The dentist is gentle and thorough. She angles mirrors and lights so I can see inside my mouth and get a good look at the tumour.

'You know,' she says, 'you won't believe me, but when people come for check-ups at one year, five years, ten years . . . they say, what year was that, now, when I first came . . .'

I'm surprised by tears. 'Thank you for that "ten years".'

No one has gone further than five before. Not even me.

I've to go and have some X-rays. When I come back we wait to go back into the clinic. I text Jackie, to tell her where we are. She texts back to say we'd better behave or she'll come in and sort us out, so we say, *come on*, and she does.

When I've gathered all the letters and appointments I need

and we're free to go, we leg it over to the National Gallery for lunch. It's like mitching from school, right down to bumping into people I know in the queue. I don't know what to say to them: I'm on day release? It's awkward.

There's a woman crying over by the coats. Gallery staff are trying to help her but she doesn't seem to speak English. They call an ambulance. It arrives just as we're leaving. I limp past, holding my sore stomach. Jackie is going to bring me back to the hospital. I have to drag myself to her car, which is parked a short distance away, on the square. It's funny how short those green man sequences at the lights seem, now that I need more time.

Back on the ward, people talk me through the same old questions. They say I'm not to drive myself mad with how I got this, it's just bad luck. No one would have predicted that someone my age or with my general profile (e.g. having given up smoking eight years ago) would get this cancer: it is very rare.

Plus, I have learned, it has a genius for disguise. It's unclear to me whether my carcinoma began as a benign condition that changed, or whether it was opportunistic, and found a fertile site to grow. A percentage of cases like mine occur in places where leukoplakia or lichen planus have been. One doctor refers to 'the lichen planus stage', but I'm not quick enough to ask him exactly what he means.

Here's a thing: consultants don't intimidate me. I grew up with them and began my working life with them. I have a modicum of basic medical terminology, and an understanding, even if outdated, of how hospitals work. And yet, for all my note-taking and lists of questions, I still forget to ask the crucial ones, or don't think of the one revealing piece of information that I need until after they've gone. I write down what they tell me and then forget to look it up when someone else comes round. What is wrong with me?

The head-and-neck nurse comes to meet me. Her name is Sinéad. She has an easy way about her, but she's direct, talks me through everything I've already heard. I've noticed that people ask what my understanding of my situation is – so that they can gauge how much I've taken in? How much I can handle?

My voice wobbles down the rutted track of my recent history. I'm mortified. I've only just met her and here I am, teeth rattling with nerves.

She says not to worry. She'd be more concerned if I wasn't emotional about it.

I draw up another action plan in my notebook, involving exhortations to myself to eat well, sleep, squeeze my rubber ball and stay positive. They don't sound fierce enough.

A new patient has come to the bed beside mine. She is beautiful. Paper thin, she holds herself erect and glides along, clavicles like razors. Her pyjamas probably weigh more than she does. She is refined, pared back to the bare essentials, bone and breath. She looks neither right nor left but straight ahead.

Someone has left a scratch card on my bed, a gift. Or a sign. I'm afraid to play it. But if I don't, what does that say about me?

When I do, it's a €4 win – double the money. Where's a fortune-teller when you need one?

Sometimes I break when I talk to Simon. Speaking is an emotional trigger. Words fracture in my mouth, unlock me. I can think 'I have cancer', but when I say it out loud my voice rebels.

26 April 2006

I feel the murky outlines of a formless cloud, a vapour that is terror, rising. What I can't get over is that people learn to live with this, adapt to it, absorb it and move beyond it. To live so close to death. To be dangling over the edge. But I'm lucky. What about when death is a certainty? When there is no hope?

How does a condemned person get his legs to carry him to the scaffold? How do soldiers move into battle?

I've a stream of visitors, and then a medical person comes to see me and they all go off to wait in the coffee shop. Some of them have to leave before I can join them.

When I get back to the ward, the woman in the next bed has a crowd of visitors. Three women and a stolid man who sits on my bed with his arms folded across his broad chest. It takes him a while to realize that I'm asking him to move, he's so engrossed in the racing on TV.

Through a window at the end of the ward I can see a block of flats, Fatima Mansions, being demolished. Wallpapers and fireplaces exposed. Under the walls, piles of rubble are being broken up to make new earth.

27 April 2006

The operation has been put off until next week, when the plastic surgeon will be available. I'd be on my way down to theatre right now if they were doing it today. Instead an antechamber the size of a week has opened in front of me and so I enter it. We all do. We have no choice. Time moves in one direction only. What will I do with it? If I knew now what the outcome was going to be, what might I do differently?

You can't finish writing a novel in a week.

As I write that, I hear an echo of the boy on the train: Is that *really* what you'd wish for?

David has been called back to St Michael's and then transferred to St Vincent's. A pelvic fracture has shown up on his X-ray. We commiserate with each other, via text. Con, his father, is at home again, but Jackie keeps him in this loop of goodwill as she circles between the three of us.

A stooped, elderly man with wild hair, who makes me think of a hermit or a preacher, comes close to my bed to get a good look at me. I tell him that this is not his ward. He asks for directions to the door and leaves, his attendant three paces behind him. I've seen them walking around before. Sometimes he carries a walking stick across his chest, reinforcing the idea of a preacher, striding through the desert with slippers for sandals, clutching his staff. There is something venerable about him, despite his pyjamas.

I'm let out for the day. When the nurses say things like, 'Do whatever you want,' or 'Have a good time,' I wonder if they mean, *Run, girl. While you can.*

28 April 2006

This week feels like the end of a pregnancy, when you are ready to go through anything to get to the other side of labour. All the work is done. We are just waiting. We play endless games of cards. As soon as someone comes in, we deal a hand and go.

I have to stay close to my bed because I still have to meet the tracheostomy nurse, who will explain all about the tracheostomy and answer any questions I have. I can't go home until I've seen her. I'm afraid to miss her, so I don't even go to the coffee shop. I ask a nurse if he can find out when she might come, but he's too busy. After lunch I ask again. The day drags on while I squeeze my squishy ball in my left hand to build up the muscles in my arm. My mood sinks. I ask again. I'm close to tears by now.

In the end someone rings up for me and it turns out that the tracheostomy nurse is off today. I ring Simon, pull the curtains around my bed and have a good cry.

That's one whole day wasted.

They let me out for the evening. We walk to Bulloch, where the tide is low and the seals are lazy. Big crabs lie belly-up in the tidal mud. On the pier we find skeletons of fish, picked clean and scattered. There is a live crab in the patch of sandy water between pier and rock, pale and still, lethal. All of these are signs. Then I see a shattered crab shell, picked clean – pearly creamy white inside, muddy pink outside, no trace of the living creature left. Nearby, there's a group of them (is there a collective noun for crabs? A disease of crabs? An eruption of crabs?) in low water. Waiting for some lucky gull.

29 April 2006

When I woke up the morning was bright, if subdued, the sky more blue than grey. A cloud mass moved in, with, wouldn't you know it, a long thin pincer that closed in to shut down the blue. Well. That solid mass is only temporary. I know the sky is still there. Clouds can come and go, but the sky returns.

My sister Clair and her husband Sean are here from America, on business. When they told us they were coming, we all expected that they'd be here for the post-op vigil. Now we have the pre-op nerves instead.

47

We meet them in the restaurant Emma works in, have a slow lunch. The chef has bought in fish I like. We're given plenty of space to talk. Later we go to the harbour for a walk, with the little family, who've come up for the day.

I feel Lyn behind every word Clair and I say to each other. Saying goodbye is hard.

30 April 2006

Most days I'm the first to wake up in my part of the ward. I get to have the first shower and I can take my time, knowing no one is waiting to use the bathroom. One of the nurses comments on the perfume I use.

'It smells so good in here in the mornings,' she says. 'We can tell that you're up.'

I know what she means. As the ward wakes up it breathes out the sour smells of the night, smells of human waste and decay and loneliness. I deploy moisturizers, shampoo and cologne against them.

Out again for a few hours: we go for a walk around the old reservoir. It's littered with plastic rings from cans. I pick them up – I can't pass them by. It's a small thing, still within my power. There's no bin, though. Simon takes them from me and puts them in the pocket that's not already occupied by my hand.

1 May 2006

I'll lose salivary glands, jaw, teeth. My senses of smell and taste will be compromised, or lost. What I think is – if you had to lose two out of the five senses, which would you go for? Which would you keep? I think about sight and hearing. About touch. I'll take these.

For a while I won't be able to eat or talk – or even breathe – for myself. But I'll still be here, with my people around me. I'm stunned by what the surgeons are willing and able to do, and that so much expertise will be marshalled on my behalf.

Sometimes when I wake up the crab is sleeping, nestled in against my jaw, a swollen weight, but quiet. Sometimes I still wonder if I'm faking it.

Nessa is moving out of her flat today, coming home. The college year is all but over.

2 May 2006

The symbolism of low tide. All it reveals: what was there all along, but hidden.

I get out for the afternoon. We go to a solicitor's office to figure out the power of attorney issue, in case I emerge from the operation in a permanent vegetative state. I am supposed to be at a workshop, with the novelshop. The contradiction between what my normal self would be doing and what my new self is up to is acute. Into traffic and out home: a last walk on a gorgeous evening, past Joyce's Tower, half-tide. A couple sit on the wall having dessert and a bottle of wine; there are a lot of young people hanging out and staring at the sea. We used to do all those things too. The traditions and habits of a place continue, no matter what. At first I find that comforting. Then it terrifies me.

David is still in St Vincent's. They are going to do an operation to repair his pelvis, the day after mine.

I am more and more ready for my operation. The pain gets worse, a hot knife in my cheek, sour pincers under my teeth. Now the lump in my neck is huge, hard, like stone. I fear it's sliding under the chin and out towards the lips. I feel it under my top teeth as well and hope to God I'm imagining it. Stay away from my eye.

There's such a tide of goodwill flowing towards me, I really feel it, that it will carry me through.

3 May 2006

They have given the woman opposite me a zimmer frame and I meet her out for a morning walk on the corridor – I barely recognize her, upright and beaming. She can go home now. The unknown woman dozes.

My team come around and go through it all again, patiently. The plan is to split my lip, which may result in permanent numbness; lift my cheek open, open out the jaw and remove the tumour, which is 'big'; most likely they'll have to remove the parotid, the large gland under the angle of my jaw – but it'd probably be damaged by radiation therapy anyway. They'll try to preserve the upper branches of my facial nerve (which controls opening and closing of the eye) and the lower ones, but the middle ones (affecting the smile and other movement) will most likely go. They talk about adjusting to what I've lost, when I come round.

I wish I could see through the veil of the next three days or so. I wish I was on the other side of them. On the other hand, my jaw is still intact, the blood in my veins is still my own. The news that I'll have a tranfusion rocks me. It never dawned on me that I would need one. I feel a strange pity and regret for the two wisdom teeth on the other side which have to go, just to make housekeeping easier – it's not their fault.

Simon and the girls come in, with Ryan. We head off to IMMA (the Irish Museum of Modern Art). Then the hospital rings – I have to go back and sign the consent form. The procedure is explained yet again, but this time they up the ante a little – they might have to go for my upper jaw too. I wish everyone would stop talking about what might happen and just get on with it.

We are offered a tour of ICU to see how it works, because I'll have to go back there after the operation, for at least a day. I'll find out all about it soon enough, so I stay in the waiting room with Ryan and we make up stories about the ghosts who live in the Roancabin below us. Back in the ward there's a flurry of activity, of people coming to wish me luck, cards and letters delivered to my bed.

Here's a thing to remember – I have my last bar of chocolate before the operation, a Mars Delight, and it hurts. The flavour is there, but it hurts to chew. That old thing – by the time you realize that you're about to lose something, it's already gone.

When all the visitors have left I find a letter from a schoolfriend, hidden under my pillow. She must have come in while we weren't here. Her words make me feel elastic, full of hope. I wish I'd seen her, but I know why I didn't. Later still, when the ward is going to sleep, another schoolfriend creeps in. A sad *Hello?* from the bed across the way alerts no one. We look through the cards and letters and talk in whispers.

'Did you know how many people love you?' she asks.

Now that this night is finally here it's easier than I thought it would be. I think I'm ready. The crab insinuates itself slyly between my teeth, ready to rupture, and I know it's past time for it to go, even if it does take half my face with it. This may be unreal, but I feel okay about it. Let's do it.

4 May 2006

6 a.m. First thing when I wake up I hook up Nessa's Discman, plug in to the Buddhist meditation CD, and allow its chant to calm me. I have a shower, not thinking about anything other than its minor melodies. I'm not allowed to use moisturizers of any kind, have to remove all nail varnish. I sit on the bed with wet hair and wait, squeezing my rubber ball. We won't know for sure if the operation will go ahead until ICU can confirm a bed for me afterwards.

I send a text to Jackie: *See you on the Far Side.*

Simon is on his way to wait with me. To pass the time, I read back through these notebooks before putting them away. What I have written seems inadequate, scattered, superficial, partial and egocentric. It doesn't say enough about love or about hope, those moments when I think I can see the way ahead: long and difficult, but a way. I feel its failures, but it is at least a record. If I'm lucky, there will be memory attached to the root of each word when I come back to it . . . It will be a long time before I can write again.

Chapter 2

Now, while the surgeons are busy, seems as good a time as any to fill in a bit of background.

I am no stranger to anaesthesia, or to medicine. I spent more time in casualty departments and operating theatres than your average suburban child, not because I was sickly, but because my mother was an anaesthetist. Our kitchen cupboards were crammed with medical samples in vials and blister packs and boxes; there were stethoscopes on our hall table where other families might keep their keys, a sphygmomanometer beside the phone. My first notebooks were the bulky Warner's medical diaries my mother discarded at the end of each year, barely used. My own first entries and later my early lines of dialogue, character sketches and maps of fictional places were drawn amid pharmaceutical advertisements under lists that were cryptic to me, written in her flowing blue hand. Names and times, the odd chemical formula, partial grocery lists mixed in with the scientific and commercial names of drugs.

Our night-time rituals included late-night phone calls from the hospital with the surgical list for the following morning. I can still hear my mother's voice reciting dosages: *One tenth of Omnopon. One sixth of Atropine.* Atropine, one of her more frequently administered drugs, is an extract of belladonna, or deadly nightshade. I was intrigued when I learned that it was named for Atropos, a mythological figure empowered with choosing how a person would die. But while I was entranced by metaphor and allusion, my mother was all for science and the hardest of hard facts. This difference would be a source of bitter conflict between us as I grew up.

My mother was the first person in her family to go to university, so far as I know, and it was an unlikely path for someone of her background to pursue. Her father, Edward Hart, was a butcher on the corner of Parnell Street and Riddle's Row, a street which no longer exists, having been replaced by a shopping centre during the clear-out of Dublin's inner city in the 1960s and 1970s. She was born there in 1914. Two years later, rebellion broke out just around the corner and British guns pounded the area where they lived. Within a couple of years, the Spanish flu would kill her three little brothers: Paddy, who was two, and the three-year-old twins, Ned and Joe. Her parents moved out of the city centre with their two surviving daughters as fast as they could. They had five more daughters and then another son, but it would be impossible to overestimate the effect of losing those boys, on any of them.

Disaster would strike again when one of the younger girls was in an accident. The nature of this accident is unclear – stories differed according to who was telling them at the time – but legend has it that Gabrielle was pronounced dead in casualty and carried off to the hospital morgue. A passing dignitary, being conducted on a tour of the hospital by a nun, stopped to take a closer look.

'But – that child is breathing!'

Gabrielle was revived and rushed upstairs to a ward, but her brain had been deprived of oxygen for a long time and she was never the same again. This was a subject on which my mother would never be drawn unless she was issuing warnings about the dire consequences of doing this or that. She never talked about her lost brothers either.

Eventually the family moved back into town, and settled

in the smoky flat in Merrion Street where I remember them best, my talkative, sharp-eyed aunts with their pillowed bosoms, their cigarette holders and their easy laughs.

My father, too, was the first from his family to attend university, where he met my mother. His father was a confectioner and a caterer, as was his father before him. They made sweets and sold them, and their business grew until in the end they were giving parties and dinners for the great and the good of Dublin. I could say that my grandfather entertained royalty, but what I mean is that he once provided tea and sandwiches for King Edward VII in a marquee in Kingstown, now Dun Laoghaire. My sister Clair has the teacups to prove it.

Such unionist dealings were not to be advertised in the Ireland where I grew up. I don't know what my grandfather's politics were, but I do know that he was Church of Ireland and that my grandmother, who was his sister-in-law before she was his wife, was Catholic. Trouble in the house. These things mattered, back in the 1900s.

My father was a clever, thwarted man. An engineer by trade, he was a Ham radio fanatic and spent long hours in a shack behind our house, communicating with people all over the world. He claimed to have been the first person in Ireland to know that JFK had been shot, because he was speaking to a friend in Dallas when it happened. He believed in global communication and in miniaturization; he designed a prototype for a television you could wear on your wrist. People thought he was cracked, but if he'd been born just a few decades later we might have been rich.

Instead, he and my mother went to war against Hitler. He joined the RAF within months of their getting married, in 1939, and when he left, she went with him. I think they had an exciting time during the war, but when they came back in 1945, with two children, it was one more thing that couldn't be talked about. As far as Ireland was concerned, there hadn't been a war at all, it was just an 'Emergency'. My father was twenty-nine years old and had already been diagnosed with the emphysema that would eventually kill him.

He went to work for the ESB, at the beginning of the rural electrification scheme which would transform the country over the next thirty-odd years. My mother returned to her medical training, which had been interrupted first by marriage and then by war. All that remained of the catering business by then were a surplus of salt cellars and cut-glass soda syphons and several intriguing, but rather tarnished, silver spoons.

By the time I came along, the youngest of six children (five girls and one boy), my father was chronically unwell. His condition coloured all our lives. He would be all right for a while and then deteriorate, rally and deteriorate again. He would smoke through violent spasms of coughing, smoke while hooked up to his oxygen tank.

My mother had her work cut out for her, keeping us all going and him as well, while working as the only anaesthetist in our local hospital. She put in 48-hour days, or that's how it seemed to us. The phone rang every night with the surgical list for the next day, shrilled in the small hours of the morning when my mother was needed. If we went out anywhere, as we rarely did – to the cinema, say, or for Sunday lunch somewhere – she had to tell people who she was and where she was sitting, in case the hospital rang up looking for her. And when they did, we'd all get up and troop out, no matter how thrilling the moment in the film, or if hot food had just arrived on the table. Years after she retired I met one of the porters who had known her. 'They have four men up there now, doing the job your mother used to do,' he told me.

I was six when my father died. Later, in my unruly teenage years, the nuns tried to curb my more anti-social tendencies by reminding me that my mother (who was considerably older than the mothers of my friends) was not going to be around for ever and that she worried about what would become of me after she was gone. I thought they meant that she was literally about to die – after all, I'd lost one parent already, so why not another? My mother did nothing to correct this belief of mine, but then I was an extremely difficult, self-destructive teenager and she was alone, she was not a young woman, she was tired. Who's to say that, in her shoes, I wouldn't have done the same? She suspected that I was inherently feckless, and thought writing an unreliable way to make a living (she was right on both counts). She knew that a woman needed to be able to support herself, and in that, as in so many ways, she was unusual for her time. We had spectacular rows about what I would do with my life in the future and what I was doing with my life at the time. The fear that she would die did little to make me more tractable; it just stoked my inner rage.

I probably would have been a morbid teenager anyway. I read a lot of poets who'd led sickly lives or died young, novels like Sylvia Plath's *The Bell Jar*. I flirted with the idea of suicide, as many teenagers do. I thought I was depressed, but my mother would have none of it. She said that mental illness, like literature, was a luxury of the immature.

Two of my sisters, Clair and Trudi, qualified as doctors. I wouldn't study medicine, as my mother wanted me to do, but I did train as a radiographer, in St Thomas's Hospital in London. I liked hospitals. I was comfortable in them, having spent a significant portion of my childhood hanging around in waiting rooms and clinics and hospital car parks; my early summer jobs were in casualty departments and in the consultants' rooms where my aunts worked as secretaries. I was admitted for minor ailments like ear infections, because there was no one to look after me at home. I had my verrucas removed under general anaesthetic which I slept off in geriatric wards, had my ears pierced by a casualty officer on duty and, along with my sister Jackie, who was as pale and thin as I was, endured lengthy sessions of ultra-violet treatment in the days when Irish people would speak no ill of the sun. I quizzed my sister Trudi and her friends from *Gray's Anatomy* and Robbins' *Basic Pathology* before their exams, and I did the same for my mother, when she studied for her ECFMG – the qualifying exam for doctors wanting to work in America.

My mother never went to live in America, but my oldest sister Clair did, and so did I. I went with Simon, soon after we were married. Our daughters were born there.

Simon and I met when I climbed in through his bedroom window, wearing a deerstalker hat, a black velvet skirt and the red-and-yellow striped rugby socks of a local school (not his). He was in bed with a broken back, having fallen out of a tree while trying to retrieve a shuttlecock. I was fifteen and he was eighteen.

As a child I had a habit of trespassing in local gardens, the grounds of schools, outbuildings and empty houses where I had no business being. This is the way we carried on in those days, when nobody thought much about where children were or what they might be up to, and so long as you turned up on time for tea there were no questions asked. But I had more or less abandoned this pastime by the time I met Simon, and had legitimate reasons for clambering through his window unannounced.

His cousin and my friend had arranged to go out together that afternoon, but at the last minute my friend brought me along. Maybe it was the socks, but the cousin took one look at me and revised his plans for the afternoon.

'We'll go and visit Simon instead,' he said.

Simon's parents were out. He couldn't get out of bed to let us in, but his window was open, so we climbed through it. We already knew who each other was, through the networks of schools and discos and the pairings and ruptured pairings of friends.

We were friends in a loose and easy way while he went out with a schoolfriend of mine and we continued to be friendly after they broke up. It wasn't until I had qualified as a radiographer in London and he was working as a geologist in the United Arab Emirates that we began to see each other differently. Maybe because we were both away from home, we started to write to each other, and kept the correspondence going after I went back to Ireland.

We arranged a holiday, with a mutual friend, on the island of Corfu. By the time we came back Simon and I were inseparable. He had left the UAE and was coming home to start work with an oil services company which had opened an office in Dublin, lured by tax breaks offered by the government of the time. I worked in the Mater Hospital, just down the road from his office. We found a flat together within a month of coming home from Corfu, got married nine months later. In short order, a series of strikes – bank, electricity, postal – brought the company Simon worked for to its senses and they packed up and left, as many others did in those times.

We left with them. I was twenty-two years old and pregnant.

We spent the next few years moving around the States, from Texas to California and back again, with our daughters, first Zita, then Emma, then Vanessa. After ten years, when Nessa was four, we came home. A recession in the oil industry meant that the work was running out. Simon got a job on one of those international contracts where a person works for two months and then has a month off. The girls and I could be based anywhere except wherever he was, while he worked offshore near Tierra del Fuego and in the Caspian Sea, spent months in the Sahara Desert and in the Altiplano in Bolivia. Families were not part of the deal.

It seemed like a good time to come home. The girls and I have been here in Dublin ever since, while Simon has been away for long periods of time on temporary or extended contracts. Currently, his job is based in London and he comes home at weekends.

While we were still in Texas my sister Lyn, who lived in London with her husband, Adam, and their two small daughters, was diagnosed with cancer.

Lyn had discovered a painful lump in her breast a year previously, but the doctors she consulted assured her that it was nothing to worry about. They never bothered to do a biopsy. The rest of us, who were scattered around, in Dublin, England and America, were relieved to hear that her lump was harmless. We thought nothing more of it.

The consultant who saw Lyn advised her that one of two things would relieve her painful lump – menopause or pregnancy. She wanted more children anyway, and got on with her life, as advised. Soon she was happily pregnant, but her baby died *in utero* and labour had to be induced.

When she could not drag herself out of the pit this left her in, her doctors told her that she felt rotten because of the miscarriage and advised her to 'get over it'. She became jaundiced. Having had enough of GPs and consultants advising his exhausted wife to pull herself together, Adam brought her to their local casualty department.

The cancer that had been in her breast all along had spread to her liver. She died three weeks later. She was thirty-three years old. Her daughters, Zoe and Kevi, were aged four and two.

After we buried Lyn, it became clear that my mother was suffering from Alzheimer's disease. It would take fifteen excruciating years for her to waste away and die, years when the shadow of illness and the expectation of the imminent death of a parent returned to claim us. It's worth mentioning that in the mid-eighties it was difficult to find a doctor who would admit to recognizing the early symptoms of Alzheimer's in a colleague. For my sisters who were here and had to deal with it, this professional reticence made an unbearable situation even worse.

We came home from the States in 1990. At first we stayed with my sister Jackie and her husband, David, on the street where she and I were born. Then we moved into their basement, where we lived for the next five years.

During that time Jackie was also diagnosed with breast cancer. She had a lump which had previously tested as being benign. When she changed to a new GP she was advised to get the lump re-checked. This time they found not one but two different types of carcinoma. Luckily, both were still in the early stages of their development and her treatment was successful.

After Lyn died, I discovered a lump in my own breast which was investigated and found to be nothing. When I turned thirty-three, the age she was when she died, I discovered another one. It went away when I was thirty-four. Somewhere in the back of my mind an expectation lurked, although I told myself that lightning doesn't strike the same place twice.

Well. When Jackie got her diagnosis, we learned that it did.

Since my own diagnosis, people have asked if I am angry, if I think: *why me?* It feels like the darkest secret to admit that what I really felt was, *why not me?* It is what I thought when Lyn, who didn't smoke or drink, who ate the uninspiring salads of 1970s Ireland with determined enthusiasm and who was usually in bed by ten o'clock at night, got cancer. It's what I thought with increasing ferocity when Jackie got it and I had to watch her treatment from the sidelines.

One way or another, medicine and illness were the joint themes that I inherited. My early childhood was inflected with illness and the expectation of death. But when I began to suspect that there could be something sinister at work in my mouth, I remembered my earlier false alarms and hesitated. I didn't want to be a hypochondriac, I didn't want to be wasting anyone's time. I had been brought up as a doctor's daughter, after all, and we all know about the cobbler's children, their bare and calloused feet. I had a superstitious dread of reaching the age at which my father died, forty-eight, and part of me registered that this sore could be serious, but another part dismissed it as nothing to worry about. I'd never heard of cancer of the mouth. Even when I went on the internet and learned how real it was, I didn't think that it applied to me.

But when I got my diagnosis, some tiny hidden part of me uncurled and stretched and said *hello*. I was shocked, but not surprised. What's more – and this is more difficult to admit – the depressive tendencies that I have fought throughout my life now assumed that they'd been vindicated and could take over. This was my birthright, what I had been primed for all along – a fatal illness.

Except that cancer is not necessarily a fatal illness, not any more.

★

In the months leading up to the opening of this story, I had a golden time, despite the canker in my mouth. Emma and Nessa were both in college – Emma in her final year of an engineering degree, Nessa studying communications and specializing in video production. Zita, her partner Eoin, and their son Ryan, had recently moved to a new house in a town about an hour's drive away from us. Although we missed them, we still saw them often.

Friends of ours (he Australian, she Ugandan) got married in Kenya and we had the holiday of a lifetime, travelling along dusty, treacherous roads at speed in those terrifying white vans, exploring Masai country in a loose social caravan of other people who'd come to Africa from all over the world for this wedding. We delighted in the drama and beauty of the landscape; we had excitement and fun and friends; hippos at our window, elephants at the water-hole, giraffes in the tall distance – and then the wedding itself, which was held in Karen Blixen's garden in Nairobi. There were monkeys in the trees. Acholi dancers wearing ostrich feathers entertained us and danced with us through the day and the night. They were there because they were family, not because they were paid. It was unforgettable.

During the next few months I launched a collection of poems for one good friend and opened an art exhibition for another. I worked on my third novel and on non-fiction pieces for an anthology, went to workshops with different writing groups. I belong to three such groups, which makes me sound promiscuous (maybe I am).

Then my novel *Nothing Simple* was the surprise, wildcard addition to the shortlist for novel of the year at the Irish Book Awards. The dinner was held in March. John Banville won the prize and no one was surprised, least of all me, but I had all the more fun in the weeks leading up to the dinner for knowing that I was unlikely to win. It meant that I didn't have to be nervous or write a speech, and best of all, I didn't spend the money in advance.

Stories have their origins in simpler but more dangerous times. In *Aspects of the Novel* E. M. Forster writes that the storyteller in primitive societies had a precarious position. Gathered around the fire, our ancestors liked to be entertained, diverted from the sure and certain knowledge of icy winds blowing across the tundra, wolves howling at the moon. If the storyteller failed and the audience got bored, Forster says, they either fell asleep or killed him.

The dread and exhilaration that writers know when they face their audience can still feel extreme. Reading aloud or putting words on paper, you can sense the flames at your face. They might kill you. You might live for ever.

At my friend's opening in the Hallward Gallery, I was nervous. Many of the people who were gathered in the room earn their living making speeches of one kind or another. But I also knew and believed in what she wanted me to say, which was about how we had both started out as wild and irresponsible teenagers, leading each other astray, and how we wandered down various career paths before finding our way to where we'd always wanted to be.

'Life is short,' I lectured the assembled group of barristers, politicians, speechwriters, actors and psychotherapists; 'if you have something that you love doing, burn to do – what are you waiting for? Look what can happen!' And I invited them to look around the walls of the gallery, to see what can be achieved when we take chances, abandon the safety of the familiar and go for what we really want.

There was laughter and generous applause. I felt such exhilaration. They would not, after all, feed me to the wolves. Not this time. I was riding high.

Pride goes before a fall, they say. I don't know about that, but I was brought up to throw salt over my left shoulder and I still do it, when no one is looking. I bow three times to lone magpies, cross my fingers, touch wood. I have reason to know that life is unpredictable, just as I know that it's a thrill, a miracle, a matter of pure luck. And we stumble along in our daily lives, oblivious. Just as well, or we'd get nothing done.

But there's no harm in remembering from time to time. No harm at all in appreciating what we've been given and what we could so quickly, so perilously easily, lose.

This story begins one week after the Irish Book Awards dinner. My careless bluff, issued in the Hallward Gallery a few short and busy months earlier – *Life is short . . . what are you waiting for?* – had been called.

Now, look.

This is what the surgeons did while we've digressed.

First the tracheostomy. They cut a hole in my trachea (windpipe) and then inserted a tube in my throat. The tube was attached to a ventilator.

My face was opened up by surgically splitting my lip, tracing a line down the middle of my chin and along the underside of my chin towards my ear, and a large area of tumour was removed from the inside of my cheek. A section of my lower jaw was taken out, with its teeth still attached. A smaller section of the maxilla, or cheekbone, also went, as did half of my parotid gland (the large salivary gland close to the ear) and all of the lymph nodes on the right side of my neck. These excisions brought quantities of muscle, nerve and sinew along with them, but the major blood vessels, the carotid artery and the jugular vein, were left intact. Two drains were inserted into my upper chest.

During the same operation, a different team of surgeons opened up my leg and removed approximately half of the fibula, the slender bone that runs parallel to the larger tibia, between the knee and the ankle. This was then artfully placed in the oral cavity, in combination with a titanium plate, to rebuild my face. A significant patch of skin and fatty tissue, along with arteries and veins, was 'harvested' from the same area of leg to establish a soft tissue lining for my cheek. The blood vessels were joined to the existing blood supply by reconstructive microsurgery.

Throughout all of this, the input and output of various body fluids were scrupulously recorded along with vital signs. I was given two units of blood. The whole procedure took the best part of fourteen hours.

Then I was sewn up again and brought out to recovery, of which I remember precisely nothing, and then to ICU.

The various suspect bits of me were subsequently staked out and measured in an approximation of their original contours; photographed, noted and recorded, converted into slides and dispatched for various tests to find out the extent of their incursion into surrounding areas.

Meanwhile, at home, Simon and the girls and their young men, Eoin, Peter and Mark, played cards and watched the clock while they waited for the call to tell them the operation was over. At around 1 a.m. I was transferred to ICU. Simon and Nessa drove in to see for themselves that I was alive, albeit bruised and iodine-stained, inclined to tug at my drains and try to speak. Even if I had been able to enunciate through the tubes, I wouldn't have made any sense.

The room began to spin, for Nessa, as she took in all the lines and drains that I was hooked up to. She listened to me honk and choke and thought she'd never be able to understand me again.

The keen-eyed nurse distracted her by describing how the last young man she had taken care of had been intubated for three days. She tried to calm his apparent and increasing agitation by giving him a blow-by-blow account of Ireland's progress in the Six Nations rugby tournament.

On the third day his tube was removed. The first words out of his mouth were: 'At last! Get me out of here! That was a nightmare – I can't stand rugby.'

I, on the other hand, am partial to rugby. They knew I was in good hands.

So they went home again, where Simon gave such a realistic impersonation of the sounds my drains made when they were suctioned by the nurse that he caused Emma to faint on the stairs.

What do I remember about my post-op stint in Intensive Care? Euphoria ('I'm alive!') and vomiting, in roughly equal measure. Trying to pull out my drains. Not being able to talk because of the tracheostomy and writing what I needed to say in rough, uneven letters on scraps of paper that I would never see again.

Simon, Jackie, Zita's partner Eoin and the three girls appeared and disappeared. They smiled at me and stroked my matted hair. I drifted in and out of sleep. Whenever I woke up, someone was always holding my hand.

On the way back to the ward, I was wheeled out of the dimly lit unit into a bare white tunnel of light. This was just the corridor leading to the lift, but a joke came to mind – *don't let them wheel me into the light!* I found this hysterically funny, but I couldn't say it. Trapped, the words rolled round my head like marbles in a collection box.

Two tall shadows at the mouth of the tunnel resolved themselves into Emma and Peter, her boyfriend. I choked out my insane punchline about being wheeled into the light, and they were kind enough to act as if they'd heard it and found it funny too.

A bout of vomiting put paid to that little bit of hysteria as we sped along the empty evening corridors, back to the ward.

The first few days passed in a fog of pain and panic, the latter because of discomfort with the tracheostomy and the dryness of my mouth. I was forbidden to drink for at least ten days, to avoid infection and promote healing in my mouth and neck. Even though I was on IV fluids I had a desperate need for water. The loss of salivary glands added to the dryness, as did the morphine. I often woke up fighting for air, begging for water.

Morphine can cause panic as well as dry mouth, and this vicious circle of panic and pain caused trouble for days until we hit the right balance of medication. Things improved when they switched from intravenous morphine to a trans-dermal patch.

After a while I was allowed to swab my mouth with a pink sponge moistened with sterile water. Imagine sucking a piece of styrofoam blended with cotton wool and you're close to the experience. I sometimes cheated, sucking on the sponge and swallowing whatever water my greedy tongue could extract from it. Never much, which was probably just as well, but it gave me an illusion of control at a time when I had control over nothing else. I was still catheterized. I couldn't speak because of the tube in my trachea. I couldn't walk and even if I could, what would I do with the drains that were stapled to my chest, or the intravenous lines in my arm?

I was hooked up to bags of 'feed' as well. They hung in neon green bags from a drip stand beside the bed. The rate of flow was kept low, initially, while I got used to it. It made me burp and feel sick. Sometimes it made me throw up and they turned it off for a while, but I had to learn to tolerate it.

Because I was always in a state of panic and dread when I woke up, I was afraid of going to sleep. I asked Simon to stay on the second and third nights, so that I wouldn't be alone. On the fourth night I sent him home, but asked the nurses (via my notebook) to leave my door open and the lights on.

The thread of my pulse in those early days was fear.

My notebook became my lifeline. I had to write down every request, every question, every anxiety. Before the operation I used to note the date above the entries, but now I started recording the hours and minutes, as if the notebooks formed a rope ladder upon which I could haul myself, rung by rung, out of the pit.

I had a strange lack of understanding of my actual physical condition, of the extent of what had been done to me. Forgetting that I was catheterized, I was afraid that I'd wet the bed. The new configuration of my mouth confused me, painful and swollen as it was. My tongue was heavy and immobile and it burned. I could feel the weight of my new cheek falling inwards and I was afraid that I would bite the graft. I wrote this fear down, showed it to different people. No one thought to remind me, and it was days before I remembered myself, that I had no jaw there any more, no teeth to bite it with.

I wrote a note to Simon: *Did they take out some of my tongue?* He didn't know.

★

Sometimes my voice was so loud in my head that I wasn't sure what I had said and not said. But if no one was looking, I had to wave my arms or bang on the bed to get their attention. Then they waited while I scrawled my need. *Water*, or, *Pls open the window*. Sometimes I thought, *This is too hard, I can't do it*. Giving up and letting go seemed far more attractive than the impossible, hopeless, painful effort to keep going. It would certainly be easier. As I sank further and further, each return to the surface was more weighted with dread, more of a struggle. I lapsed into a state of exhaustion that felt as deep and dark as midnight water. On the third night two faces shone above me like moons, not letting me go. Simon and Dudu, my nurse for the night. I swam towards and away from them. I couldn't decide. *I can't. This is too hard*. But her eyes and Simon's voice held me to the surface, fixed me in place and I stayed.

In a bizarre side-ward in my head, a weird cast of characters came and went, including my own several ghosts. I wasn't sure what their intentions were. I had conversations with the dead, but looked for the living. I exhorted myself the way a PE teacher bullies scores of girls on to a freezing pitch on winter mornings. When I felt most exhausted, least capable of effort, I urged myself to try one small bit harder: to reach the notebook and lift the pen. To push myself a tiny bit more upright, towards sitting. It was a surprise to me, how hard I had to push myself to do the smallest things, like move an arm. Each change hard-won, but worth it.

Being there was like being held underwater. I could see what was going on around me, but my hearing had been affected, maybe by the swelling on that side of my head. I couldn't speak or breathe. I could easily drown.

Later, reading my notebooks, I would be surprised by how 'up' I seemed, by how I lifted myself to the surface for visitors, who cajoled, coaxed and soothed me but could not be down there with me. I begged for news, for stories from the world outside of the one I was trapped in. When they left, I sank back, exhausted.

Sometimes I couldn't wait. I'd drift away. When I came back, I'd find their handwriting in my notebooks: *I had to go; I couldn't wait; I didn't want to disturb you; Goodbye.*

Do what you have to do, I had said to the max-fax team beforehand, and I meant it. When they mentioned the possibility that they might harvest the fibula, I barely heard them. In most of our conversations it was the ulna, a bone in the arm, that was discussed for the graft – hence my arm-strengthening pre-op exercises with the rubber ball. But when I woke up, it was my left leg that was bandaged, strapped to a backslab, heavy and sore. It turned out that when they opened up my face, the extent of the tumour made them remove more bone than they had originally intended. That meant they needed more bone for the graft.

Right around the same time, Simon heard someone say that they had been able to 'save the eye'. He hadn't realized that my eye was under threat. But I had willed the tumour to stay away from there – I thought I could feel it in the upper reaches of the maxilla. And they'd warned us about damage to the facial nerve, which would probably affect the eye as well.

I was relieved that my eye was still there and that I could open and close it at will. I thought about the quest for a clear margin and shrugged off the unexpected damage to my leg. They told me I would be able to walk and drive. I would have full use of it, sooner than I might think. I figured that a scar on my leg would be the least of my problems.

Then I saw it – a deep, purpling mass just above my ankle,

about six inches long and two inches wide, of something raw and not remotely resembling flesh. A thin red line ran above it, almost to my knee; there were two livid squares on the calf, where layers of skin had been peeled off and used to line the inside of my cheek.

'What about the hair?' I asked the plastic surgeon, thinking about the skin of my leg, transplanted to my mouth. It was not a happy thought.

'What about it?'

'Doesn't it grow in there?'

He looked aghast. He shook his head. But once my shocked tongue recovered some degree of mobility and probed the inside of the cheek, I could swear it discovered light, frondlike strands of hair flowing from the new wall of my mouth, like seaweed from a rock at half-tide.

Ryan came in one morning while the dressing on my leg was being changed. He did a double take when he saw the wound.

'Did a shark bite you?'

I relaxed about it, then. He'd given us a way to joke about it. I put less emphasis on its ugliness after that, more on its dramatic potential.

Chapter 3

9 May 2006 (fifth day post-op)
I'm back in my old ward, but in a side room, on my own. It's like I've been through the looking glass. Here, it's the men who shout. The max-fax team have relaxed, as if we've come through a trial together, I have proved myself, we are allies at last. Or am I the one who is more relaxed?

At any rate, my team are friendly and warm. I'm proud of them and they seem pleased with me. The nurses call them the United Nations, because they come from all over the world. This adds to their allure. I'm half in love with all of them.

I'm aware of life going on beyond the hospital, but it seems very far away. David has been discharged from St Vincent's and put on complete bed-rest. They decided not to do an operation in the end. Lucky him. My brother, Joe, was here from England at the weekend, but I was too out of it for visitors. Emma's finals started yesterday. I fret about this. I feel as if I've sabotaged her chances of doing well.

My body feels carved up, bruised and stained. I lust for basic things, like air and water. To see the sky.

When I cough, gloop comes out of my throat. I have mild hallucinations: in a wide, warm, wood-panelled room people bend over me to see if I'm okay, but when I open my eyes there's no one there.

The phlebotomist says, 'Your poor old veins, they're worn out. We're at them all the time.' She touches my disgusting hair and tells me I'm great.

There are staples and stitches on my chin and neck and on my chest. Two tubes emerge into circular plastic drains full of serous fluid. Another one connects my stomach to a lurid green bag on a drip stand. I wear pounds of soggy bandages. I mishear what people say to me:

'Did you say "rip"?' I write, to a nurse. 'As in "rip" out the catheter???'

(No, that's not what she said.)

The young Polish woman who cleans the ward comes in to wash the floor.

'Oh Lady!' Her voice is sorrowful when she sees the new me.

For once, she doesn't complain while her mop circles under my bed, behind the locker.

Seagulls fly low outside the window, as if lost. I don't blame them. These buildings are armed like starfish. They look like steel containers. It could be a deepwater harbour.

Sinéad, the head-and-neck nurse, drops in. It feels like a social call, I'm so glad to see her. She asks if I worry about how I look. I tell her (in writing) that I do sometimes, but I care more about how I feel and what I can do.

'I can always live at home in the dark,' I write.

'It doesn't look so bad,' she says.

I write that it feels gross and spongy, not like a face at all. That I'm frustrated by being so weak. I tell her that I don't know if I'd have done it, if I'd known how bad the immediate post-operative period was going to be. But I'm glad I did do it, now.

She asks if I had enough information before going into surgery.

'They explained it all. But information is one thing. How it feels is something else.'

74

I can't describe how it felt. It's as if I dropped the thread that was leading me through the labyrinth and couldn't find it in the dark.

A doctor takes out his phone and uses it as a torch to see inside my mouth. This makes me laugh. I can't wait to tell Simon. We've used our phones to text people across the city and on several continents about what's happening to me, to send and receive pleas for help and messages of support, to store information and jokes, but this raises their potential to a new level.

10 May 2006

2.35 a.m. I feel more dead than alive. I have a shocking sense that this is how things could end: hot, dishevelled and sweaty in a hospital bed.

I am heavy, muzzy and isolated. My sight is fuzzy. Breathing is an effort. I am deaf. My skin feels repulsive and alien, not mine at all.

And yet, I'm so much better off than other people are. How long would I have lasted without surgery? Do I even have the nerve to ask?

Tomorrow it all starts again for someone else. They could be prancing up and down the corridor outside this room right now, for all I know. Just like I did. I had such arrogant health, and didn't even know it. What would I say to them if I had the chance? Good luck? Fight hard? You'll get there?

Six days ago, five, I'd have said, 'Don't bother.'

8.30 a.m. Small red worms of phlegm come out of my throat when I cough – all those nice suits could be destroyed when the teams come in. Professor Stassen is so like my brother-in-law that it's absurd, as if David is actually here, when in fact he's on complete bed-rest, at home. The resemblance is comforting and unsettling all at once. It makes me cheekier than I might be otherwise.

Today's revitalization programme: try to sit up. Read a bit. Start up your phone. Get into Sudoku.

They all think I'll be traumatized by my appearance, and they tell me it's not as bad as I imagine. I haven't thought about it as much as they think I have. Just as well I've grown my hair. I've been considering adopting a Speranza-like approach to the whole business. One hundred and thirty years or so ago, Speranza – Lady Wilde, Oscar's mother – used to hold literary salons with the curtains drawn, veiled lamps in strategic corners.

Another thing they are fond of saying is that I must be sick of writing everything down. How little they know about me.

Simon and the girls have started to decorate my room. They have made a collage of photos of the flowers that people have sent, which I'm not allowed to have in here, and of the ones that Simon is growing out on the deck, at home. They add photos of all of us, including the cat (Lizzie), the dog (Oz) and of the view from our bedroom window. They put up all the cards. Three walls blossom with these images. Now, when medical people come in, they stop to look at this picture or that, ask who the people are, make comments on the photos. The room is a friendly, colourful place.

A doctor comes in and changes the tracheostomy tube. If I cover the hole in the tube with my finger, I'm able to speak. My voice comes out abrupt and startled. I have to practise this.

They switch the oxygen off and take my notebook away. They say I don't need it now.

I take it back as soon as they've gone.

I still have hallucinations of touch – my hair is brushed back from my face, fingers probe my jaw. There are whispering sands in my ear.

In the opposite wing of the building, I can see the flickering images of a TV. Someone must be watching it all night. I like this distant flicker. It's company.

11 May 2006

Waking up is different here. A wash of vivid orange rises behind my eyes like a sunrise and then I'm awake, but not fully.

I'm afraid that I'm turning into a tyrant, handing dirty tissues to my own children to dispose of, inviting them to help me to the commode. I have such limited stories to tell – this leak, that delay.

We'll get the pathology results on the tissue samples they took after surgery in ten to fifteen days.

I wonder why the potassium I have to take is such a lurid shade of pink. When I ask why I have to take it, I'm told it's to do with muscle connectivity in my heart. You get arrhythmia if the level is too low or too high. I make a note so I can tell Simon when he comes in. He might be interested. It has to be better than the ninety-ninth story of how my PEG leaked.

I ask Nessa to buy me a mirror in the hospital pharmacy. It's been a week, and I haven't been curious about how I look, but now I want to see for myself. Whatever my face is like now, I know it will change as the swelling goes down. I want to see it so that I'll have a baseline to compare it with later.

Nessa comes back with one of those pocket-mirrors with a lid, the only one they had. I can only see bits of me, in stages. It's probably just as well. I take a quick look, clock the staples, the stitches, a deep gouge where my cheek used to be, a massively swollen and distended chin. Like Desperate Dan in the *Beano*, with stitches for bristles.

Okay, I think. Okay. I've seen it now.

I close the mirror and put it away.

Then I try to brush my hair. My fingers come across a wodge of something disgusting on the right side of my head. Revolting to touch.

I prod it, wary. 'What is it?' I ask Nessa.

'What's what?'

'Here . . . There's a clump of tissue, or skin or something rolled up here. I think it's pinned to my head . . . Is it a clump of hair? We could cut it . . .'

She has a look. 'Oh, Momma,' she says. 'That's your ear.'

I have to write 'tell me about *you*', over and over. People are reluctant to talk to me about themselves and what's going on in their lives. I wonder, are they afraid to tell me good things in case it makes me feel my own situation more acutely? Do they bite their tongue on whatever irritates them because it might seem trivial? I want *news*.

12 May 2006

Morning cocktails have arrived. Prune-coloured iron, a white and a citrus antibiotic, sticky orange Calpol and cherry-coloured, fizzy potassium. They get mixed up in a glass until they turn sludgy and brown, then injected into my stomach through the PEG tube. I get anti-emetics when I ask for them, still wear the morphine patches. God only knows what my real mood is. I forget ideas as fast as they come into my head.

We are all melting. It's going to be a hot day.

2.30 p.m. Textured white, green and yellow dozes. Running passage of grains of light. Someone sighs in my ear, draws her finger along my jawline.

I wake up as a physiotherapist bustles in and find a message from Simon. 'I love you', in red ink on my hand.

The physiotherapist says that it's time to try walking.

I ask for the commode first. A nurse suggests I might try going to the bathroom instead. She says to wait, she'll cover the mirror for me. I tell her not to worry, I've already seen my face.

They are helping me to the bathroom when a woman wanders in to ask where the ward fridge is. She hovers at the door as if she has every right to be there while I shuffle past her on my one good leg, supported at each shoulder. The nurse steers me to the loo and goes off to look after your woman.

The joy of running water to wash my hands! I swear I will never take water for granted again.

When I straighten at the sink, my whole face rears up in the mirror in front of me. It is stitched and stapled, and a prominent column of stapled flesh is raised along the length of my neck. I look like my mad grandmother. I've never seen this resemblance before. It's as if I was handed from one side of the family to the other while I was asleep.

The younger nurses are at the desk, smiling, when I come inching out of the room on a zimmer frame, a plastic drain clipped to each pocket of my striped dressing gown. There are people on the corridor but they move out of the way, faces averted. Dudu appears and I give her a hug – and then I have to turn back. I'm wrecked. It's been ten minutes or less. I covered about ten yards and my blood pressure is up.

They come and remove some of the stitches from the incision wounds. I can't wait until those drains are gone.

4.30 p.m. A nurse comes in to give me my meds. She's in a hurry. I feel nauseated already from the feed and when this mixture hits my stomach I throw up, violently. Crud every-where, around the incision and on the skin of my neck and chest.

A lot of the time I'm not even thinking. I just lie here and breathe while bells ring, fans whirr and heavy doors are swung shut and locked for the night. There's a whispering voice in my ear, like a radio left on, white noise. My ear still has this thing of not belonging to me, but it throbs all the same. My throat hurts. It's lucky that one of the nurses warned me that it would feel like having a hot spud in my mouth. It helps to know that this is normal. But I worry about my tongue. It burns, as if flayed. As if it could be swallowed.

Have I really let myself think about the nature of what's happened to me? It happened so fast. A little girl stared after me, earlier, when we passed her in the corridor. A thing I will have to get used to. I wonder what they did with the tumour. I wonder if I could see it. I've asked to see the scans as well. I'll ask again.

13 May 2006

2.50 a.m. I can't sleep. One of the nurses perches on the zimmer frame to chat about my new feeding regime. They want to stop the continuous feed and replace it with controlled amounts, given at intervals. They'll increase the amount of feed I take and the length of time between feeds gradually, until I reach a point that approximates normal intervals between meals.

He says that I'll have more physical independence when I'm disconnected from the PEG for a few hours at a time.

'Don't go too far at first,' he warns.

I think of my face and know that I won't.

The wing opposite is closed for the weekend and makes a dark and lonely barrier between us and the city. When we look, a light appears and we cheer, thinking that someone has found a way in and colonized a room, but no, it's the reflection of my lit window. We wave at our projections.

Vanity is a funny thing. You can be realistic about your looks and still care about things like hair, or a specific style of clothes. You might get a shock when you see yourself in photographs (just as you can hear a recording of your voice and think: *I don't sound like that!*) The greying, bulking figure that peers back from the mirror bears no resemblance to the sharp eyed, fiery being who looks out. But you can still feel a definite liking for the oddest things, like the curve of an arm, or the sensation of a particular fabric against your skin, or the shape of your legs in certain shoes. In my case, it's not that there's particularly much of a face to guard, but that it has to be so particularly guarded, now.

I've worn my hair short for years but now I'll have to count on it to shield my scars. It grows fast and thick, but recently it falls out in clumps at the sight of a brush. It is ten days since it was washed, ten days since the operation, and it still rains a black soot of dried blood.

★

5.34 a.m. The birds have started their curling, morning flight. They settle on uninhabited eaves but I can't hear them. Today it is a full calendar month since I walked in here with my purple backpack, apologizing to Jackie for wasting her time, saying that she could still make it to her Italian class, and that I'd find my own way home . . . Emma teases me about what I said to her that morning when she left for college: 'There's a slim chance I won't be back tonight. Could you make sure the dog has enough water?'

6.30 a.m. A roaring begins outside on the corridor. The man who looks as if he's escaped from the Old Testament, like a preacher on the run, is chucking chairs around. Hello, day. They'll be in to me next.

Simon arrives with a paper and we have 'breakfast'. He drinks coffee, I suck illicit drops of water from my pink sponge-on-a-stick. We go for a short walk along the corridor, make it about twenty slow yards before I have to turn back.

My team arrives, to remove the tracheostomy tube. As they pull the tube out, there is that sense of choking pressure that I hate. I cough and a clot flies across the room and sticks to the wall. It misses the Get Well cards by inches.

'Good shot!' they say, admiring.

I've a strange wheeze when the tube has gone. They warn me to hold gauze to the wound when I cough – which I do, quite a lot. I've only one drain left now, plus the PEG.

The new feed regime turns out to be a bit of a circus but we get through it. There is an endless round of exercises, mouthwash, cleaning, feeding, etc. Time flies.

The preacher comes in to the room while I'm dozing. He's after my zimmer frame.

'It's mine,' I tell him, feeling like a kid in a playground. 'You can't have it.'

His mild expression doesn't change. His attendant leads him out again.

Later, the incision wound under my chin opens – like a zip, Simon says. I don't feel it, but I see horror in the faces around me as it happens.

14 May 2006

3.30 a.m. I'm still coughing up all kinds of interesting phlegm, but into my mouth, rather than the tube. This is progress, of a kind. I'm wary of the stitches at the incision site, of a certain leaking air effect from the hole where the tracheostomy tube was, and of ongoing ooze from this wound or that. No one here seems to mind what emanates from where. 'Oh, that's normal,' they say.

Even the student nurses are blithe as they tease sodden masses of gunky, snot-coloured gauze away from the edges of my wounds. No one wrinkles so much as a nostril. Chunks of comfy, fresh bandage are cheerfully cut to cover the worst of the damage. Given time and sterile water, a student can unpick the bits that are stuck to my skin, thread by thread, and barely cause a wince. These people are miraculous.

My every lying-down has a sense of fatefulness, a mortal expectation. While I sleep, it's as if my body believes that I'm destined for something significant, like a transfer to another ward, or theatre, or to a terminus. Waking, I'm stunned to find it isn't so.

I'm more awake than I have been for a while. All of a sudden I want to know everything. I want lists and diagrams – of the changes they've made to my body, and the plan from now on. Did they keep any of the tumour? Where is it now? How much bone, how many teeth, what else did I lose?

5.08 a.m. I wake, splayed, in the same position I went to sleep in. This is how I sleep now – beached. Someone is crying out there, hard and fast, as if she's given up the long struggle to hold it in. Ghost hands fix the oxygen tube at my neck, the one that's not there any more. Friend or foe? There's an engine room running in my ear, but it is comfortable not to move; to allow tiredness to overtake me. I give in to it, let go and float in a gorgeous daze . . . but I wake up anxious . . . is someone I love leaving the room because I wouldn't look at them?

We walk to a window that looks out on to another wing of the hospital and see three floors of women in purple uniforms, one above another, each standing at a sink, preparing to co-ordinate lunch. I think of that scene in *Edward Scissorhands*, where all the suburban cars reverse out of their drives at the same time.

There are family dynasties working in this hospital, along-side migrants from Eastern Europe, Russia, the Philippines, India, Pakistan, Africa. It's like a microcosm of what's happening throughout the country, without any fuss.

The preacher is less amusing when he storms in and uses my toilet to crap in.

In an act of pure kindness, one of the nurses brings me down to the big bathroom and we wash my hair, giggling like runaway schoolkids. We tape a large green incontinence pad around my neck, plonk a towel in my lap. I peel off my pyjama top, clutch wads of coarse paper tissues to my eyes.

The water runs black and sludgy grey. It must be disgusting, but she takes her time. My drains and dressings survive unscathed.

Look at all the paper that I use up, the latex gloves and gauze. In other parts of the world you wouldn't get so much as a sterile needle. And there's no recycling that I can see, except for newspapers.

My new, ropey columns of swollen flesh squelch and squeak when pressed. There's a small pocket of infection in the incision wound, a sinus. My team frown when they look at it, say they'll keep an eye on it. I hope to God that it won't turn into a major setback.

15 May 2006

3.25 a.m. I have a lot to think about. For a start, there are the possible complications due to the sinus that has opened under my chin; my uncertain future; my ruined face, which won't move properly again. No matter how hard I try, one side will have no expression. The nerves have been cut. Ryan has already imitated my drawn-up mouth, my new lisp. The girls froze when he did it, but I laughed it off. There's no point in being precious.

Then there's the very fact of my illness. The sorry state that I'm in now has been brought about in a bid to 'cure' me of this enormous, virulent creature, my tumour. It would be easy to forget how menacing the crab really was, given that I didn't know that I was ill until they told me so. But it's a fight to the literal death for one of us. This fucker emerged from the depths with me as its target, moved stealthily and fast, rooted itself deep and spread as wide as it could. I'm lucky to have found my way to people who are brave and ruthless and brilliant enough to root it out.

I wonder if I'll need radiotherapy and to what extent it will be my decision. It all depends on the pathology results. Radiotherapy uses lethal doses of radiation to destroy tumour cells but has a terrible effect on healthy tissue too.

When people talk about my face, I don't want to hear their reassurances, their 'barely noticeable's. I've seen it. I know what it looks like. And I know something they don't: the effort speaking takes, how words are like rocks in my mouth, harder to shift as I get tired. But I can't really think about it when there are more urgent questions, like survival, to deal with.

My team come in and check the incision. They tell me that there are now two sinuses there. They might have to go in and fix it. When they say 'infection', I want to weep.

The plastic surgeon is more optimistic about the neck wound when he comes. Put in plugs of dressing and change them often, is his advice. No need to panic. The pain team come around, a couple of anaesthetists and an anaesthetic nurse. Their voices are pleasant and have a narcotic effect all by themselves. They could bottle them and make a fortune. They say they'll get things sorted out. I hope so. Pain makes me tetchy, vulnerable and paranoid. I don't think anyone believes how bad it is.

More of the staples are taken out. I save them in a sample jar, for Ryan. They look just like regular staples you'd use on paper.

Nessa stops in after her exam. She's free now for the summer.

She asks about my sister Lyn, who she never met. I tell her the stock family stories. When Lyn was three, she was pretending to smoke. Being naturally fastidious, she used a hairclip as a cigarette holder and blew out for all she was worth. Advised to suck the imaginary smoke in, she inhaled the clip by mistake. She had to have it surgically removed.

That wasn't her only childhood emergency. Another time, a circus came to town. The star attraction was a 'human cannonball'. Our family was there to see it, sitting in a leggy row, breathless with excitement, fingers sticky from candy floss. The fuse was lit, the man erupted from the cannon and flew across the Big Top to land in the safety net . . . at which point one of the posts which anchored the net to the ground came loose and flew up into the air. A dislodged bolt struck Lyn on the head. The drama! The fuss! Off with her to hospital in an ambulance, lights flashing.

She was a little accident-prone, our Lyn. She was also one of the most loving people I've ever known. I miss her still.

I'm crying a little when I finish talking. Nessa is alarmed, but I tell her I don't mind crying about Lyn, she deserves to be cried for.

9.45 p.m. I talk to one of the nurses tonight about her child, left behind on another continent. Her sadness is something hard and bright. She tells me not to 'put up with' pain. She tells me I should ask for the maximum dose of everything, take anything that's going. She says the wound looks better than it did this morning. The drain is almost empty, which means that it can come out soon.

Simon has to go back to work, in London. He's leaving on an early morning flight tomorrow. I won't see him again until Thursday.

16 May 2006

6.30 a.m. I wake up and Nessa is brightening the room. Every morning feels like a gift, a bonus. Seagulls are calling through

87

the open window. The sun is in the sky, with clouds so light they are barely there.

My team say the wound is better this morning, but it will take time to heal completely. Everything else looks fine. They might take out some more staples today.

I think someone is using my loo. Maybe I'm imagining it. Sometimes people come in and use my bin, or the hand-disinfectant, because I'm so close to the nurses' station. I have to remind myself that this is a public space, I just happen to be in a part of it.

I take another walk on the zimmer, by myself. It's safe enough to exercise my deformities here, on the ward. I pass the preacher on the corridor.

'I'm doing my best,' he tells me.

'That's all we can do,' I say.

He puts his hands up, palms wide, and shakes them.

Maybe tomorrow I'll venture down to the lobby – but not alone. Not yet.

6.57 p.m. I get a text message from Zita. It's taken them three hours to get home after their visit, the curse of the M50. I tell her not to come again unless by helicopter. I'll meet her on the roof and let her in.

There's a line of pain that slides along under my jaw, like a pickpocket looking for a place to scoop something out of. My throat stings and my tongue burns. The elephant-skin of my ear feels rubbery and alien. There is a constant noise, like currents of air or water going past me. The missing glands feel squeezed. Phantom pain.

Pain in the face.

17 May 2006

4.37 a.m. Everything is quiet. The lovely student nurse gives me a painkiller. I'll try to sit out the burning of my tongue, which no painkiller seems to touch.

I wonder where the tumour is now, and in what condition. I wonder if it has left sleeper cells inside me and if so, where? But if it survives and spreads and I die, what happens to it then? It seems to me that cancer is a bit like a suicide bomber. It may be going down, but it'll take me with it if it can.

Well, *that* feeling is mutual.

One of the many things that surprise me is how completely I handed myself over to people I didn't even know. I walked in here with a sore growth in my mouth, a little scared, tired, but otherwise me – and little by little I have been surgically transformed into something else, all tubes and drains and missing bone, and I still don't know the names of many of the people who see me for one reason or another. There are so many people on different teams: maxillo-facial surgeons, plastic surgeons, radiation oncologists, pain specialists, dietician, speech and language therapist, psycho-oncology people, tracheostomy care . . . I'm lucky I have Sinéad, the head-and-neck nurse, to help me make sense of it all.

7.36 a.m. I go for a walk up and down the corridor, sit and look out the window for a while at what's left of Fatima Mansions, the demolition work. On the way back I pass a group of large, stunned-looking people who troop in to the desk and stand around, waiting for news. At least two of them smell strongly of drink. More trouble for someone.

We inch past them, me and my zimmer frame. I have to laugh when I think back on my enthusiasm on my ward mate's behalf, the morning of my operation, not dreaming for a second that I would need one too. I watch the floor as I go, glad of the solidity of the zimmer, its broad base, firm handle, the way it gives me permission to take my time and the *huge* freedom of being able to go to the loo without having to wait for help.

About the fact that they harvested a bone from my leg instead of my arm: Zita points out that no one could have held my hand after the operation if they'd gone for the arm. Also that I'll be able to get back to work sooner.

Clare Boylan died yesterday. We'd all known she'd been ill, we'd been asking each other for news, and here it is. I'll miss her smile and her boldness. I'll never understand why her novel *Holy Pictures* has been so underrated. I remember the sheer exhilaration of reading it, when it first came out. Someone who could make us laugh at ourselves, at last.

18 May 2006

Two weeks since the operation.

I wake up with two sore legs. I make myself go for a walk on the zimmer and in minutes the soreness has gone.

Another lesson learned. Keep walking. They've given me a walking stick but I'm not allowed to use it on my own yet.

There's a smell of shit on the ward. I hope it's not me.

It's a gorgeous day – I've clambered around a bit to sit in the big chair beside the window and feel the sun beating on the glass, stirring us all up.

I go down to Outpatients to get my neck checked. There is a new sinus, with bone exposed, behind my ear. I have three sites of infection in the neck wound now. They dress it and warn me to be careful. The threat of MRSA hangs over all of us.

I'm back in my room, sitting on my bed, when a nun comes in. 'I see you're fasting, I can't give you Holy Communion.'

I tell her that I'm not fasting and I don't want it.

She frowns at my scars. 'That looks severe enough. Well, the Lord bless you.' And she's gone. But I'm the one who feels dismissed.

I can't help wondering about MRSA and these women who go from bed to bed administering Communion. I know it means a lot to the people who want it – but shouldn't the nuns wash their hands between patients too?

When I flush the loo, I feel a sympathetic gurgle in my own neck. My body is developing a weird affinity for this building.

19 May 2006

5.27 a.m. It's a damp, grey-green morning. In the near court-yard the young trees pull in their leaves and shiver. There is a sculpture of a female figure there. Zita derides this figure, says she looks as if her head is wrapped in a towel. To me, today, she looks as if someone has 'just gone to get something', and left her there. Ha! She could be waiting hours and the rain is only beginning.

A physiotherapist comes and gives me a pair of crutches to walk with. When we go for a walk to try them out, Emma mentions, in passing, that my leg is broken. I'm startled. *She's right, it is!* There's half a bone missing. The leg is sore today. I hope it's mending right.

A psychiatrist comes in to say hello. The psychiatric nurse

beams from one of us to the other, as if he's finally managed to get us together at a party. I can think of no questions or worries when she enquires, but I do love her smart little black-and-white check suit.

The truth is, I don't know how I feel. I'm putting myself back together, one piece at a time.

The swelling is going down and I'm losing weight, so my face is thinner. Everyone says how well I look and it makes me feel cold. I think I look awful. But I do know it hasn't finished changing yet. I'm aware of how they might feel, watching me inch along on a stick. I've felt that grief too, for a living person who has been irrevocably changed.

8.50 a.m. The max-fax team are here. I ask them about the soreness and weakness of my shoulder. They say it's due to nerve damage during surgery and will be long term.

'Will it get better?'

'No. In fact, it might get worse – and then recover a little.'

I'm beginning to think that they deliver small doses of information as and when they think you're able to tolerate it. What more is to come?

The intern comes back to talk about my shoulder. He says the damage is to the spinal accessory nerve – and that it's too early to be so pessimistic. About the wound at my neck he says that the sinuses will delay the start of radiotherapy – we'll have to wait until they have closed. The incision site won't look as good as they had hoped it would. The situation is not great, but I feel better when he's gone.

He leaves me a roll of tape for the dressing, along with the strong-smelling Whitehead's varnish that they use on the wound. If I keep supplies in my room, they won't have to gather everything each time they come. Tape is a valued commodity on a ward, people are always borrowing each other's rolls and not returning them; it's worse than Biros, or Sellotape on Christmas Eve.

One of the nurses comes and takes the tape away.

'Bring it back when you've finished with it,' I say.

I can't read her look. 'I don't see your name on it,' she says and off she goes.

Simon is beginning to talk about going back to work full-time. I know he needs to go. I can't imagine what it will be like when he does.

20 May 2006

6.30 a.m. Small doze, deliciously comfortable. For the first time post-op, I'm not fully on my back – I'm favouring my left side, bent into some lucky air hollow. The ear that hears is turned into the pillow so there's a cushioned silence. I float in this narcotic daze – so much luckier than someone on a doorstep in the damp of a slow Dublin dawn.

Out on the ward, a man is shouting, 'The last is done now!' as if it's time for us to leave, or he wants someone to come and inspect his work. I've heard him call out before. The name he calls is his daughter's. She never comes. His accent is broad Dublin with maybe a tooth missing. He sounds cheerful, but there's an undertone that comes from knowing that no one will pay attention.

His tone becomes more urgent, hoarse: 'Oh, oh, maybe it's a bedpan situation!' He's in full voice today, speaking in complete sentences.

My brain curves down, but the shouting man is loud and agitated. I may as well go for a walk on the crutches, wake up the leg. I can sleep later.

'Are yez still in the bed?' he calls, as I go past. 'Hold her up! Would you hold her up, please?'

'Be quiet!' someone shouts back.

'I want to go home,' he says.

Don't we all?

8 a.m. Washing myself, I wail into the soapsuds because of the pain and restricted movement in my shoulder. Even the smallest things make me want to howl with frustration. I change into clean pyjamas with such effort and then someone gives me meds and spills sticky goo all over me and I have to start again. My shoulder throbbing.

My young cleaner is on her holidays. The people who come to clean my floor don't talk to me. I hear anonymous rustlings and the metallic bang of the bin lid when they change the lining, but that's it. No sighs or sad looks. I know she's moody, but I miss her.

The physio swaps the crutches for a walking stick. It's less awkward to use.

Out on a walk, I come across a woman who makes a bid for freedom.

'Get away!' she bats the nurse's hands. 'Leave me alone!'

She makes a run for it, screaming. Her footsteps get caught up in the sound of a gaggle of children in communion suits who appear around the corner, as if her footsteps have turned into theirs and she has come back, younger, plural, scrubbed and hopeful-looking.

I concentrate on walking along these long, empty corridors on one stick, building up strength. I listen to the sound of my heart washing past my ears, the sound of the sea. It's like being in a diving bell, an aqualung, the amplified sound of breath.

★

Today is the day of the Heineken Cup final. Munster are playing Biarritz, in Cardiff. The little family come to watch the match with us in my room. Another visitor comes and suddenly there's too much going on, between the chat and the game. I go for a walk with my visitor, venture into corridors where I haven't been before. I'm learning new parts of this hospital every day. Getting braver.

We get back just in time to see Munster win.

21 May 2006

I dream about wind. The colour blue. I wake to a cold wash of rain on the broken wing of the building opposite.

'Hold me!' is the shouting man's latest mantra. 'Hold me, please.'

I can't listen to this, so I walk some more around the quiet upper corridors of the hospital.

One day, shortly before my godfather died, I was adjusting pillows at his back when he groaned and leaned into my hands. I began to rub the grooves beside his spine, the wings of his shoulder blades. He closed his eyes and relaxed, more at peace than I had seen him for days. It made me think about lonely older people I have known. How touch-deprived they might be.

A haughty woman with a pointed chin sits on the big chair outside her ward. She gives me the evil eye as I pass. She glares at my face. I say hello and she says hello back, but when I've passed her a stream of invective follows me, directed at my deaf ear.

If this was a medieval village, I'd be seen as having the mark of the devil. I'd be run out of it.

★

When people come in for the first time they look wary, not knowing what to expect.

A friend says the most gorgeous thing. 'But, you look beautiful!'

I know it's weird, but I can see that she means it.

'I never noticed your eyes before,' she says.

They feel huge, I strain so hard to reach people through them.

People have sent me angels made of silver paper; they spill out of cards when I open them. Some fall on the floor and get mopped around, so that every day they appear in a different part of the room. They progress through the door and down the corridors, but I still see them, in different places every day. No one else seems to notice. Maybe no one else can see them? I don't ask. I find them comforting. I like the fact that they move around, appear and disappear.

22 May 2006

6.05 a.m. When I was doing the mouthwash routine just now, I did a near-normal spit for the first time since the operation. Almost at once, I was seized by the desire for a good solid yawn and came up against my limitations straight away. My mouth won't open wide enough. An advance, then an immediate setback.

10 a.m. We find a wheelchair stashed in a back stairwell. Simon and Nessa take me for a 'walk'. We go in to the chemist's for nail varnish and spend a fortune. Then we go to the café. It's my first time in a quasi-public environment in a wheelchair. It's not easy to get around, even though this is a hospital. Some people move out of your way and others

don't. People avoid looking at you. We park at a small table overlooking the lobby. The noise-level is a problem. I can't hear Simon and Nessa, keep having to ask them to repeat themselves.

We look at photos on the camera. I'm shocked by my appearance. I look stunted, crooked, drawn. We come back along a first-floor corridor that has a collection of paintings and prints on the walls. We find work by friends of mine and people I have worked with. I'm glad we've found them. When I get braver on my feet this is where I'll come to spend some time.

The bossy physio takes me out to the stairs and shows me how to use them, one hand on the stick, one hand on the bannister. I've to take each step like a child, bringing one foot to join the other before I go on to the next one.

When I've got the hang of it and we're back in my room the physio talks to Simon instead of me. He mentions starting to walk without a stick, he thinks I should be doing it by now. Stung, I say that I already move around my room and the bathroom without it, because I have things to hold onto.

'I can stand on my own,' I say and stand up to show him, but he's already turned his back. Still talking to Simon, he goes out.

When one of the team comes to change the dressing, he lets me use a mirror and I see the infected incision wound for the first time. It extends from the midline out behind my ear, with three pockets of infection. The wound is very ugly. It yawns and weeps pus and hurts like hell. The bone behind my ear is exposed.

He says it will take at least three weeks to heal. If the infection finds a track into the graft in my mouth and it breaks down it will have to be done again, using skin from my chest this time. Worse, it will delay radiotherapy, giving crab remnants a chance to scatter and take root.

A new nurse asks what kind of day I had and how I feel about everything. So I tell her about the shoulder. My voice cracks. I'm thinking about work.

'And they just dropped this on you, did they?' she says, in the voice of one who knows.

'Pretty much.'

She nods. No exaggerated sympathy, but recognition all the same.

The other day, a different nurse gave me a shoulder to cry on and a warm look. This sort of thing keeps me going. They say I can ask for the psych team, but I don't think I need them. I don't know what I'd say. The pleasant psychiatric nurse looks in from time to time, calls me Mrs Mills. Mrs Mills is someone I've never met but know by reputation. She is a stout, full-bosomed tweedy woman who used to sing on *Songs of Praise* when I was a child and there were fewer channels to choose from and my mother had charge of the remote control.

I think I'll wait until I get home to find someone to talk to.

23 May 2006

3.27 a.m. The silver angels are still here. They look clean and cheerful, blowing their little trumpets in different directions around the floor.

5.30 a.m. I wake up in pain, fighting for breath. My eye goes out of focus. I go for a walk through the stirring, waking ward. Two African men, ward attendants, stand guard at the preacher's door.

When I get back, I do my morning wash.

Here I am, one leg carved up to look like a shark bite, a plastic tube coming out of my stomach, staple scars on my neck and chest, a dressing like a beard on my chin, half my face caved in, blood caked in my hair . . . and what do I do? I paint my toenails blue and shave my legs.

Nessa finds a bockety wheelchair out on the back staircase. She wheels me down to the max-fax clinic.

On the way back up to the ward we stop in a quiet waiting area, and I look through my chart. Passing doctors and nurses seem to stare and I feel furtive and underhand, as if I'm doing something I shouldn't do. So I stop. Eejit.

Back in the room, the radiation oncology team are waiting, including the consultant, Professor Hollywood. One of them takes my chart away.

They tell me that cancer cells were found in eleven out of the forty-nine lymph nodes removed during surgery. They say I will definitely need radiotherapy now, but it will be delayed because of the infected wound. Handshakes all round and they make off with the chart.

Before the operation we knew about that one enlarged node, beside my ear. The scans suggested the cancer might have spread there. But I'd no idea so many others were involved. If it had spread so far, could it be anywhere else?

I'd love some time to absorb the news about the lymph nodes, but a lot of people are due to come in and see me today.

After Nessa goes I have a small hissy-fit while I struggle with the intricacies of feeding myself.

The feed is a beige liquid with a consistency on the watery

side of paint. It has a smell that's hard to describe, but there's dust in there somewhere, with the kind of cloying overlay that you know is designed to cover something nasty. I've written step-by-step instructions for myself so that I won't forget something crucial:

1. Load 50 cc syringe with sterile water
2. Clean cap of tube with sterile wipe
3. Clamp tube (so stomach contents don't flood out)
4. Open cap & attach syringe loaded with sterile water
5. Open clamp
6. Inject water (to 'flush' tube)
7. Close clamp, load syringe with feed
8. Open clamp and inject that
9. Close clamp
10. Reload syringe
11. Go again until the right amount has been injected.
12. Flush again
13. Close cap
14. Clean up

I take 250 mls of feed (five syringe-loads) six times a day. We're building up to 300 mls five times a day, at which point I'll be getting close to normal meal intervals. I'm awkward because of the arm that has no power in it. I'm still getting confused, or missing a stage. Plus, my clamp never seems to work properly and there's always backwash of one kind or another. Cleaning up takes nearly as long as everything else put together.

When I'm finished, the nurses come around with meds. By now, I give these to myself as well. Capsules are broken open into liquids and they are all mixed-up together but their consistencies vary. The one I hate most is the iron I have to take to build up my haemoglobin levels after surgery. It is a foul-smelling, sludgy substance the colour of rust. It clings to everything it touches.

I've noticed a strange cycle in myself. I start out by wanting to be taken care of, and that leads to a kind of sullenness. I sulk, then realize *I'll* have to do whatever it is, like feeding myself. So then I do the thing in a slow fury. But once I've done it I feel better, more competent and ready for the next challenge. This is my own small, intensely personal war: independence versus dependence.

In the afternoon, a friend brings in tidbits, including the Dublin Writers' Festival Programme. I'm not in it, now, since I had to cancel my gig. I try not to sulk about this, not to hate my replacement, although I'd be open to hearing adverse opinion if there's any going.

There's no way I could have done it. Look at the state of me, I can't even talk properly yet. Small shivers of lightning flash down my lip and chin. There's thunder in my ears. I am a weathervane.

I wonder if radiotherapy is really necessary. I talk to the nurses about it. One of them says she'd go for everything they offer. Another says she'd go along with anything Professor Hollywood says. They both think he's the business.

I pout at the prospect of more surgery to repair the graft, more scarring – to be followed by the systematic destruction of my mouth, saliva and senses of taste and smell through radiation. But the nurses coax me along. They say, 'You've come through so much already,' and 'You're doing so well.'

24 May 2006

6.56 a.m. I've discovered that I'd rather be awake than asleep. I rush towards wakefulness like someone underwater heading for the surface. My relationship with air has changed – I love it, now. The first thing I do when I wake up is struggle across the room to open the window and feel it wash through me. It tells me that I'm alive.

It's our twenty-sixth wedding anniversary.

Last night I asked for pain meds and a nurse said, 'They're on their way around.' I was dazed by the time they arrived, two and a half hours later.

This morning, a different nurse explains that the extra medication is supposed to be given to me on demand. 'You should get it when you ask for it, it's separate from the med rounds,' she says.

She helps me with the OxyNorm, a synthetic opiate I'm given as a supplement to the morphine. It's such a tiny (2 cc), sticky dose, it's hard to manage with my temperamental clamp.

A doctor comes in. 'Do you not do this for yourself yet?' he booms. 'You need to develop your confidence!'

Even the nurse stiffens. 'She's great,' she says. 'She does everything – it's just this little dose of OxyNorm.'

He doesn't even hear her, with his easy smile and his fresh suit.

After they've gone I feed myself. I have a spill during the clean-up and have to change pyjamas. My shoulder aches and drags. I cry involuntary tears but keep going, feeling thoroughly sorry for myself. I'm just back in bed when another nurse brings in the iron and the soluble Panadol and I have to get up and start all over again.

It's like the breakdown of personality through pain. You become childlike. You wail, and then you drag yourself together to clean up, clear away, carry on – and soon enough you slip back into the shadow and the form of yourself and hope the rest will return later, when the coast is clear.

8.30 a.m. I ask my team if I can go home for a few hours at the weekend. They say no, because of the infection. They say I might need an operation to insert a muscle plug in the wound. They are getting blood ready 'just in case'.

I ask about the 'eleven out of forty-nine' result, what it means. They look at each other. Consternation. It's the first they've heard of it. They hunt through the notes and find the report. The result won't change the treatment plan, but my classification goes from T4 N1 to T4 N2b. This means little to me, but I know it's not good. Someone will come back later to go through it all with me.

Trudi rings to say that she's coming in to see me later today. She has been sick, but she's better now. She just has a bit of a cough. I mention this to one of the nurses. 'Tell her not to come,' she says.

It hits me that I'm sick in a fairly significant way. That there's an element of danger in it. I keep forgetting that, it seems like news every time it surfaces.

Then I think – but I can't die. I have books to write. An old joke comes back to haunt me: 'The graveyards are full of people who thought they were indispensable.'

9.32 a.m. One of the max-fax team comes back, to insert a cannula into my arm. They've ordered more blood for me. I'll need a transfusion if I spring a leak from the major vessels near the wound. I've to watch for blood on the dressing. A bleed like this is rare, but they want to be ready if it happens – that's why they don't want me going home for a few hours this weekend. I'd be too far away from medical help in an emergency.

Scenes from *ER* flicker across the back wall of my mind.

The registrar comes to explain the operation to me. I know he's under pressure, but he's patient as he describes how they removed the tumour and where from. This has been explained to me already but I didn't take it all in.

He explains that removing parts of the parotid gland is a tricky business, because not only the facial nerve but also the external carotid artery pass through it. Because the nerves were cut, half of my face is paralysed and has no sensation, while the lip is weakened and numb. 'Radical neck dissection' means that all forty-nine lymph nodes were taken from my neck – also the nerve that moves the shoulder, and the sternocleido–mastoid muscle which protects the greater blood vessels of the neck. He tells me that there was 'extracapsular spread' in two of the eleven lymph nodes that showed signs of cancer. I don't like the sound of this.

They are concerned about a suspicious node on the left but not really worried. We need to keep an eye on it. He describes the tumour as an 'avid neoplasm'.

Even I can see that the pathology results are not great. But they could be worse. Every single node could have been affected. Radiotherapy looks inevitable now.

After this I need a bit of diversion. Simon and Nessa put me in a wheelchair and bring me out for a walk. We coast through the smokers, over to the grass. I pretend that I don't see the surreptitious glances that come my way. It's lovely to be bathed in air. It feels luxurious, profligate.

Sometimes, like now, the revolving main door of the

hospital stops moving. People wait patiently, stuck within its arc. It happens because someone who doesn't know the way it works has pressed forward in their eagerness to leave. We watch while they figure it out. The door starts to move again.

Outside, taxis wait for fares. Patients and visitors are gathered at the bicycle shed to smoke. Rumour has it that drugs are bought and sold out here. People make phone calls. This is where I came to ring my friends and tell them the news, pacing the rectangular path away from the crowd, not feeling the cold, not caring that I was in my pyjamas. Simon says that he's seen men sitting on the grass who are cuffed together, waiting for the paddywagon. The guard standing to one side, trying to look as if they have nothing to do with him.

25 May 2006

5.22 a.m. Today it's three weeks since the operation – altogether I've been here six weeks and a day. I make lists, obsessively: things to do, people to ring and/or write to, organizations to look up when I go home.

6.09 a.m. I go down to the window at the end of the corridor for a quick look at the demolition across the way. In the early morning light, Fatima Mansions looks less demolished than . . . ruined. The damp on the walls looks like despair. You can see traces of how someone shaped their life, or at least gave it colour when shape eluded them. There are red walls, a trace of blue, cream – amid the drab greys and browns and blacks of rubble, an anti-colour. On the gable end of the exposed block, a window hangs open, incongruous. It reminds me of the doll I once saw, left propped on the balcony of one of the four storeys in Ballymun. That doll haunted me for the whole year that I worked there, part of a regeneration programme just like this one.

The morning is cool and full of promise. I walk down to Outpatients on my own. There's a milestone.

When I walk along the corridors alone, I could swear there's someone behind me, impatient to overtake – I move out of the way, look back. There's no one there. My ghosts are in my head, fed by echo.

Ryan plays with the echo in the lift, then says the word, testing it. He draws me a fabulous picture – greens and browns and orange with a flash of red, a tall shape that could be a tree or a forest or a building or a city, with a lone road and a blue car driving away.

People wonder if I'm feeling down. If I am, it's the way a bull's head is down in a ring, ready to charge whatever comes at him. It's a bit of a shock, after all these years and my own gloomy self-image, to discover that I'm something of an optimist at heart.

26 May 2006

There is something dark and lonely about injecting yourself, with meds or with food. About the speed of a meal.

This is the swampy thought under the topsoil where I stand: the words 'extracapsular spread'. What if the cancer has escaped into the wild? What if it's taking root somewhere else right now? Baby crabs – and vengeful. We all know this plotline so well. The disinherited, orphaned-at-birth killing machine.

The disembodied voice of the PA system comes on to call out a registration number and advise the owner to return to their car, because they've left their lights on. This seems uncommonly civil. It reminds me of our maiden aunts, who had an exit code for boring parties. One would say to the other: 'I think we may have parked with our lights on.' They never owned so much as a bicycle between them.

I let my tongue probe the new skin inside my cheek. I decide that there's definitely hair in there. Maybe I'll become the bearded lady and go and live in a circus.

The preacher pays me a visit and lifts my blanket, as if he'd like to get in beside me. I tell him this is my bed. His attendant leads him out again.

Professor Stassen comes in and introduces a new, junior doctor, who shakes my hand. Professor Stassen warns him against the dangers of MRSA and I assume that he's joking. Then I see that he's not. He's defending me. He reminds me that I have to be super-careful of my neck.

In the max-fax clinic a man with cropped hair, taut arms and a worried face speaks rapidly into his mobile. When he's finished, he turns to me.

'Have you broken your jaw, love? Was it an accident?'

'No, a tumour.'

'Oh God. And they took it out, did they? Get all of it?'

'I hope so.'

'Well, that's good.' His eyes go down to his phone.

'They took bone from my leg,' I say, testing how a stranger might react to this. 'To replace my jaw.'

'It's amazing what they can do.'

'Amazing.'

He starts to text someone.

'What about you?' I ask. What the hell, he started it.

He puts the phone away and tells me that his jaw is broken.

He has a holiday booked next week and he doesn't know if he'll make it. An action holiday. We start to go through possible alternatives to their plans. His girlfriend sounds hard to please. He sighs. 'You have to have a positive attitude, don't you?'

I think about sticks and walking, the small targets I set myself.

Inside, they tell me that I'm doing very well. 'You can get back to writing your book now,' they say.

27 May 2006

I'm beginning to understand that the feeling of an alien growth on the right side of my head may be permanent. It feels monstrous to me, but it looks like an ordinary ear. Every day I touch it, to see if I can reclaim it, but no. And I'm still deaf on that side.

These are surgical outcomes – nerves and muscles were 'sacrificed' when they rooted the crab out from under its rocks. They warned me. They said it loads of times and I nodded, cheerful and co-operative, with no idea what they really meant.

The mouth, this morning, is a swollen hot box. The tongue is curled inside it like a captive creature, too large for its confinement and damaged along the side. It's too big and too small at the same time, fizzy. The box itself is rigid. And heavy, dragged down towards the corner where the trouble is. A hot spot, like a volcano in a burning desert of small fiery cones. Lightning forks across my chin, random squiggles like small electric shocks. The leg is sore but not too bad.

Outside, the wind is rising. It sounds wild and wonderful, an airy, thermal sea. A single magpie flaps around, baleful, on the grass. I wish he'd find himself some friends.

★

It's a big surprise to see David when, released from bed-rest at home, he comes in to visit. I shake my stick at him and he shakes his crutches back at me. Then we set off for a walk along the halls with our metal props, while the others take photographs of our shared lameness. I think it's funny, that we must be a vision with these accoutrements. But when someone asks if they can bring a friend of theirs along to see me, I say no. I'm not an exhibit at the local zoo.

As time goes on it gets harder to say goodbye to people when they leave. It gets harder to be here. I'm missing a meeting of the Women Writers' Web this afternoon but that's not even what bothers me. I just want to go home and hide.

I walk down to the corridor where the paintings are and spend some time there, thinking about that other life. The one I will get back to. Writing and travel and readings and workshops. The novel that was interrupted by all of this.

Back on the ward, one of my lovely doctors checks out the wound. This wound has brought them all round to see me more often than they otherwise might. It's given me a chance to get to know them differently than in the tense days pre-surgery, when they gave me information carefully and in groups, when I was rigid with fear and suspected everyone who came near me. Now I ask them about where they come from, their lives at home. They are from India, Pakistan, Egypt, Sri Lanka. This man's face comes alive when he talks about home.

He says the wound is clean, that it's shrinking. It seems that the graft is taking.

But the pain tonight is bad. Near midnight, the nurses call one of my team to come and order new meds.

28 May 2006

It's tricky to wash when half of my face and the front of my neck are bandaged; not to mention the lignocaine patch, about four inches square, under my right collarbone and the PEG tube coming out of my stomach above the navel. It requires technique and a number of separate, disposable items – gauze swabs, tissues, Q-tips.

One leg is bandaged below the knee and, depending on the nurse who did the dressing, the bandage might be wrapped around my foot as well. I wipe my distant toes and resolve to touch up my nails, brighten the view.

The other leg sports a surgical stocking that leaves hard ridges on my skin. I know I'm being ridiculous, given the battlefield that is my left leg, but I shave the healthy skin around the scars. Then my hand slips and I cut myself. Spots of blood appear on the surgical stocking when I put it back on. This causes confusion. Everyone wants to know why my other leg is bleeding. I'm half-sheepish, half-defiant when I explain.

I have a line in my left elbow – a needle with a long, proboscis-like cannula embedded in a vein and taped into place. It looks sore and immobilizing but it isn't. Still, I have to pay attention. I don't want to get it wet or dislodge it.

The other arm has two transparent morphine patches stuck on above the elbow. I could go down and sell them at the front door, except that I'd probably scare the junkies away with my face.

At least the drains are gone.

In here, they have a 'scale' for measuring pain that seems so arbitrary as to be useless. They ask, 'If you were to place your pain on a scale of one to ten, ten being the worst pain you can possibly imagine, where would it be?'

But doesn't that depend on a person's prior experience of pain, their pain threshold, the power of their imagination? Ten, for me, is the peak in the clouds, the one you've never reached and hope not to. Ever. Like, say, having a train run over your leg. Or a hot needle rammed into your eye. I don't know where these nice people want me to put my ten – with the leg under the train? Or with something I've actually experienced?

No one ever mentions that pain can have its pleasures too. It can become your familiar – especially as your experience of it broadens. It can be welcome, even, as the numbness from surgery wears off.

The solitary magpie reappears between the two trees. Furious, I make my three quick bows. I might want to go home, but I don't feel ready.

An escapee from another ward comes in, sticks his head into every room and asks us to call 999, while a young Chinese girl and a nurse try to coax him away.

He tells us that he's afraid: 'If I go back to that room I'll be shot in the morning!'

In the end, they have to call Security to bring him back to his ward.

I swear, sometimes I think I've woken up in someone else's screenplay.

There's a man dying in the room next to mine. His relatives stand around, tense and silent.

29 May 2006

My mouth gets harder and harder to open but I'm not allowed to do exercises yet. The intern won't be drawn on how long I've to stay here. He doesn't know when radiotherapy will start either, but the end of June seems likely.

The preacher clasps my hand. 'I don't think I'll be going anywhere anytime soon.' His face is sad. I feel the same. One of my writing groups meets this afternoon, without me. I probably won't be able to go to the week-long workshop we've planned in Connemara this summer because I'll be in the middle of radiotherapy by then, or just finished. My cousin has a story in an anthology that's being launched tonight, and I was meant to go and talk to Trudi's book club about writing.

This life I'm in seems just as crowded as my other one but I'd be hard-pushed to say exactly what it is that fills it.

I text Brendan to ask if the *Dublin Review* might be interested in a piece about this experience.

Nessa has gone off with a bag of pyjamas to launder, a list of messages. I hope I'm not turning her into a daughter-slave.

30 May 2006

The PA voice is in a good mood. 'Good morning. There will be glucose-monitoring training in the seminar room from ten until eleven, eleven until twelve and twelve until one. Thank you.'

It sounds like *M*A*S*H* or *Good Morning, Vietnam*. All hell might break loose any minute, but let's not forget to monitor our glucose.

I feel dizzy and lightheaded, probably because the dose of OxyNorm has leaped from 5 mg to 40 mg. I also have two lignocaine patches instead of one and they've increased other things as well.

Brendan texts back to say, yes, he'd like to see a piece about all of this. Now, dopey as I am, I wonder if I'll be able to write it.

Emma has another exam today. I wish I was there to bring her cups of tea, see her off. I text her to wish her luck, again. More texts about another event I'm missing, a friend's launch, tonight. Dinner in the Dáil restaurant afterwards. I think of them all there now, celebrating a book that's long overdue.

31 May 2006

A cheerful new phlebotomist wants all my details. She whizzes around, she works like a dowser, hunting for a vein. She keeps up a running commentary that seems to be addressed to the air rather than to me:

'Would you believe that? This site does not want to give – and it's a good vein – listen to your sister . . .' and she goes for the usual vein, gnarled and sclerosed as it is.

With the needle safely in, she looks around the room. 'What are you reading?' She bends over the books, then straightens to examine the cards on the walls. 'Your friends are very creative. Some of these are very enlightened. Some are religious, if you don't mind my saying so. Can I ask what you do?'

'I'm a writer.'

'I could have guessed.'

'How?'

She doesn't miss a beat. 'All this.' Her sweeping gesture includes the chaos of notebooks, papers, books, the cards and photos on the wall. She laughs. 'Well, now that I've finished analysing your room – I observe a lot, that's what *I* do.'

And she's gone.

Down in the max-fax clinic they tell me that the wound looks so good they might let me out for a while this weekend and that maybe I can go home on Monday. Did they really say that? I'm not sure that I'm ready for it.

They say that I don't need the stick to help me walk any more. Then we do a swallow test. It's my first full swallow since the operation. The sterile water slips down my throat. No problem at all. I walk back to the ward, swinging my stick, with a note to put over my bed which says 'Drink Sterile Water Only'.

We laugh about the notice, as if I don't need it, but I tape it up there anyway. Then a nurse brings me OxyNorm in a plastic cup instead of a syringe.

Luckily the dietician is there and she reminds us about the sterile water – it's in case whatever I swallow pushes out through the wound from the inside. Saved. Again.

The joy of water. It slips, cool and silky and clean, along my tongue and slides easily down my stiff and gritty throat. In America, I saw many dried-out river beds, the earth cracked and bleached, like bone. Later in the season they would fill with water and course along, the levees barely able to contain the flood, green flushing the banks. The air itself seemed saturated, the trees sucked water from it and flung their arms out wide, fingers draped with lacy Spanish moss. People talk about the brilliant foliage of New England, but in Texas it's the grasses that turn, flushing up in the spring, erupting with the colour of wildflowers, bluebonnets and Indian paintbrush. None of it could happen without water.

★

A phone call from Emma – she's finished her finals! Great girl.

When I'm on the phone to Simon, he describes what he sees through the window of his flat in London: a single pink balloon against a blue sky with grey rainclouds underneath. I tell him about the wood pigeon on the grass outside. Pretty, its white ring vivid, its green head rising.

1 June 2006

The team come round to say I'll probably go home next week, to let the wound finish healing away from the threat of MRSA. When the wound has healed, I'll have radiotherapy. They stress that I'm to push for it.

I wonder, have I lost my place on a list?

I've noticed that the pulse in my ear accelerates with certain stresses. As if it's trying to tell me something. I should learn to pay attention.

I go down to the max-fax clinic. The corridor is crowded. I lean against the wall to wait but a man with a battered face and dark glasses offers me his seat. Later he sits beside me. It's his first visit, he's not sure which doctor he'll see, he doesn't know the system. He says all this to the floor, although I'm right beside him, my pyjamas incongruous with his suit.

Milestone of the day: they took off the surgical stocking, now that I'm walking so much. And I can use toothpaste!

The nun who 'can't give you holy communion because you're fasting' comes in and studies my wall.

'If cards could make you well . . .' she says. Her tone suggests how unlikely this is. Then she leaves.

She reminds me of someone. An ill-wisher, from the past.

'Is this the way down?' a frail, elderly woman asks at the top of a flight of stairs.

'You'd better ask a nurse,' I say, directing her back to her ward. Traitor. Poacher turned gamekeeper.

I'm allowed to use the stairs normally now, taking my weight fully on each leg. But I'm still slow.

2 June 2006 (Zita's birthday)

I wake late. Washing my teeth feels like scrubbing a bare concrete wall. I've barely finished when the max-fax team arrive. I ask when I'll have the other wisdom teeth out. I don't know how they'll do it, when I can barely open my mouth. They tell me to start stretching it. They say that the wound looks good and that I can move on to semi-solids. I'm thrilled – just in time for Zita's party. Now I can have yogurt. I text the girls and ask them to bring some in.

I go to Audiology to have my hearing tested. Bad news. My left ear is okay but the right one is not. The audiologist doesn't know if the change is temporary or permanent. She brings me in to a doctor, who tells me that it's probably permanent. My eyes fill.

'Are you okay?'

'Yes.' What the hell else am I going to say? We caught her heading off with an armful of files, in a hurry, but she was nice and came back in to see my results – not to deal with my emotional trauma.

I feel sick, clogged with tears as I limp off, holding my bulging file and my notebook. I put a smile on my face when

I come in to the chaos of Zita's party. It's mad in my room, getting everything set up and me having feeds and meds in the middle of it. They have their sandwiches and crisps and I have *yogurt*! M & S vanilla, it tastes gorgeous. We teach Ryan how to play Snap.

A friend comes and we go down to the coffee shop and I have an actual bottle of water, delighted with myself, while she has coffee. We natter away. When I tell her about my deafness, she makes a dismissive sound and says: 'But no one will notice that. You can't see it, your ear.'

I raise my voice for the first time in ages. 'Well, I fucking notice it!' and launch into a lament about the effort it takes, the energy, how tiring and isolating it is, etc.

But inside, some sleeping part of me opens an eye and blinks, astonished. This sleepy eye considers the impact of what it sees. I *have* been concerned about other people's reaction to me, but this exchange has made me understand that my changes are more deeply urgent and internal. I'm jolted into knowing that these things – the hot boxy weight of my mouth, the drag on my neck, the numb ear, the combined silence and throbbing pulse that is my deafness – may be with me for as long as I live. I have to take this in as part of my future. But that knowledge brings 'the future' with it. Something has lifted and I feel free. Giddy, even. As if something has been settled. That's it then. Let's get on with it.

Back in my room, I make notes for the *Dublin Review* piece. I feel happy to be back at work.

Tomorrow is Nessa's birthday. We haven't told her that I'm getting out for a couple of hours. We want to surprise her.

3 June 2006 (Nessa's birthday)

I feel as though there should be an audience, ready to applaud my first proper meal – a bowl of hospital porridge and a cup of stewed tea. Instead I come face to face with the intricacies of swallowing – bits get stuck in my mouth, my tongue is stiff and awkward, out of practice. It can't manoeuvre the food to the back of my mouth. My weak lips sag and I drool the porridge all over my chin and down my front. After a while my throat and oesophagus are sore, so I stop. Glad, after all, that there are no witnesses.

Never mind. My real first was yesterday – that scrumptious yogurt, the girls and Ryan cheering me on, and laughing when I drooled, helping me to wipe my mouth, much better than this grim and silent struggle.

I've never been aware of my oesophagus before.

We have a *brilliant* day. I creep up behind Nessa, who's lying face-down on the grass, and slip a card under her bikini strap. Her shock is total. She gets another surprise when Zita and Eoin and Ryan arrive. We have a rowdy lunch, salads put together from supermarket packs and cooked chicken. And then all those summery things like badminton on the grass, water pistols, lying out in the sun, hilarity. It's bliss to be home. Mark and Peter are here and Jackie drops in for a little while. Even Oz is excited, bounding around with Zita's new dog, Gus, as if he's a puppy, too.

I slobber and drool a lot. We use up all the kitchen roll mopping up my face and neck, but who cares? I'm here.

I begin to crash right around the time I have to go back. Nessa begs off coming with us in the car because she wants to see a film on TV.

Then she hesitates. 'It's the first day I won't have been to the hospital!'

I didn't realize she was putting that much pressure on herself. Maybe it *is* time I came home.

When we get back, I'm so tired that I have to lean on Simon's arm. We take the lift to the ward and I lurch in, my new gait. When Simon has gone, a nurse asks if I had a drink while I was out and I realize that they think I'm jarred. I have to laugh. Water is enough for me, these days.

I do feel euphoric, though, a sense of freedom.

4 June 2006

When I wake up, my right arm is totally dead. All of me is stiff and sore, but when I start to move, the rest eases except for the arm. It's incapable of supporting any weight, won't lift any higher than the elbow. Have I had a stroke during the night? Dread rushes through me. I think about Nessa or Emma's shock if they come in to collect me and hear this news. I want to ring Simon to tell him to come instead.

Then a lot of things roll in on me, heavy waves in a sluggish sea – what might lie ahead of him, of me, of all of us?

Seagulls wheel overhead, calling *whaa*, *whaa*.

After a while I hear a nurse's voice at the desk and go out to tell her. 'My arm is dead. I can't move it properly.'

'Oh, no!' she stares at it. 'Did you lie on it?'

'I don't think so. I don't think I moved all night.'

While we're standing there it begins to give a little.

'It's probably just stiffness, after all,' I say.

I go back to my room and make myself do the exercises,

work my fingers, curl my hair with them and get some movement in the end. Eventually I get my arm back.

The drama in my head dies down again and then Nessa arrives to collect me. She's in flitters. She thinks she got a speeding ticket on the Long Mile Road.

5 June 2006

It's a bank holiday Monday and I get out for the afternoon again. I have an awful moment while I'm eating scrambled egg, then yogurt with a spoon. Simon is beside me. I'm drooling and mopping my mouth and I'm struck by the fact that this is what he's landed with, a woman who drools, for the rest of his life – or mine. Suddenly I'm in floods of tears, apologizing, but not really able to talk; and that makes it worse. He says loving, reasonable things about adjusting. I know he's right but it has nothing to do with what's hurting me, which is the fear that I may have years of this ahead of me. And that's if I'm lucky.

I can't bear it that they see me like this, so pathetic and messy and useless. I don't want to be fussed over. At the same time, I know I couldn't survive without him, without all of them.

It's my last night on the ward.

In hospital, my pyjamas give me insider status – people move out of my way, give up their seat at the clinic, try not to stare at my oddities. Out in the world, I'll have to fend for myself.

Tonight I think: okay, I'm a woman with a mortal illness – but so what? Life is a mortal condition. We all have it. Some of us have to face it more acutely, is all. The treatment has saved my life, or at least prolonged it. I am irrevocably changed – I walk with a limp, inject myself with food and drugs like any addict. My face and neck are swollen, distorted and scarred; my shoulder movements are severely limited; I am deaf in one ear; and my right eye is weak. I eat like a messy baby, drink with difficulty. Sometimes I have to fight to stay awake. My family watch my every movement with concern – and yet, I am as alive now as I have ever been. Maybe even more so.

I am not invalid. I refuse it.

I hear a familiar sound and look out on to the corridor. A middle-aged woman moves along on slow crutches, learning how to walk again. She's just like I was, on my zimmer frame, a few short weeks back, walking up and down the ward corridor, pushing a bit harder all the time.

That has been my big lesson here. I need to push myself harder all the time, not take the easy route. It's a lesson I've learned over and over again. Painfully, but well. I walk free now, I don't even need a stick. That much of me has been restored.

6 June 2006

Everything falls away in a haze of packing, sorting things out, stocking up on medications, dressings, prescriptions. Simon makes several trips to the car with my stuff while the intern writes my discharge notes. I hug everyone I can find, say goodbye and thank you. These people feel like family. I'll miss them.

Then there's a moment when I stand in front of the nurses' station and don't know what to do next. The nurses are smiling, but they have work to get back to. Simon is waiting. I know what everyone expects of me. So I wave, turn my back on my empty room, take Simon's arm and walk out of there.

Chapter 4

7 June 2006

I love waking up in our oddly shaped attic room, the way light pours into it from both sides, the views framed by its windows. On one side, trees and sky. On the other, the fall to the bay, and Howth across the water.

But I can't stay here all morning. We have to go in to the hospital, to the max-fax clinic, to have my dressing changed. On the way downstairs my leg is rigid and cramped. I creep down like an old woman, clutching what I can – Simon, the edge of a chest of drawers, door handles, bannisters. Pain darts through my leg. The thought that I might still die bobs up, like a cork in water.

We do the drugs. Simon makes gorgeous porridge full of cream and honey; I make the coffee. We're switching over to a regime that's half liquid feed and half semi-solid food.

Lizzie, the cat, has a blade of grass in her nose. Simon pulls it out and she sneezes hard, then goes on sneezing in the sunshine. The birds mock her with their different songs.

Simon fills a Jiffy bag with drugs for lunchtime and a carton of the food supplement I have to drink between meals. My OxyNorm is drawn up and ready. I imagine slinking into one of those blue-lit loos with my loaded syringe.

The cat has another bit of grass in her nose but this one won't come out. She goes mad when we try. We ask the girls to take her to the vet, and off with us to St James's.

★

It feels completely different to be here as an actual outpatient. I've no file to carry, for a start.

The pain in my ankle is so bad that I'm hobbling. It hasn't been like this before. A little sore on the stairs last night and then again this morning, but it's vicious now.

We're seen in a succession of rooms. The petite dietician advises me to eat all the things I usually feel guilty about: desserts, full-fat yogurts, lots of dairy products. She says not to worry about sweet things or chocolate. They want me to keep my weight up because I might lose some during radiotherapy. I may be starting to eat again now, but it's likely that I'll stop again if my mouth and throat get sore from radiation.

The speech therapist checks the movement of my tongue, my swallow. The social worker is putting together an application for a medical card. She says that I'm entitled to one, now that I have a long-term illness. When I get it, I'll get free medication, free visits to the GP. It will be a load off our minds. I haven't let myself think about money yet, but I know I'll have to, sooner or later.

In the main examination room, there's a lot of banter. The nurse with green eyes stands up for me, the way she does. I don't think I've ever seen her stand still, but she manages to inject an air of calm and rationality into the proceedings, no matter how rowdy the rest of us get.

When I ask if I can go to the hairdresser yet, they say that I can if I want. But they describe the dangers to the neck wound and its exposed bone in such a way that we all know I won't. None of us points out that having my hair done would belong in the category of bolted horses and locking stable doors, so far as my appearance is concerned. We talk about the leg. They say to let pain be my guide, keep it raised as much as possible when I'm at home. We head out. I hold Simon's arm and try not to whine.

On the way home we stop to buy a walking stick.

The cat has cancer too. That lump in her fur turns out to be an aggressive tumour, about to rupture. We thought it was a knot of hair. They'll operate first thing in the morning. Before I was diagnosed we had that worry about the dog. The vet thought he might have a sarcoma, but it turned out to be arthritis.

I hoped that when I came home I'd go back to being me with a few changes, but my throbbing ankle has put paid to that. My invalid status interferes with everything. The girls are great – affectionate and willing – but they can't keep curtailing their plans to fit in with mine.

I even behave like an invalid – asking for this and that, whining and whingeing in a demoralizing way. I don't know how any of them can stand me, but when I say so I cringe even more, it's such an invalid-y thing to say.

They point out that it might not be the worst thing in the world that I'm forced to lie on the couch and do nothing. They tell me that they've spoken to our GP and have written away for an application form to get a temporary disabled parking sticker. They didn't say anything before because they didn't want me to get upset by the idea.

'You need it,' they say, when I protest. 'You'll only have to use it for a few weeks.'

Simon is ambivalent about going back to work in London next week. We talk about which days he'll go and how long he'll stay away. I'm thinking: *help!*

8 June 2006

Ankle in agony this morning. The more upset I am, the louder that pulse beats in my ear.

I'm exhausted. It's because I'm anaemic, after the operation. That's why I have to take the iron. Then I get constipated because of the iron and have to take laxatives. We're trying to get the balance right.

The biggest crash, ever.

A friend's young child reacts badly to the sight of me, won't stay in the same room, speaks only to Simon. I say meaningless, brash things in an effort to ease the tension but it doesn't work. When they leave, I cry the most violent tears I've cried in a very long time.

Then the girls and Ryan arrive home from the vet with the cat. Between them all they dust me down and get me going again. It's time for meds. I'm still rattled and forget to clamp the PEG tube. When I open it, stomach contents squirt into Nessa's face. That gets a laugh, from her sisters.

I have to fight for breath tonight. That terror.

9 June 2006

I drag myself out of bed early for the trip to Outpatients. I kneel on a chair and Simon washes my hair at the kitchen sink. We manage the feed and meds, all without bickering. We load the car with the goodies I want to bring up to the ward to say thank you. Better late than never.

In the max-fax clinic we have to wait a while to be seen. I tell them how sore the leg is and that I can't put any weight on it. They send us to the plastics trauma clinic, because they did the surgery on my leg. My leg is their preserve.

It's a long limp over there, outside and down to the back of the hospital. I feel like a Monty Python skit, with my spanking fresh bandage like a ruff at my neck, uttering poodle yelps as we go along, trying not to cry. When we get there, a nurse brings me in to lie on a trolley in what looks like a storeroom – sterile supplies, gloves, gauze, Mepore – everything. The beautiful young woman doctor comes in and asks a few questions, prods my leg, seems cross with the other crowd for sending me over. I think there should be a ban on beautiful people working in plastic surgery, it's too unfair. We wait for another doctor and I go through it all again. I tell them how sore the leg is, how useless.

'What do you expect?' they say. They describe the extent of the surgery.

'But I could walk when I left the hospital,' I remind them.

They don't seem interested in anything except the flesh wound, where the fat pad was taken, to line my cheek. It's healing well. They give me stern advice: walk so long as it's not causing you discomfort; always have your leg up when you're sitting; exercise it gently.

This is confusing. I'm to push myself, but not to do anything that hurts. I can't put my weight on it now, but they send me home. I'm glad of the information and the instructions, but they don't change the pain. The nurse gives me more dressings to bring home with me.

I wait at the door while Simon gets the car. We come straight home, our goodies still in the boot. I'm too knackered to visit the ward.

Gorgeous lunch of scrambled egg and baked potato with avocado while we watch *Home and Away* with Nessa. It's a younger, less glossy version of *Baywatch* meets *EastEnders*, set in Australia. Then I have a nap.

Lizzie, the cat, is here too, sleeping off the after-effects of her anaesthetic.

A parcel of books arrives from Penguin. Lots of people have sent me books. I have my own library, waiting for me to start reading again. Other people have given me scarves, just what I need for my gory neck. I'll have one for any occasion, any outfit. A cousin sends pyjamas from New York, a writer friend sends recordings of poets reading their own work. I get a gorgeous scarlet silk robe in a purple box from Liberty's in London. Lotions and potions galore. Simon puts a lot of work into dinner and setting up my laptop. I'm spoilt rotten.

Strange sensations play across this non-face. I hit it, to see if I'll feel the blow, but I don't. I have to struggle to stand. I cannot believe this is me. I hate what it reduces me to.

10 June 2006

I want to go in to the ward, even though it's a Saturday. I want to bring the presents, which are still in the boot of the car.

'You're not up to it,' Simon says.

'Yes I am.' I can't do it alone. He'll have to help me.

He throws his hands up in the air and yells: 'It's too much!'

He goes over to the dishwasher and starts unloading it.

'Wait, I'll help.'

'Stay where you are. Get some rest.'

I struggle to my feet and across the kitchen, but by the time I reach the dishwasher, he's finished. He swings the door shut.

I'm too late.

Outside, the flowers he's growing flare on the deck, a storm of gorgeous colour and smells. Begonias, fuchsia, African lilies, trailing ivies. There are herbs in pots out there as well: basil, oregano, thyme. Several types of mint. He's done this for me.

There are vases on every surface. Fat bees hover and drone.

The large, smooth ball in my mouth still burns. My leg aches. I hope they are right and the pain is normal. It's turned into an ugly day. The river runs edgily below ground, wind rushing with it. Leaves and the outline of a boat pole. A tunnel with hatches in it, the mouth closed. Underground events. Ugly, ugly.

Here's something cruel – when you have the runs from hidjus laxatives and have to get to the loo on a bockety leg.

The girls steer me into the living room, coax me onto the couch. They organize my feed, give me my meds and I complain. I'd rather do it later because people are waiting for me in the kitchen. The girls insist.

I'm overcome by a sense of unreality.

When a friend comes to say goodbye my throat flares with panic – she's going away for the whole summer. Will I be here when she gets back?

11 June 2006

Last night I had the runs and my ankle was killing me. I hobbled and lurched around. Then I felt horribly sick and had to go to bed. Simon came with me. I dreaded lying down. We had one of those 'I want you to marry again' conversations I always swore I'd avoid, they seem so clichéd.

This whole situation seems like a cliché when I look at it in the cool misty light of morning.

Another day.

12 June 2006

Last night there was so much tenderness between us, I broke wide open. When I turned in the dark, Simon seemed to glow beside me.

This morning he leaves early, to go back to work in London. When he goes I'm in the middle of a dream about snow and ice, fire and art. I wander in and out of sleep, not knowing if it's night or morning.

Nessa and I go through the whole feed-and-meds ritual, then set off for Outpatients. We're nervous, because it's our first time doing all this without Simon. She is fantastic, coaxes me along. But then pain in my leg and more pain and worse pain on the long walk from the car to the clinic. The corridor is narrow and hot and full. Stares. Consultations. By the time we get back to the car I'm almost crying openly. I want to bleat, *This is too hard*. But I put one foot in front of the other and keep going.

They say: no stairs, lie on the sofa, do nothing. So that's what I do. And drift in and out of sleep, visits and phone calls. The leg looks deformed to me, its alignment seems wrong. But the swelling is down, so there's hope. I learn how to hop up the stairs using the stick and the bannisters for support. I have to rest at each step. It takes a while.

On the phone, a friend who knows about these things says that from what she's seen, it's the people who take it easy and do absolutely nothing who do best. Maybe the leg is trying to tell me something?

★

I print off tables from my laptop to keep track of what I eat, what I have to take, and the exercises I have to do. Here's my regime for each day:

Exercises: leg, mouth, eye, shoulder, neck six times a day
Feed: 250 mls, twice a day
Flush tube: once a day
Diet: soft food building to more normal regime, twice a day; supplementary diet drink, 2–3 times a day
PEG: clean and change once a day
Neck dressing: Outpatients three times a week
Leg dressing: moisturize as often as possible
Medication: Difene, OxyNorm, pregabalin, anti-platelet agent, paracetamol, lignocaine patch (daily), diazepam, amitriptyline, iron, laxatives, fentanyl patch (every three days)

13 June 2006

I've moved down to sleep in Nessa's room because it's one less flight of stairs to deal with and it's beside the bathroom. The trees are a sea of green outside the window, a riot of birds' wooden clacking. I have a lovely, relaxing lie-in: I don't have to go in to the clinic. A day off.

The proofs arrive for an anthology of work I've contributed to. Changes have to be made by the end of the week, if at all. I take them out of the oversized brown envelope and hold them, but I don't have the energy to read through them. I worked on these pieces intensely a few months ago, now I can't even look at them properly. I set them aside, say I'll deal with them later. I have never done this before. Proofs are usually an occasion for the kitchen table to be cleared at once, demands for quiet, pints of coffee. Now I can't bear to think about them. They are stacked among the bills like a bad conscience.

Emma rings from college. She got her results. When she tells me that she got a first and that she's won a prize, I laugh and cry so hard that Nessa has to come and hold me.

Tom from the pharmacy appears with things I need. Jackie comes to help me to wash my hair and to lend me David's zimmer frame, because he doesn't need it any more. This day keeps getting better.

I have to learn to listen to my new body. My leg improves when I do nothing, but my neck muscles constrict and I hear strange noises, a steely wind in my ear. This wind polices the border between then and now, before and after, safety and danger. When I stretch my jaw a pulse pounds, warning me to back off. Might that vein in my neck still go? Sometimes, when I do the mouth-opening exercises, I get a sensation at the hinge of my jaw as if it is held together by thick rubber bands. As if they could snap.

I'm afraid to go in to the max-fax clinic on the zimmer frame tomorrow in case they slag me about giving in. I like it that they tease me, make me think in terms of strength rather than weakness, but I don't think I could laugh about this. I don't have much choice – I can't walk without it.

14 June 2006

In the clinic, they are surprised by the zimmer, but they don't laugh. They check out the leg. They apologize in advance, say that if it's broken it will hurt like hell when they try to move the joint. I brace myself, but I don't feel anything worse when they pull on it.

They tell me that the wisdom teeth on the other side can come out now. They'll do it in Day Surgery next week.

As I hobble out, a doctor turns to the nurse. 'Is it really that bad?' he asks, about my leg. I see her nod. The door closes.

15 June 2006

I nearly lost it yesterday when we got home. Sank into a pit of depression. It felt like those early days after the operation. Near the end and not caring. Nessa took care of me. She put me to bed in her bed, borrowed a fan from next door to stir the heavy summer air. She pumped feed into me at the right times, then got me up to watch mindless TV. I felt better by the time she persuaded me to go to bed for the night, arranging duvet covers and pillows to make me comfy.

I feel rotten this morning, but Emma does the early morning meds and feeds and my strength begins to come back. Simon comes home tonight.

I've to psych myself up for Tuesday, when my wisdom teeth come out.

Ryan says, 'I wish your mouth would get better.'

'I do too, sweetheart.'

He sighs, a heavy sigh. 'If I find a magic stone to wish on, I will.'

16 June 2006

In the corridor outside the max-fax clinic we sit beside a bristling gang of teenage girls supporting one who is rigid with fear. On our right, three battered-looking men talk about how they broke their respective jaws. One of them was jumped by a gang of women in the west. I don't stand out from the crowd in here. I can see a stitched cheek here, a flattened profile there.

Young women who work here prance past, well put-together, a world apart from those of us who skulk against the walls waiting to be seen. Porters in scrubs and runners, suited men with an air of power and assurance. Cleaners dressed in blue *tsk!* as people walk on their newly washed floors.

Inside, the max-fax team are happy with the wound, say I can have Monday off. For three whole days, I'll be able to laze in bed as late as I want. They tell me I should wean myself off the pain medication but they don't say how. I've an appointment to come back and see the pain team in a few weeks. They show me exercises to stretch my jaw with tongue depressors. I've to put a stack of them between my teeth, close on it, then open as wide as I can. The idea is to try to accommodate an increasing number of sticks. I start at three. It seems pathetic to me, but they say if I keep working at it, it will get better.

There's some uncertainty as to whether the wisdom-tooth extraction can be done on Tuesday – I've to ring on Monday morning to check.

I wonder how they'll manage to get in to my mouth to do it, since I can't even fit a biro between my teeth. They assure me that it's no problem. They've even done it in this room, it's that routine.

'Tell me how.'

'You don't really want to know.'

But I do, I do. I'm not worried about their ability to do it, but about my ability to withstand what it is that they do.

I plead for a general anaesthetic, but they point out that it might be a problem, because my mouth doesn't open wide enough to accommodate the ventilation tube.

I hobble off to find Simon, and nearly sideswipe my friendly intern on a corner.

'How are you?' he says.

'Don't ask,' I wail. 'They're going to take out the wisdom teeth on the other side!'

He makes vague, comforting noises.

'I can't open my mouth,' I remind him. 'They won't be able to do a general anaesthetic. And how will they get at the teeth?'

'There are ways.'

'How? They won't tell me.'

He looks off through the window into the empty courtyard and frowns. 'Let's see, I think they go up through the nose . . .'

Oh God, they were right, I don't want to know. I tell him never mind, and stump off.

In my head, I see those fairground machines, Cosmic Cranes. A lever with pincer-claws hovers above a container full of soft toys. It's harder than it looks, to grasp the toy and manoeuvre it to the drawer that leads to the outside. The pincers always seem to fail at the last minute, so that the toy falls back into the pile. I imagine those claws going up through my nose and down into my mouth.

I'm deeply sorry that I asked.

We go up to the ward. I wish I was stronger on my feet, the way I was when we left. Not bent double over a zimmer frame. But I don't want to put it off any longer.

The pale physiotherapist gives us ice packs for my leg. She seems worried.

'Has a doctor seen it?'

'Yes. They say it's okay.'

'Keep an eye on it.'

On the way home I realize how the M50 has opened up the hills to us in a new way – there's seriously good-looking scenery up there.

Charlie Haughey's funeral is on TV. One of my friends is somewhere in the crowd, reporting on proceedings. Bloomsday celebrations are getting underway in Glasthule. Another friend rings to say that she's already dressed up and hunting through old jewellery for something flamboyant to wear. Her book club is heading down there for lunch, wine and pageantry – a brilliant day, brilliant thing to do.

I love knowing that friends of mine are out there, that these wonderful things exist to be done.

Next year, maybe.

Is the crab still at work in the dark?

I went cold when I read in Lance Armstrong's book that his brain tumours were necrotic. Necrotic means dead. If they'd been lively and aggressive, he says, they could have gone on to carry him off.

'Avid' is the word they used about mine. Avid means eager, greedy. I think: *voracious*. I don't like the sound of a voracious crab, not one bit. Did they get it all?

I've been told that someone has to come off Tuesday's 'elective surgery' list so that I can have the wisdom teeth out. I muttered something insincere about hating to take someone's place, but they said that these decisions are based on relative urgency. Why is this urgent? Because these teeth have to come out before radiotherapy starts. Once it does, dental work will become a risky business. They also need to come out because it's hard to reach back and clean them with my mouth as tight as it is. I have to do my best to keep my mouth super clean, to reduce the chance of damaging the graft or getting any kind of infection.

The team's urgency about moving on to radiotherapy makes me think that they're concerned. There are no radiotherapy facilities at St James's and I have to go to St Luke's (a smaller hospital which specializes in cancer care) for treatment.

I've had a letter from St Luke's and an information leaflet which explains in broad terms what will happen from now on. At my first visit, I'll be seen by the radiation oncology team, who will explain my treatment plan. It's important that I am in the exact same position each time I have treatment, so they will make an immobilization 'mask' or 'shell' for me during this visit. Then there will be a 'simulation', where they'll pinpoint my treatment area.

After that first visit, it will take at least four weeks for the calculations to be completed and treatment to start. This means that, even if I get an appointment soon, I'll have time to work on the piece for the *Dublin Review* and to read enough about radiotherapy to understand what's happening.

We talk about converting the living room to a bedroom, in case the stairs get to be too much. It's tiring, hopping up and downstairs on one leg. We also need to figure out how I'll get over to St Luke's every day. It's in a suburb about seven miles from here. Public transport is not an option for me – I'd have to take three buses – and I can't drive with my leg like this (not to mention the chemical cocktail that passes for my bloodstream).

17 June 2006

A group of small girls comes to the door with flowers. Last time this happened, they'd put a stone through the window of Emma's car, while I was in hospital.

'Would you like these?' they ask.

'Why?' Simon teases them. 'Where did you get them from?' He pokes his head out the door and looks up and down the street, as if to check whether the neighbours' gardens have been trampled.

From the kitchen, Emma calls out: 'Did you check your car?'

They sigh and scuff their feet and then admit that the flowers are for me. I call out to thank them.

The girl from next door comes to the window, shy. Half-looking. Taking her time. I wave and she waves back. Solemn.

A salesman comes to the door. We know him well, we've bought food from his van for years. He's in the kitchen with Simon, looking through his list. He knows I'm here. I decide to go in and face it down.

Emma comes with me. The zimmer leads the way, metal on wood.

'Hello,' I say. 'I'm not as fit as I was when you saw me last.'

He looks right at me, shocked but not looking away. 'Lord, you've had a bit of a bang there.'

'I've had cancer.'

'They're rearranging your face, then?'

I prattle my way through this. 'Yes, but it'll be okay . . . takes a while . . . get there in the end . . .'

It's excruciating. I can't bear to hear these meaningless phrases coming out of my mouth. He's a nice man, he deserves better.

'I'd no idea,' he says.

'Neither did we.' Then I back out, zimmer clicking, and leave them to it. I'm glad I didn't hide, even though I could have.

Nessa and Mark are off to the Dundrum shopping centre for the afternoon. They ask if I want anything. I hesitate – there might be books on cancer. But I look at her sparkle, and I think, no, let her go and have an illness-free afternoon with her boyfriend.

Later she rings to tell me that she's found a really pretty skirt. Breathless and happy, she describes it. 'Got to go,' she says. 'Love you. See you later.' For the space of that phone call, it's as if the last two months didn't happen.

By this evening I can fit six tongue depressors between my teeth. Twice as many as when I started.

The long difficult slog of radiotherapy is still ahead and I'm scared stiff at the prospect of the tiny operation to take out my wisdom teeth. I'd turn and run if someone gave me back my leg, shout for freedom if my mouth worked. But it's too late. I'm already here and the only way out is through.

I try to remember what I'm fighting for. Not the treatment but the cure.

18 June 2006

Lyn died twenty-one years ago today.

My leg is sore. The swelling has gone down so that the hard knob I've been pointing out for days comes into relief. Surely everyone can see it now? There's something wrong.

A blue pain strips the lining from my spine. It's blinding and gleaming all at once. Will Sunday always be diarrhoea day? I clack and shuffle through the house. There are so many steps, obstacles and corners to negotiate, the dog's bed in the way, chairs and doors. I feel black-robed, veiled and ancient, the hag reinventing herself.

Then a friend arrives with a pair of crutches, shows me how to use them. They make such a difference.

One of my schoolfriends brings Sunday-morning scones. She asks what it was like, in hospital. I tell her it's like being held in a different world, underwater. You struggle to breathe. You can see everything that's happening around you, all the chaos, but your sights are set on being released back into the world of air.

Simon is up in the attic, working. He says that he's pretending to be in London. He comes down and cracks jokes to visitors about it. In the end I say, 'You'd want to watch it, or people will begin to think you were up in the attic all those sodding years you said you were away.'

I sit on the sofa with tongue depressors skewered into my mouth – I'm up to eight sticks! I can now fit my thumb between my teeth – who can I ring with this news?

Nessa comes in to play the piano. The sun slants on to me from a blue eye in a rushing black sky. Passing neighbours shed layers of clothes. The blue eye widens.

A friend drops in with books and a lovely journal. She's calm when she sees the shark bite, but says, 'That'll be an end to the mini-skirts, then.'

'I don't know. If I have to take the face out, I may as well bring the leg.'

At least I can still make people laugh.

★

Jackie brings some books on cancer. She tells me that nine out of ten books in the local bookshop were on breast cancer and she had to go into town to find a better range. I wonder why this is. When we're out and about I see those pink ribbons everywhere, on the backs of cars and pinned to people's clothes. Breast cancer awareness. I wish I'd been aware that you can get cancer in your mouth.

The clinical oncology book brings me up short. My disease was a lot more advanced when they found it than I'd realized. The cold tongue of fear slides down my throat, wraps itself around my heart and squeezes. I let this fear ride me for a while, then I put it away. You can't let it win.

I've been trying to cut back on the morphine, but when I left one of the patches off I paid for it with pain and weakness, being squeezed by the hot python that has replaced the crab at my neck. One of the books explains my mistake. The patches are my base medication – the others are for 'break-through' pain. Would it be better to cut back on those first? I should wait and talk to someone who knows.

19 June 2006

In a fit of optimism I make a 'to do' list, the first in ages. It shows the change in my life as clearly as anything could. Now I plan things like cutting my nails or washing my hair the way I used to plan conferences, workshops, even books.

My leg is stiff again this damp grey morning. A disappointment, but there you go. I've slept well and I feel better. That'll have to do.

I ring the health insurance company to see what would happen if we wanted to upgrade our coverage, now that I have cancer. A helpful rep explains that a two-year pre-existing condition rule applies: you start to pay now but the benefits don't kick in until two years after the diagnosis.

My new laugh, like a dog's bark, comes out. I say I'd be happy to settle for the two years, all by themselves, thanks. He laughs too, God bless him.

The school bus pulls up and one of the girls from next door gets off. I wave but she doesn't see me. I've become a woman-at-the-window.

I get a text from a friend who's under stress, saying that all she wants is for this week to be over. I think about what's ahead of me tomorrow when they take out the remaining wisdom teeth. I think about wishing your life away. What I want is for time to settle and slow. All I want is to be here, now.

The prospect of this operation, minor and all as it is, terrifies me. I calm myself: there's no need to be afraid *now*. It's not happening *now*.

20 June 2006
The day of the wisdom teeth.

It's extraordinary, how empty the unit is, after all that fuss about having to cancel someone else. I'm the only patient in a recovery room with eight gurneys. Eerie. It turns out there are more patients somewhere else, but not many.

I ask if there's any chance of a general anaesthetic. The anaesthetist explains that it's out of the question because the movement of my jaw is so restricted.

When he goes away, Sinéad, the head-and-neck nurse, tells me that she's been on to the physiotherapy department about my leg. They say I should have been referred for outpatient treatment sooner. They'll see what they can do, but there's a waiting list. They'll send me an appointment in the post.

I can't help thinking that some of the nurses who wander in come to get a look at me. They seem bored. One of them sits a few yards away from me, reading through my notes. I might as well be naked out on the street.

Professor Stassen comes along as I'm being wheeled in to theatre. He's with a short dude with bristly eyebrows bursting out from under his green surgical cap. I wonder if they might be persuaded to spend the afternoon in the pub instead, but I don't say it out loud. The routine of needles and sticky monitor pads and blood pressure cuffs begins.

I remind him that I need huge doses of anaesthetic and he laughs at me. 'Don't worry.'

Whatever the sedative is, it works. The next thing I know I'm in recovery, euphoric, extraneous teeth gone. And I didn't feel a thing.

In the evening, Nessa tells me that she's decided not to get a summer job. Instead, she's going to look after me and drive me wherever I need to go, she'll take care of the house and the shopping, she'll be the constant presence I can count on. I'd never have asked her to do it, but it's a huge relief.

21 June 2006

I have an appointment with the radiation oncology team in St Luke's, the cancer hospital, tomorrow. I have one whole day free. How will I spend it? Here, on the sofa, with an ice pack on my throbbing leg.

I'm afraid that I might never be able to have a general anaesthetic again, because my mouth won't open wide enough for a ventilation tube. The idea frightens me. What if I need surgery for some other pressing reason? The irony of it, given that my mother spent her life putting people to sleep, is not wasted on me.

I hear that a friend dedicated her reading during the Dublin Writers' Festival to me. It's as if she's reached down and hauled me out of this pit up to the podium beside her. But ladders of pain bring me right down again to where pain waits.

The big question of the week – well, one of them – is whether I'll be able to go to the Women Writers' Web meeting on Saturday, two days from now. I'm desperate to see everyone, to do something that isn't related to illness, to get back in touch with who I used to be. But even I can see that it might not be possible. There are a lot of stairs involved, for a start.

I do what I can to rotate and stretch the foot and wonder how long I'll have to wait for a physiotherapy appointment in St James's. A growing rage is interrupted by a phone call from a writer friend. He is hilarious about the nuns in the convalescent home down the road, where he's recently had a stint himself, following a heart operation

When he went to check out, the nun at the desk asked if he'd rented a TV.

'There was one in my room,' he said. 'But I didn't use it.'

He describes how she peered at him, over her glasses. 'You didn't look at it at all?'

'I think I watched the news one night.'

'That'll be eighty euro,' she said.

22 June 2006

Today we go to St Luke's.

My foot and ankle are sore, but a bit more flexible, maybe. I'd love to be able to walk into radiotherapy when it starts. To be able to go down to the sea right now.

This morning is laid back, almost as if we have nowhere to go, nothing to do. I even do some work. Then suddenly it's time to go.

There's no room in the hospital car park and we have to go back out onto the street. When we find a space it turns out we have a puncture. You couldn't make it up. I stump along on my crutches. At least it's not raining.

I've been to this hospital before, for breast checks, but this experience is completely new. We're in a different part of the building for a start.

St Luke's is small and it never seems as crowded as other hospitals do, although today is a busy day. It's a bright place, with fish tanks in the waiting areas, good art on the walls. People smile more in here than I've noticed in other hospitals. They're more relaxed. I feel less defensive about my face. Water coolers are in evidence at every turn, and they never run out of water or paper cups.

I clunk down a long corridor to a waiting area short of chairs. We have to sit beside the TV, facing all the people who watch the screen. *Big Brother* is on, then Ascot. A yellow sign encourages us to change channel if we want. It's mostly the people who accompany patients from other hospitals and nursing homes who watch. The rest of us just sit and talk, quietly. A fish tank competes with the TV for attention – it takes a while to spot the single doleful blue fish who slinks around at the back of the tank.

We're called in to a tiny exam room. Someone takes pictures of my face and leg for ID purposes. Professor Hollywood explains the treatment plan. I'm a bit confused at the end of it all, despite copious note-taking. There's a lot to take in. They still have to decide where to concentrate the treatment and how many sessions I will have. There's a risk that the surgical graft in my mouth might react to irradiation.

I ask if I'll be having chemotherapy as well. At some stage over the last few weeks, I'm sure that someone mentioned the possibility that I might have it, but I can't remember who, or when. Professor Hollywood says that chemo is not particularly effective for the kind of cancer I have.

In the mask room, the radiation therapists ask me to lie down on a narrow bed. They take a rectangle of yellow plastic mesh with a hole in the middle for my nostrils, soak it to soften it, then push it gently down onto my face. Their hands push and feather and sculpt the plastic to my immobilized face and neck and the upper part of my chest. Then they let me sit up to see my negative, the print my features have made in the mesh. This includes the sunken cheek and the rolled swelling at the line of my chin. Ghostly and alien.

I look from the shell to my injured foot and think about a line I read once in a story: If your foot was severed in an accident, would you recognize it out of hundreds when it was shown to you? I thought my answer would be yes. I've always liked my feet. They've carried me a long way, even when I've given them dog's abuse with bad shoes and long hours of dancing.

I don't think I'd recognize this foot as mine if someone showed it to me now.

They soak the mask in cold water and ask me to lie down again. They reapply it to my face and check that the fit is good. Then we are brought to another waiting area; another fish tank. There's a long queue for the scanner. Rumours that the machine has broken down.

I go into an X-ray room and strip off yet again, this time for the scan where they'll set up my treatment field.

I lie down and they cover my face with the mask, which they anchor to the table with some sort of clip. Voices, hands, bright lights on my eyelids, darkness. A calm, indifferent voice asks me not to move, tells me when they leave the room. I breathe through the plastic mesh. They put tape on the shell and draw on it with markers, a target for the beam of radiation.

When I shift my aching leg I'm given out to. 'You moved your whole head there,' someone says.

The lights come on and they say they've finished. The controls fail and the table won't lower, so I have to climb down via a chair.

'My leg hurts,' I say, to no one in particular. 'It's hard not to move it.'

The radiation therapist is impassive. 'Take a painkiller before you come the next time.'

Then they say that I have to come back for another scan tomorrow.

'I've to be in St James's tomorrow morning,' I tell them.

'Come here in the afternoon, then.'

Out on the street Simon changes the wheel and we drive to a garage. I sit in the car, feeling ridiculous, while they jack it up and fix the puncture.

We hit the worst of the traffic and it's late when we get home. I'm wrecked. We talk about what we heard today, about balancing the need for aggression against the risks of treatment, especially because of the infected wound in my neck. I'm worried. What if they're holding back, not being aggressive enough?

23 June 2006

Two different hospitals to go to today. The plan is to get home and rest between appointments. Today all Emma's applications for grants and for her Ph.D. have to be in. She's getting everything together as we leave.

In St James's, the max-fax team send us off to the plastics trauma clinic to get the leg checked again, because I'm still 'complaining' of pain. I know this is the language of medicine, but it annoys me. Why can't doctors say 'report' or 'describe' instead? There is the long hunt for a wheelchair, the bumpy journey over to the trauma clinic.

We wait in a tiled hall with sleepy people. Simon has to park me in front of the water cooler. I always seem to be causing some obstruction these days. A weary-looking family walk straight past everyone into the treatment room. The hallway bristles with resentment. Then we hear their story. They've been here since eleven last night with their son, in A & E, exposed to weirdness and drunkenness and all sorts. They tell us that a man came over to them and said, 'It's not right, your boy having to see all this.' Then he vomited all over them.

Inside the treatment room, there is general disbelief at the suggestion that there is anything wrong with my leg. I show them its new alignment but they're unmoved. The perfectly pleasant doctor says that he'll order an X-ray anyway, to keep me happy. We leave with an appointment to come back for an X-ray when we're next due in Outpatients, on Wednesday morning. That's five days away.

On the way back to the main hospital, every jolt is excruciating.

There's no time to go home, so we go straight to St Luke's. We struggle through lunch in the coffee shop – I make crumbs from a blueberry muffin, drink a glass of milk. Simon mashes a banana for me and wets it with one of those yogurt-like drinks. We go round and wait. The radiation therapists are still at lunch.

They call me in at last. I lie down, they put the mask over me, fasten it in place. I don't even have time to get uncomfortable. The scan lasts three minutes or less. Then I can go. Is that all?

There's no one else waiting. I ask what happened yesterday, why I had to come back for such a short time today. They say that the other machine broke down. They had to fit in as many people as they could on one machine.

I could weep by now, with tiredness and frustration.

On the slow shuffle to the car park I stoke up a rage. Who gets to decide whose time is more valuable than anyone else's? But then the opposite arguments start up straight away: maybe everyone else was up from the country, what about that? Maybe we had to come back because we're from Dublin.

My time doesn't belong to me any more. I decide then and there that I will go to the writing group tomorrow. I say so. Simon objects. He says look at the state of me, I'm too tired. We get in to the car and have a screaming row.

Actually, I'm the one who's screaming. 'If I have to spend so much time on this shit, I'll do what I want for the rest of the time I have!'

I'm crying as hard as I did when that child was afraid of me. I have to fight for air. 'You try to make it easy for me to go along with all this, please don't make it hard for me to do what I need.' Then I calm down, ashamed of myself.

On the way home we talk about how we can arrange it so that I can go to the meeting, as if nothing has happened.

24 June 2006
A shower! It's Simon's idea. He helps me. We put one of those green plastic garden chairs into the shower and I hop in and sit on it while he hoses me down with warm water. The sensation of water falling onto my parched skin is a blessing. He stays well clear of my neck. He's a saint. I feel more human.

A friend from the writing group drives me to the meeting. Sitting there listening to people read, I feel the reassurance of hearing this work, its continuity – it's so comforting not to be the focus for a change. To think about other things besides illness, even though I've brought no work myself.

Then it's time for me to go. Simon is waiting outside, in the car. They all get up to say goodbye, the reverse of a receiving line. I love these faces, these smiles. Cards and letters and texts and phone calls from these women have been a mainstay for me over the last few months. I try to tell them so. I'm not sure they realize what it means.

The drive home is a wavering dream of rain, my sore weighted leg. Now I'm on the couch with an ice pack, dozing while Simon makes dinner and Nessa plays the piano, softly.

Inspired by exposure to so many ideas, I sit on the sofa with my notebooks and my laptop. *How much time do I have?* is the big question. From now on, when I start a book, I'll wonder *will I finish it?* and *will this one be my last?*

26 June 2006
Tomorrow is Emma's graduation. I feel sorry for her because everything is going to be so low-key. It's my fault. She says it's all she wants, to have just the family, and Simon's parents, for lunch. She'll go out with her friends later.

The house is quiet. You'd never think there were five people in it, a sleeping dog and a cat on a bed somewhere. I'm down here on the sofa writing meaningless sentences in front of the window. Outside, all the greens stand full and quiet and ready. A single line of birdsong and the high buzz in my ear are the only sounds. Then the faraway rumble of a man's voice, Oz breathing. It's good to be alone and not-alone.

Our GP calls round. When I wail to her about the issue of the general anaesthetic, she says, 'But look at the speed of developments in medicine. Who knows what changes might happen?' And I know she's right. You can catch someone else's belief like a germ. It can ignite and lift you.

I ask about chemotherapy. I understand that they have to be cautious about the graft, but I've read that chemo might increase the effectiveness of treatment. She suggests that I ring Professor Hollywood's office, so I do. I explain my question to his PA, who says she'll give him the message.

I can't go to Emma's prizegiving ceremony. When they leave without me I feel sad and abandoned on the doorstep. But after dinner I haul myself upstairs to the computer to catch up with some emails. I write to my friend, the oncologist in Canada, to bring her up to date with the latest developments and see what she thinks. Then I write to people who have invited me to give a residential workshop in Andalucia this summer to say that I definitely won't be able to do it. It hurts to do this, but it's a relief to have it settled.

There's a build-up of affectionate and encouraging messages in my inbox and I respond to as many as possible and make it downstairs again – sitting, and bouncing from step to step – before the others get back. They get stern when I do things like hop upstairs on my own.

27 June 2006

The girls have hunted out a suit I used to wear to work and bought me a pair of low-heeled summer shoes for Emma's graduation. The bad foot is twice the size of the other one, but I squeeze it in there all the same. The trousers of the suit trail along the ground.

On the way out to the car we meet our postman.

'What happened to you?' he asks, so I tell him.

He gives me a hug, tells me I'm great and that everything is going to be fine. He's the kind of person I have faith in, so this is a good start for my first public outing in a non-medical setting.

Emma looks beautiful and Peter is a revelation in a suit. Then they put on caps and gowns. We take photos before they go in to the hall and I dread this part but what the hell, I'm here. I do my best to smile for the camera.

After the ceremony they are swept away by their friends, for group photos, and to set up the party for tonight. My leg throbs, so we decide to give the tea-and-chat part of the proceedings a miss and head home to finish getting the lunch ready.

I have never felt so utterly useless in my life. I stump around the kitchen holding onto counter tops and chairs, getting in the way. I insist on chopping, or washing leaves, or whatever needs to be done to get this lunch together. Simon asks me to do them a favour and pretend that I'm a guest, just this once, to let them do all the work, but I refuse. I know I'm behaving badly but I can't stop myself, even though my leg screams a protest at every effort to put weight on it.

We are at the absolute loudest stage of the meal when the phone rings. It's Professor Hollywood. Slightly shocked that he's on the phone himself, I go out of the kitchen and sit on the stairs to talk to him.

He asks what's bothering me. I'm afraid that the treatment won't be aggressive enough because of the complication of the wound at my neck. He explains that my particular carcinoma doesn't respond very well to chemo in the first place, and that the marginal gains are probably not justified in my case. Not just because of the wound, but because of the potential toxicity of the treatment. They have to weigh up risks and benefits in each individual case. It's probably exactly what he said to me before, but he doesn't hurry me. He's a patient man.

When he hangs up I sit there for a minute and think about the implications of what I've just heard, and listen to the party getting louder in the kitchen. Then I pick up the crutches and swing my way back in there to join them.

Chapter 5

28 June 2006

We arrive in the X-ray department at St James's while they're in the middle of introducing a new, computerized storage and retrieval system. It turns out that the appointment we have isn't valid. The upheaval is so general that they agree to take me anyway.

I ask if I can see the image. I want to know exactly how much bone was taken out during the operation. I imagine the slender, elegant fibula broken and crossed at my chin like those iconic images of Celtic saints.

I get a shock when I see the X-ray of my leg. Not because of the creepy missing length of fibula, or the small staples where blood vessels have been clamped off, but because of the angled split and splinter of the tibia, the knuckle of new bone that means new growth. Not only is the tibia broken, the break is not recent.

I lean on the borrowed crutches and look at the ghostly image.

'Have you been walking on it?' they ask eventually.

'Yes.'

We look at it some more. I have a wild desire to laugh. 'They told me to exercise it.'

'How long have you been using it?'

'Three weeks.'

I haul myself out of there and go to find Simon, back in the general waiting area. I'm really banjaxed now. But as I think about what to tell him, how he'll react, I begin to doubt what I saw. Was that someone else's X-ray? Did that conversation really happen?

'It's fractured,' I blurt out when I see him. And then: 'I think.'

We go round to Outpatients and wait. It's a friendly morning. There's enough goodwill on this corridor to sink a nuclear submarine. I feel vindicated, like a child who's been wrongly accused of malingering.

'Wait till you see the X-ray,' I babble, when I shuffle in to the room and plonk myself on the dental chair while they call the image up on their screen. My left lower leg appears in front of us – plundered fibula, staples, broken tibia and its clumsy, misshapen effort to mend itself.

'See? It's gone,' I say. And laugh.

I can laugh because I am here now, in this room, with people who will sort this out. I'd trust them with my life.

This is the sort of thing people say all the time, without thinking what it means. But in my case it's true. Before I came into this clinic I was in free fall. These people, this consultant in particular, put out their safe and clever hands and broke my fall. I know it. I owe them my life.

Plus, I like them. We have a laugh in here. Most of the time.

They are taken aback by the X-ray. They say they've never seen that happen before. If anything, they seem more stunned than we are.

Their surprise makes me feel better, for some reason.

So long as I'm in here, I feel all right. But no matter what, I'm going to have to go on the long trek down to the other clinic, to see the other team, because my leg is their business, and they ordered the X-ray.

While we're here, we ask to see an X-ray of my new, bionic jaw. The titanium part of the graft looks a bit like a bicycle chain. Simon takes a photo with his mobile phone.

Before we go, Professor Stassen talks us through the pathology results from the operation. He explains that 'spread' doesn't mean, as I'd feared, that my cancer cells are running wild through my system, it means that they've grown on the outside of the lymph node capsule. There is a slightly worrying reference to 'perineural invasion' but we're not to dwell on it. We got a clear margin, albeit not quite as big a margin as they'd like.

I tell them I'm writing about the experience and we shift into general information mode. We talk statistics. Oral cancer is equivalent to cervical cancer in its prevalence, but people don't know about it, just as I didn't. It's important to get stubborn sores checked. What seems to happen is that dentists refer their clients to doctors, doctors refer to dentists and so on, when they should be sent straight to the Dental Hospital.

In my experience, you might have to wait a ridiculous length of time for an appointment like that. But I also know, because I'm tired of hearing about it from other patients out on this very corridor, that a well-placed phone call from a dentist who is on the ball can get you into a clinic on the same day.

We talk about my leg. Professor Stassen is going to be away for a couple of weeks, on his holidays. I have to concede that this is allowed. We're out of time now. People are waiting on the corridor outside, other doctors have come into the room. They stand by the door and wait to be recognized, like courtiers.

Before we go down to the other clinic we slip in to see the petite dietician so that she can weigh me and change the troublesome clamp on my PEG tube, yet again. She and the nurse who sticks up for me when I need it fill a bag with dressings and other fixtures. We're like children leaving a macabre party, with our goodie-bag. I even need a buggy – they insist that I need a wheelchair. It takes ages to find one. In the end Simon asks a porter, who lends us one from a store room. It's broken, missing a side. We have to swear to bring it back. Simon says it's a pig to drive. It won't steer right and we jolt along, every snag an agony.

Over in the plastics clinic they tell me I have to be admitted.

'No!' I wail. How could I not have seen this coming? I thought they would do a quick reduction of the fracture, maybe put plaster on my leg, then send me home.

'You'll have to have surgery.'

'No!' But I can already see that it's no use. Across the room, that deformed tibia looms on another screen. I've been walking on it for too long, making it worse with every step. It will need to be re-broken and set properly.

The first doctor we see is leaving to get married; the next is off to Oxford on a research grant. I could not have timed this worse. Anyone who's worked in hospitals for any length of time knows that the two most dreaded dates of the year are 1 January and 1 July, when the various rotations rotate. It's as if the different disciplines and teams play musical chairs. New personnel end up in new positions and have to find their way around.

The way back over to Admissions is a surreal journey in that bockety chair across the now-familiar pitfalls of the uneven pavement. I try to bleep Sinéad to tell her what's happened. A staff car is parked across the ramp. I have to stand up and hop around it, drop my bulging file and my phone. A small crowd gathers, waiting to cross the road behind me, while we scramble to pick everything up, with me hopping on one leg.

Simon parks me in Admissions and goes off in search of food and a drink so I can take my meds. A nurse I know rushes past on the main corridor. I call her name but she says, 'sorry-I-can't-stop,' and hurries on. I feel stupid. Then a nurse from my old ward appears. I feel a mixture of terror and relief. What if he rushes past as well? I'm almost afraid to say hello, but it turns out that he already knows what's happened – he met Simon in the hall. I'm the reason he's here.

He goes into the office to see if they can get me back onto my old ward but it can't be done until tomorrow. In the meantime, I'll go back to the very first ward I was on.

Same bay, different bed. It feels so different, ten weeks on. The call of the peacock has gone. Everyone is more mobile than the last group, except for the woman beside me, who's in a bad way. I'm relieved when Sinéad turns up to say hello. I think things can't go too far wrong when she's around.

The pink-skinned lady in the middle bed who smells of face-powder talks to everyone. She's the one who looks out for my neighbour and I'm glad, this time, not to get involved. I'm too slow anyway, with my useless, deformed leg, my crutches. I'm beside the window, near a sturdy rustling tree, the slanting open windows of another wing. Air. Sky.

The woman opposite me has been reading a box of Kleenex for an hour and a half. She has a familiar body type, round, with sloping shoulders. Iron and steel in her hair. She reminds me of my aunt, Gabrielle. She moves in the same dreamy way. She wears a black and white houndstooth cardigan over tracksuit bottoms, owl glasses.

'Obsessive-compulsive disorder,' the pink lady informs me, in a whisper, from behind her hand.

I'm admitted by a nurse who's in a hurry to get through the questions on the admissions sheet before the change in shift. 'Any fears that you express?' she asks, pen poised above the boxes she has to tick.

No, sweetheart, none that I express. Not so casually, at any rate.

'What about body image – what do you feel?'

'Pity,' I say. Then I change it to 'Sympathy'. It bothers me that I don't know which she wrote down. When I was getting ready to have my wisdom teeth out they asked if I had any fears and I said 'dentists', only half joking. I was surprised when none of the max-fax team followed up on this at the time, they're usually quick to pick up on a joke. I wonder if anyone ever reads these things.

(Later, I find out that the nurse wrote: 'She says she's sorry about the situation, herself.' What is the point of these questions if there is such a huge gap between what you mean and what a person hears you say?)

I'd forgotten that you can't escape the TV on a ward. News headlines blare out across the room. Israel beating on Gaza; trouble about statutory rape law; two missing school-girls found murdered in Belgium. I have a sense of being stuck in a time warp, the same things repeating themselves over and over again. The obsessive-compulsive woman laughs at each horrific story. She stares at me a lot but at least she's not laughing at me yet.

The orthopaedic people are worried that the fracture might be due to a problem with bone density. They want to be sure that the cancer has not metastasized to the bone.

'If it's gone to the bone, that's a different thing,' I say to Simon. I'm thinking that if it has, I'm going home. Now.

'That's game over, I'm afraid,' he agrees.

We're already into extra-time, here. Don't even mention sudden death.

The mother of one of my closest friends died of cancer when we were fifteen. Shortly before she died, she fractured her femur walking up the stairs in their house. This image has haunted me ever since it happened. Now it comes to roost near the front of my mind. But modern medicine is different. Now they have bone-strengthening injections, all kinds of treatment they didn't have then. As our GP continues to remind me.

Simon says he feels as if he's spent his whole life learning the wrong things. I know exactly what he means. These last weeks around the hospital I have begun to feel that I made all the wrong choices in life. I was so quick to put distance between myself and medicine. What I wouldn't give to have some of that familiarity and confidence back, the unconscious and unfair advantage of being a healthy person working in a hospital, knowing your way around the system, understanding the processes of disease even in the most general way.

I don't have a water jug and the obsessive-compulsive woman has two but no one (least of all me) wants to take the extra one away from her. I ask for one of those metal contraptions that hold blankets up and away from sore limbs. I think it's called a cradle, or a cage. I had one in the other ward, but a nurse here says they went out with the flood, in a voice that brooks no contradiction.

I don't argue. The weight of the sheet falls on my leg and I settle back to familiar sounds – night trolleys, voices, monitors. Somewhere a door slams and the building shakes. You expect your hospital to be more solid, somehow.

The pink-skinned lady, who's so generous with information, directions, and physical things like pulling curtains and shutting windows, falls asleep first, a silent shape, on her side.

29 June 2006

The pink lady has a stone in her bile duct. She covered up her pain for days before she came to the hospital, so that her daughter would go on holiday. As soon as her daughter left for the airport, she headed down to A & E. She was there for eleven hours waiting to be seen.

She tells horror stories about people coming in having overdosed on paracetamol, says that once they've been pumped they're put back out in the waiting area to sleep it off. I wonder if this can be right. She describes a pair fighting behind her — a young one of about sixteen letting an old bowsie beat her. Drunks. Then she was put in an observation ward along with five men, all of them overdoses, the one beside her abusive, yelling filth all the time, about women.

She says that the nurses felt sorry for her, came in to talk to her, but she still couldn't stand it. What she'll never forget: the paracetamol overdoses, the way they begged for water they couldn't have, vomiting and blood, blood in the beds and on the floor.

I begin to wonder if she's been sent, strange messenger, to warn me of the dangers of getting it wrong.

The OCD woman is doing her personal brand of calisthenics. She strikes strange balletic poses, knocks wrists, knees and elbows against the wall. She looks as if she's dancing with it. In the bathroom, she has a routine of banging the corners and the fixtures with her stick. The pink lady tells me, in a whisper, that she washes her hands in the toilet bowl. And worse.

When the OCD woman comes out of the bathroom a ward assistant tells her to wash her hands. She does, and then plunges them immediately into the bin, right under the MRSA notice.

The pink lady is inexhaustible. She talks to everyone in the ward. She dips a sponge into drinks for my incapacitated neighbour who is, it turns out, recovering from a stroke. The pink lady instructs her to show me what she can do.

'Lift your right arm' she bosses and the woman raises a shaky hand, one eye rolling. 'See?' the pink lady says to me. 'She couldn't do that when she came in.'

The orthopaedic team appears. They're confident that the fracture is not the result of any spread of the cancer. They'll either reduce the fracture and give me a plaster, or do an open reduction, with a plate and screws to fix the bone in place. They say that the new growth of bone at the fracture site complicates it, but it means that I'm a good healer.

What it means to me is that it's been broken for a long time, all the time that people told me there was nothing wrong.

I wish I'd said 'anaesthetics' when the nurse asked what fears I have. I point out that my mouth-opening is severely restricted and ask what's likely to happen. They say I might be a candidate for an epidural. This means I'll be awake for the reduction but I won't feel a thing.

One of my schoolfriends rings to express her rage at this latest development.

'Tell me who to blow up and I'll do it,' she says. I tell her to be careful, the CIA are probably listening.

She says she doesn't care. 'Do you need anything?'

I remind her that this hospital is like a small town. I can get anything I want here. I can even rob a bank if I get bored.

The problem with people asking if I need anything is that

I don't know what to ask for. Apart from the fundamentals that my family bring – laundry, slippers, bottles of water, nail varnish, the meditation CD that I got before the big operation, a supply of medication to tide me over until the hospital system catches up with the fact that I'm here – I can't think of anything. Sometimes the right face, the right smile, appearing at just the right minute with the right story turns out to be just the thing I needed. Sometimes I want none of those things, but to be left alone.

The pink lady is back in bed, huddled under the blankets. It must be exhausting, being so concerned about so many people. Last time I was in this ward I was the one opening and closing windows, calling the nurses, preventing a distraught woman from climbing over the sides of her bed. Not any more.

A porter suddenly appears, ready to bring me to my old ward in a wheelchair. A friend carries my bags, through corridors we walked along, arm in arm, just a couple of weeks ago. I thought my leg was broken then. I didn't know what broken was.

I get a gorgeous welcome, hugs from some of the nurses, big smiles, people dropping in to my side room to say hello. No one can believe I'm back.

When the fuss dies down and I'm on my own I start to worry again about the anaesthetic. Then I remind myself how I sailed through the wisdom-teeth experience after all that fretting. A registrar tells me that an epidural is out of the question because of the medication I'm on. They can introduce a naso-gastric tube and administer anaesthesia that way. He admits that this can be unpleasant and might take a while.

I send out a storm of text messages looking for reassurance

and I get it in torrents. My friends point out that I might not actually want to be awake while the cast of *Scrubs* carry out feats of carpentry on my poor ankle. My sister Clair, who specialized in anaesthesia and who I don't expect to lie to me even if it might make me feel better, texts from America. She says that this kind of anaesthetic is often less traumatic than people expect. Professor Stassen sends reassuring messages. He seems to believe that I'll still be alive when he gets back from his holidays. For all I know he's already at the airport and should have turned his phone off ages ago. I feel better. I remind myself that other people have got through this. I can too.

30 June 2006

Being back in the reception area for Theatre is a bit like a reunion party, with nurses coming over to say hello and ask what I'm in for *this* time. I recite the list of my allergies: penicillin, Solpadeine, seafood. Then they wheel me in. I stare at the ceiling and concentrate on breathing.

When all else fails, it's surprising how comforting it is to feel your ribs rise and fall, air flowing in and out of you. Sometimes, when this is the only thing I seem able to do, it's enough.

An anaesthetist appears beside me. 'I hear you might have a problem with this anaesthetic?'

'Yes.' I demonstrate my pathetic effort at mouth-opening.

'Well,' he says, all business, 'we might try something different.'

I wait for the track through the nose to be described to me again, but instead he says, 'I'll give you an injection that will put you out, and we'll see. If it doesn't work, we'll wake you up. But we'll have done most of the unpleasant part already.'

'Okay,' I say, meaning, I love you, you are amazing, don't ever leave me.

Next thing I know the operation is over.

I wake up with a brand-new set of staples and a drain in my leg, which is swathed in a salmon-pink bandage. The bandage looks like the one my mother used to wrap around the cosh she kept beside her bed, so that if a burglar came in and she had to knock him out she wouldn't hear the crunch. The max-fax team come around, in force, for a social call. Thank God they didn't arrive ten minutes earlier, with me on the commode.

The doctor who used to urge me towards independence stays back when the others leave.

'I'm sorry,' he says, 'that this has happened to you.'

It's amazing how this cheers me up. Another doctor comes back to talk about how we'll manage the dressing at my neck. At least I don't have to brave the M50 while I'm here. We discuss amassing our supplies again, the Whitehead's varnish and all that. I feel absurdly happy. We're back onside.

After they've gone I have a *Eureka!* moment, a flashback to meeting the intern in the corridor during the saga of the wisdom teeth, when he said: 'I think they go through the nose.' There I was, visualizing my teeth being yanked up and levered out through my nose. And he was talking about the anaesthetic!

I'm my own worst enemy sometimes.

It's a gorgeous, gorgeous blue evening. I have a new tree to look at, a different corner of the car park and a prefab. It's all lovely to me in the euphoria of the anaesthetic and relief. I don't mind being here, not a bit. This leg needs minding and I'm back with the nurses I know and love.

★

The World Cup is on in the main ward opposite. Scales play across my new face and my tongue drills. I'm woozy and sore and back to this: waiting for meds. My mood sinks. It's like being adrift from my moorings. I look up and see how far I am from shore, waver a little, tug the rope – it is unreal that I am here, it's so like a dream, faces snap into focus and I'm back, then I fall away again, behind a thicker veil than usual, a waterfall.

1 July 2006

What I forget is how it feels to be waiting for everything, like a painkiller, or the commode – and then the fear that one of my many teams might arrive while I am on it. How I feel like a moaner, whinger, complainer and imagine that every whisper is about me. It wouldn't surprise me right now to hear that the whole hospital has been primed to make me miserable. Even the smokers down in the bicycle shed are probably having a good laugh about the fact that they forgot to bring me lunch and that I haven't had my midday meds.

In the middle of the afternoon I ring my bell and ask about the meds. I'm told I haven't been written up for any. I break down and weep all over the nurse I haven't met before. She brings in my chart so that we can figure out what's gone wrong. I've been written up for a different schedule, and some of my drugs have been left off the list altogether.

I'm mortified to be so upset, but she says I'm crying because it's important to get what I need and hard when I don't. She says a bunch of stuff about strong women losing their independence and how hard it is to let go. She says she'll give me a phone number for someone else who had surgery like mine. I don't like the sound of this much. I scowl at her but it has no effect. She fixes my cannula and says they'll start an antibiotic soon, she'll get the pain meds sorted.

The orthopaedic team stress that I'm not to put any weight at all on the bad leg or it could go again. I'm to get a plaster-of-paris soon. I'll have it for eight to twelve weeks.

When they leave, Nessa and I talk about the problems I will have getting around from appointment to appointment. There's no sign of the application form for the disabled parking permit yet.

'Can we not ring up and see what's happened?' I ask.

Apparently not. The system is that you write in for an application form. Then they send you the form, you fill it up and send it back to them. There's no point ringing up to make enquiries. The girls have tried.

Simon is antsy about going back to work in London tomorrow. His mind is on other things when he comes in, like air fares and this being the busiest weekend of the year at the airport.

The fear of old age, of being alone when I fall, tumble in on top of me. It's as if I have been fast-forwarded thirty years or more into timorousness, deafness and failing eyesight. I am as fragile and weak as a woman in her eighties.

I wrote an opening line once: *I will die falling.* I gave it to an elderly woman. I also gave her determination, fire, friends with a sense of humour. It doesn't seem like enough now.

2 July 2006

There are so many stories all around us. They seem more acute in hospital – not just the life-and-death dramas of patients, but the people who work here too. Especially the ones who've travelled a long way to get here and have had to leave their children behind. That's what Simon does, but at least now he gets home at weekends. When we first came home from the States he used to be gone for months at a time. I have friends whose fathers came home from England maybe once a year. Emigration is the story of any country where work is hard to get, and our success is so recent here that I don't understand our collective amnesia. When I was growing up I don't believe there was a single family in this country that didn't have someone working abroad, legally or not. Now look. We talk about economic migration as if those are dirty words.

My sulky young cleaner drops in to tell me how tired she is. Her face is drawn. She's pissed off because it's raining, scowls at the rain, at the word 'Dublin'. She has this afternoon off – every chance they get she and her boyfriend head out of the city and go to places like Howth or Malahide.

The joys of flirtation, even in the ridiculous state I'm in. I'm wearing the designer pyjamas that came from New York and someone clicks his tongue and tells me I look 'seductive'. I leer at him, with my scars and my twisted leg and my bandage-beard.

The nurse comes back to ask if I've had a good cry yet. What is it about this place? They all want to see you weep.

'You found me crying yesterday,' I remind her.

'That was only a little one.'

I had a good night's sleep. I'm better today. I tell her the leg is no problem now – I'd be tempted to kick a ball with it.

'Jaysus, don't do that,' she says. Then she gives me a phone number for the woman she told me about yesterday. We have different types of cancer, but we had similar operations.

★

I'm sick of hospital food already. My choices are limited because I don't eat meat. But I have to force myself to eat what's on offer, and it takes for ever with my awkward mouth. Here we are, heading into a time without Simon, and I have to make it as easy as possible for him to go away, to stay away.

Plan the piece you want to write about all this as if it's your last. It should leave nothing of what you want to say unsaid. If it was to be the last thing you write, would you be satisfied?

I take up this notebook to unleash some languid being, the type who'd wear a silk kimono with a scarlet dragon on the back, paint her toenails, smoke cigarillos through a holder and stab an enemy general with a hairpin with lethal accuracy between one verse of a song and the next. Her, again. I can see her dressing room, stockings tossed over a screen. Who knows what'll come out of her mouth, besides smoke?

I listen to the social exchanges going on outside, on the corridor. I recognize the preacher's voice as he pleads with someone, 'Don't go 'way. Don't walk away.'

I was one of those sturdy people who walked away from him once. Now I'm flattened by my own haste. What could I have done differently? Maybe nothing. Maybe it's the universe, springing traps for me.

3 July 2006
Emma starts work today. I text to wish her luck. It doesn't feel like enough.

A consultant comes along to say hello and sorry for your trouble. He says what they all say, this has never happened before. Never.

I say something polite and he leaves. As soon as he's gone I hate myself for being so mealy-mouthed and weak. So I haul myself off the bed and out after him, stumbling on my crutches. I ask him if he'll please come back, I have something to say.

My heart is pounding, my mouth is even drier than usual. I'm surprised by how terrified I feel when I tell him how dismissive I felt that his clinic had been in his absence and that I know it's not his fault but I hope they'll pay more attention to the next person like me who comes along.

He listens as if he hears every word. I can see that he takes it all in. 'I'm sorry,' he says. 'It shouldn't have happened.'

I feel like a new person when he's gone.

Then another doctor comes in and asks the nurse to leave. We go through the sequence of events again. He writes down dates. A nurse puts his head around the door to say they'll try to get me a wheelchair from the Health Board because, 'No weight-bearing with that plaster is going to be hard work, especially with radiotherapy.'

'We might postpone the radiotherapy,' the doctor suggests. 'You will get very tired.'

'No!' Before he went away, Professor Stassen told me not to let that happen.

The doctor says, 'You know, Lia, for many people life is hard, but you are strong. Soon, this will be just a memory.'

He says it's difficult for everyone. I know he's right. He says to smile and that he knows I can do that as well.

I can, too. Metaphorically, if not actually.

I get a call from a woman I've met maybe twice in my life. She tells me that she had a major illness a few years ago. Horrendous treatment. Horrendous. She feels she has to warn me what I'm in for. Before her treatment started, she went on a trip around the world. For several months

'Why don't you do something like that?' she asks.

I count the tiles on my ceiling and remind myself to breathe. 'I have a broken leg,' I say. I don't mention the infected wound at my neck, or the urgency of radiotherapy, how we all want it to start as soon as possible.

She goes on to describe the rigours of her treatment and various complementary therapies she tried, reflexology, acupuncture and so on. She gives me some useful numbers. Before she gets off the phone, she tells me that even when she got her diagnosis she knew she'd never commit suicide. 'I couldn't do it to my children. Because that message is passed down through generations.'

My weak eye weeps but my heart is flinty-eyed, stony, while I consider the nature of messengers. These women with their stories of the horrors of overdoses and the danger of blighting your children if you sow the seeds of suicide in their minds.

'Why didn't you hang up on her?' Simon asks.

But I consider myself warned.

4 July 2006

I'm told that radiotherapy might start as early as seven days from now. I'm not looking forward to it, but I don't fear it. I want to go ahead and *do* it; the sooner we start, the sooner it's over.

I hope I can get my hair done first. It looks a fright – dry and thin, it's coming out in handfuls. But I'm not allowed, until the neck wound closes over the bone.

★

I have a bleak morning. Simon rings from London and I cry when I hear his voice.

I get so bored with myself sometimes.

On the phone again to check up on me a little bit later, he says, 'You sound as if you just moved out to sea.' It's the seagulls, yelling at the window, but it's a little bit how I feel.

I can't believe that it's my last night on this ward. Again.

I sit at the end of the corridor, rest my cast on the window ledge and watch one of those demolition machines, a cruncher, eat away at Fatima Mansions. Shells of the buildings are all that remain. A chimneyed wall with paint reminds me of the Dublin I grew up in, its crumbling walls and flaking paint, the innards of houses exposed to the street.

One night years ago we were in a restaurant and a waiter spilled flaming sambuca on my arm. The flames played, blue, on my skin. I didn't feel a thing.

Sometimes things don't happen for a reason, they just happen.

5 July 2006

I have a last session with the little freckled physio. We head for the stairs. The preacher makes a break for it, runs after us. His attendant calls to the physio to close the door. She pushes it shut, just as he gets there.

'Don't you dare!' he roars, punching the air beside her face with his fist.

She ducks back.

'She didn't mean anything by it,' I tell him.

He mutters. Lets himself be led away.

Her young scowl mirrors his.

'He's sweet, usually,' I say.

I watch him go back to his room. I'll miss him.

On the way home we go to the Irish Wheelchair Association and rent a wheelchair, so that I won't be confined to the house. It's heavy. Nessa just about manages to lift it into the boot.

When we get home, a small stumble brings my heel to the ground – black wings of fear close over me. What if I break this leg again? Just remember to keep breathing.

Before I go to bed, I get a phone call from the nurse who sorted out my medications. 'Just checking to see if you're all right,' she says. 'You can call us, you know, if you need to.'

I relax a little. It's like having an escape hatch, primed and ready.

Chapter 6

6 July 2006

I'm back on the outpatient circuit. Today it's the Dental Hospital. Emma and Ryan have come along to help me while Nessa finds somewhere to park the car. I wonder how people get through all this on their own.

The dentist who talked so casually about 'ten-year check-ups' that she made me believe in them too makes impressions of my remaining teeth. From the impressions, she'll make acrylic casts. I'll have to fill these casts with a fluoride gel and wear them over my teeth for fifteen minutes every day for the rest of my life. Otherwise my teeth would get into trouble very soon, because I have less saliva than I used to. The salivary glands on one side of my mouth have gone, and the rest could deteriorate after radiotherapy. The fluoride gel will stain my teeth.

The radiation oncology team have decided not to make a stent, a device to hold the tongue out of the way of radiation. They won't make it because my mouth doesn't open wide enough.

Emma takes Ryan to the square while they wait for me. They sit on the grass and make daisy chains but then some man comes along and takes his trousers off, so they come back to the waiting room and watch TV until I'm finished.

At home, later, a troupe of neighbourhood kids come peering at the window. They started doing this before I went into hospital. I go over to say hello and they fall back, mouths in perfect Os, and run away. A clutch at the heart.

I tell the others what's happened, trying to laugh it off.

'Result!' someone says, and then my laugh is genuine too. It's true, they stop annoying us after that.

Visitors come and go. Then I realize that I've been sitting in the same chair for seven hours straight.

Simon comes home tonight.

7 July 2006

Ryan has a loose tooth. This morning, Zita brings him in to us.

'Show Grandad,' she says. 'He's the expert on loose teeth.'

Simon used to entertain the kids and their friends by terrorizing them with the threat of pliers, or the good old string-tied-to-a-door-handle trick.

Ryan bares his bloody mouth. His tooth is skewed and loose.

Simon says, 'Oh, I think Ryan should pull that tooth out himself.'

Ryan reaches into his mouth. Fear turns to wonder and delight as the tooth comes free in his hand. Glee all round.

Now he lisps, like me. Oz shares my limp.

Downstairs Zita's puppy, Gus, is trapped under his round brown bed. He runs around in circles like a baby spacecraft, swirling and circling on our kitchen floor.

8 July 2006

I pay some attention to the extraordinary changing texture of my face, mouth and neck. There's a bizarre succulence in my cheek, a powerful fizz in my tongue. The strangest is a roll of flesh that feels like rope, at my neck. It burns sometimes, gives off heat to my fingers, but it doesn't experience itself. I could slice it open with a knife and the knife might feel the wound but the skin would not. It's a little like an elephant trunk, or a creeper, root-like, vegetable. I realized only a few weeks ago that it wasn't an external, fleshy, plastic surgery construct, but my own skin grown taut and stretched to its limits by swelling.

A writer friend brings me a great present – a signed special edition of Eavan Boland's poem 'Anna Liffey', from the reading I missed the other night at Foster Place. Another has lent us several seasons' worth of *The Sopranos* on DVD. I gave myself a present of *Six Feet Under* for Christmas, but Simon votes against watching that. He thinks that a series about undertakers may be a bit close to the bone, but then he's not a fan, like me.

We spend the evening with *The Sopranos*. Maybe there's something more high-minded I could be doing, but I can't think of much that could be better than this, sprawled on the sofa like teenagers.

It's full of abrupt departures, deaths so sudden they seem casual. Not too far below the surface, my mind races. You only get so many warnings, so much time to change. Then they run out.

Emma's coping mechanism, luckily for all of us, is baking. At any given minute of the day or night she takes down the baking trays, softens butter, sifts through flour and sugar. She's at it now. The house fills with inviting smells. Even though it's late, we're all drawn to the kitchen.

9 July 2006

The little family have come to stay for a few days. They bring me for a cool blustery walk in the wheelchair, down in Sandycove. It's strange to be wheeled along paths I have always walked, thinking nothing of swerving off onto the rocks at low tide. But there's joy in feeling the wind on my face, the smell of low tide, the gritty shapes of stone and stranded weed. I feel an inwardness as well, concentrate on the people I'm with to avoid looking out into the crotches and soft bellies of people walking past me, young ones jogging and power-walking, their ponytails swinging.

10 July 2006

Simon went back this morning. I didn't sleep much, miserable, watching the light swell and listening to the house: to Zita going out to bring Eoin to work, then coming back, Gus going crazy, wanting the day to start.

I get some time on the computer and send round a few emails. A journalist friend writes back to say that he's glad to see my name turn up on his screen outside of an obituary column. I laugh out loud.

The public health nurse asks how I feel, if I'm angry. She says that a lot has been thrown at me. I tell her I'm really okay, most of the time. Maybe it's denial, or maybe it's ahead of me, or maybe I'm too far removed from myself but I don't feel anger. I feel other things: fear sometimes, and paranoia, and pain, but not anger.

There was every chance that, left to its own devices, the tumour could have finished me off by now. But I'm still here.

What I'm beginning to feel is: *lucky*.

11 July 2006

Is this a joke? This morning, when I'm washing myself, blood comes off my neck at the incision, onto a Q-tip. Now what? Is it about to open again? What am I supposed to do?

The girls have taken Ryan to Tesco. The morphine patch is falling off and maybe that has something to do with my reaction, which is extreme. I fly into a panic, become a perfect impersonation of a lunatic, falling apart. I pull out the drawer too far, looking for a dressing for my PEG. I flap, I pant, I mutter.

Then I calm down, breathe, and think about a story with a character whose head just might fall off, any minute. She has to hold it very still, just in case. I tell myself: *You're not as helpless as you think. You're stronger than you know you are.*

I call Sinéad. She's calm. This does happen, sometimes. I can go in if I want, or wait and see what happens next, it depends how worried I am. She's at the other end of a phone if I want to wait. I can always go to the GP. So I ring our GP and she gives me an appointment at the start of her next clinic. Now, why didn't I think of that?

The GP says that the blood on my neck is probably due to me poking at it with a Q-tip. There's no sign of the wound opening. I feel stupid, but she is generous with her time.

People are super-nice to me in the waiting room, in the same way that people bend down to talk to you when you're in a wheelchair, their voices slightly raised – it's an odd experience.

I get a call from St Luke's to say that they need a verification appointment before radiotherapy starts, probably at the end of next week. The verification session is when they check their calculations, like a dress rehearsal for the real treatment.

The day falls away in a rough-splintered mood. I am so far outside of myself I can barely hold on, resentment curdles everything. Everyone seems like an enemy. I have a granulating blister at the PEG site and it's getting worse. The patches won't stick to my skin. Maybe I'm reducing my meds too fast? I'm short-tempered, frustrated and paranoid. If I want something, I want it *now*; if people are in a room I'm not in, or leave a room I come into, they hate me; if someone gives me a one-word answer to a dumb question I feel dismissed.

Simon rings to find out what happened today, but he can't hear what I say because he's crossing Kew Gardens and there's a jazz festival on. Then he can hear me but he has to go because he's hosting a dinner and people are waiting for him outside the restaurant. I let him go.

When I get undressed for bed I want to lift my head off my neck. I get this a lot – as if there's something fastened there, something I'm wearing. When I go to take it off I discover my own neck, my own chin.

12 July 2006
The woman who had an operation like mine rings to introduce herself. She had hers two years ago, she's an old hand. I can't imagine myself two years from now. We swap stories, describe our new faces, laugh about the challenges posed by soup. When she says she doesn't know what 'normal' is any more, it feels like the truest thing I've heard in ages. It's bizarre, to be so explicit with a person you've never even met. Within minutes we're trading information like the extent of our scars, the number of teeth we lost (seven in my case, not including wisdom teeth).

We talk about being glad to be alive, but what I feel is more provisional and tentative than that. I'll be in suspense until I get to the other side of radiotherapy. I'm still on the rope bridge.

We arrange to meet at St Luke's when I go for the verification appointment.

One of my schoolfriends comes out to babysit me so the girls can go out. I still can't be left alone for long – I need help getting up and down from the couch and on the stairs, can't carry a drink from room to room. She's going to do this once a week for the next few months. She's been to the sales and bought clothes that she thinks I'll like. I model them in the kitchen, prancing around on my crutches, loose trousers and long T-shirts, white and emerald green. She irons the things I'm going to keep while we talk and drink tea in the kitchen.

13 July 2006

It's a fabulous blue day. Nessa's boyfriend, Mark, is off to China on a college trip. She drives me along the Vico Road and we stop to admire the view of Sorrento Terrace, Dalkey Island, the Muglins. Somewhere below us, under the sea, is the cave where St Augustine gave his interview to De Selby in Flann O'Brien's *The Dalkey Archive*. We open the window to let the air in, but along comes a bee as well. Just as well the car is parked. When we've evacuated the bee we drive on, speculating on how many car crashes might be caused by kamikaze insects.

At Scotsman's Bay we discover that there is no wheelchair ramp from the car park to the promenade. There are steps, there are even disabled parking spaces, which we don't use because we don't have a permit yet. But there is no ramp. I decide to risk the hop to the top but then I bounce around on one leg, the other heavy with plaster, terrified I'll lose my balance, while Nessa wrestles the heavy chair up to catch me, just in time.

We won't try that again.

It may be a good-looking day, but it's bitterly cold, half-tide. There are butts and cans near the ruins of the Baths. A woman walks down to the sea trailing three kids with nets on poles. It looks idyllic. A bullet-headed man uncurls from a bench and struts along in front of us in sandals. Despite the cold, we come back to the car the long way, to avoid the steps.

I trawl through the notebooks for the *Dublin Review* piece. It's absorbing and creepy to do this. Getting to the point of fear, I get colder.

A woman I know rings to tell me that her husband has cancer too. She tells me that my family are suffering more than I am and advises me to take up something like growing flowers, something with magic attached to it.

She might have a point. During the December weeks when my mother was dying, we brought a potted baby Christmas tree to her room and threaded a single string of coloured lights through it. Those lights kept vigil with us while we stayed with her through the nights that followed.

By coincidence, I've been sent a present of a magic bean. This bean comes in a pot with the name 'Leah' engraved on the front of it. The idea is that you plant the bean and water it and watch it grow and that its sturdiness and rapid growth will represent your own health.

What none of these people know is that I have a chronically black thumb. I give the bean the evil eye, but decide to plant it all the same, bearing the spelling of the name in mind as insurance against disaster. I'm not in the mood to let things rot if they have a chance of survival in circumstances I can control.

So I follow the instructions that come with the bean. I fill the little pot with the springy black soil from its plastic bag and set it on a saucer in the middle of the kitchen table where I won't forget to water it.

Time floats away. I cross the room to phone someone or write a thank-you and – it's bedtime.

15 July 2006

For all my knowledge of St James's, I'm not sure where the orthopaedic clinic is. When it's time to go back to have a check-up for my leg, I ring to find out. I'm put straight through to one of those nightmare electronic menus:

'If you wish to make a return appointment and it's over a year since your last visit, press X . . . If you wish to make an urgent appointment, press Y . . . If you wish to speak to a receptionist, press Z.'

I press Z and go straight back to the beginning of the loop. I try the other options – most ring out. I try the one for 'If you need to make an urgent appointment' and the voice advises me to ask my GP to send a letter to the consultant and *hangs up on me!*

I'm as cross and indignant as if I really do need to make an urgent appointment. How can they treat people who are sick and scared like that?

Sometimes I think that hospitals only exist as vast employment schemes – and that being a hospital patient is not unlike being a writer. Look at the industry that's built on what we do: publishers, bookshops, libraries, reviewers, literature departments at universities. But actual writers come pretty low in the pecking order. Where would all *these* people work, if there were no patients, if no one ever got sick?

I ring the main hospital number. As the woman who answers the phone answers my question in her quick and harried way, I can see exactly which one of the women at the information desk she is: the blonde with gold jewellery who shrugs into her jacket. It's funny that her face comes to me with her voice; the whole hospital opens up behind her, the lobby, the trees, the revolving door breaking down and the people waiting patiently for it to start moving again – but she has no sense of me at all.

My sister Clair is here from America for the weekend. Everyone comes around. We sit in the garden and take photographs. I've never liked having my photo taken, but today it feels excruciating. The cameras are passed around, the photos viewed. The harder I've tried to smile, the scarier I look, my mouth a twisted gash in the blur of my face. I look as if I'm snarling. Now I have justification for talking about my 'good side'.

16 July 2006

I'm out on my own, at the hairdresser's, having my roots done!

It's the most gorgeous day outside and it's quiet in here. Some of the stylists do each other's hair in the lull. A girl I don't know is scrubbing chairs and a window-cleaner washes the mirrors. It's odd to be out 'alone' – although really I've been transferred to my stylist's care for the duration – and to be parked in front of a mirror for so long. I'm glad I brought a book. But everyone is so nice, coming over to say hello and tell me I'm great, which, of course, I love to hear. When they catch my eye in the mirror they smile and wave – it's okay being here. I don't know why I was so nervous before I came. Maybe because of all the mirrors?

My stylist tells me that they often have clients from the rehabilitation hospital up the road, people who have to find places to stay while their relatives are in the long-term care of the hospital. We talk about how isolated they are, the problems of money, of having to pay for somewhere to stay at the same time as you're not able to work. I think about our growing overdraft, and the fact that I'm here having my roots done anyway, and marvel at my recklessness. This is another version of shaving the leg around the shark bite. Small gestures to appease the stubborn remnants of vanity.

There are so many levels to this parallel universe, the underworld we only see when we are plunged into it. But this one, about money, is something you don't often hear about. All the healthy food they tell you to eat is expensive; no one has time or energy to shop around; small things like hospital car park fees and smoothies bought in convenience stores add up heavily on the debit side. I can't imagine what it's like for people when the main breadwinner is the person who's ill. Which brings me back to people who are in long-term care and how their relatives have to fend for themselves.

I feel such outrage – why does nothing happen to change any of this? It reminds me of David's story about being on the train from Galway to Dublin last week, standing for the entire rattling journey across the country, not a drink of water to be had on the train – mothers with children, in that heat – and they had paid a lot of money for those tickets. Sometimes I wonder why the entire population doesn't take to the streets and stay there until we get things sorted out.

When Nessa comes to collect me, she's worried. There

have been major storms in China, in the province where Mark is staying. She can't get in touch with him. Neither can his mother.

We decide to go straight over to St James's because we're not sure what traffic will be like at that time of day. Wouldn't you know, we get there in jig time, no traffic at all. We pass under a bridge, where two weirdly futuristic-looking motorcycle cops stare down at us, still and watchful, ready to spring.

Further up the road they come up behind us at speed, lights and sirens flashing, escorting a crowd of motorbikes who are raising money for the children's hospital in Crumlin. They hold up traffic for a while but people are good-humoured about it. Not able to believe their luck maybe, or tolerant of the cause, or just grateful, like me, for the sunshine.

In the hospital coffee shop I watch the painful progress of a man in a bright-blue dressing gown who pushes his dripstand along in front of him towards the door, step joining step, alone and determined, chin jutting towards his goal. Nessa sees a girl her age, balding as a result of chemo, with a scarf on her head.

We make our way to the orthopaedic clinic, where the plaster is sawn off. A pale and hairy leg emerges, with its shark bite on one side, its squares of peeled skin, and the long line of staples where the fracture was. If only I'd thought to bring a razor and some moisturizer before they seal it up again.

We're sent round to X-ray where we wait again. Every time someone who doesn't know the system goes straight to the desk, the whole room tenses. Will they get to jump the queue? But they are directed to take a ticket and join the rest of us. Initiates and novices.

Between the taxi-drivers' strike and the weather, hardly

anyone turns up for the clinic, so we're seen quickly. Back in the plaster room, they're all eating ice-cream, with the infectious joy of summer. I get a new plaster. They offer me a choice of colours and I pick blue, to match the nail varnish on my toes.

Back home, Nessa gets a message from Mark – they are miles away from the storms, they knew nothing about them.

18 July 2006

The bean called Leah has erupted through its soil and gleams on the surface, milky-white and kidney-shaped. I cover it with some of Simon's potting soil and hope for the best.

I'm getting tense about how long I've been waiting to hear about radiotherapy. People are suggesting that I'm not pushing hard enough, that I need to hassle the hospital more. Emma comes down on the side of the hospital and the delay. She says it takes ages to process the scans to determine exactly how to set up the treatment plan, that it's long and painstaking work. Plus, they have to wait for a time slot on a machine that does head-and-neck treatments. She says they told me when they made the mask that it would take at least a month, but that they'd try to get me in earlier.

I don't remember this. Emma says it'll be in one of my notebooks, that it was always going to be this late and I'm lucky to be in the system at all. I've needed time to recover from yet another general anaesthetic, to get stronger. She thinks I should look at this as a chance to see my friends, have fun, do what I want to do while I'm free to do it.

I sniff inwardly and think it's easy for her to talk, but of course she's right. It's how I'd look at it if I was clear in my own mind, no meds, no cancer. No broken leg.

She's wrong about getting strong, though; that's not what's happening here. I'm getting weak instead, especially mentally. I have to admit defeat to Brendan and tell him I can't do the piece in time for the autumn issue.

Oz's arthritic limp has been getting worse and tonight he can't stand up to go outside. At last he makes it to his feet. Watching him limp and hesitate at the door, his tail wagging, brave, breaks my heart. Then Zita opens the other door. He must think 'biscuit', because he speeds up, as if there's nothing wrong with him at all.

19 July 2006

We're on the M50 again. I pass the time by thinking that one day I will write about this road, its pulse, the dramas contained within each vehicle, the plundered hills. There's always a backlog at our offramp. We inch along. Each change of the lights allows only three or four cars through. A tram crosses. The lanes bifurcate and a driver who doesn't know the road holds everyone up. I can read impatience and frustration rising from the road in the heat- and fuel-shimmer of these summer days.

Men in bright vests walk up and down selling newspapers. We all get to see the headlines, but hardly anyone buys a paper. On Monday, it was 'Night of Terror'. Today's is 'Back from Hell'.

We make the long trek to Outpatients. I feel as if I age with every crutch-supported step.

In the clinic, we go through the chronology of my leg again. Someone is writing an article about it. Apparently I've made medical history.

Sinéad tells me that she rang up about my radiotherapy dates this morning and was told that the calculations are finished, my chart is on its way. She's going on her holidays next week, wishes me luck. I'll miss the reassurance of knowing she's at the end of a phone if I need advice.

They check the wound at my neck (which has nearly closed), my mouth, the glands on the other side. There are two beautiful, sleek young people in the room. Students, I think. They look ridiculous in a setting like this, both of them. They belong somewhere elegant and chic.

Professor Stassen explains my history to them, asks me to open my mouth (to demonstrate its limitations), to smile (I can't), to screw up my eyes. 'It's very disfiguring when the eye droops,' he says. Mine does, but only a little. My smile is non-existent, no matter how hard I try.

The beautiful young people follow him out of the room. I feel bleak, watching them go, like an exhibit in a freak show.

We go home and have a twenty-minute turnaround before we have to head back into town for my next appointment, in the Dental Hospital. In that twenty minutes, Eoin comes to take measurements at the front steps. He's going to build a steel handrail for me. Our street is on a hill and there are steep concrete steps down to our front door. They are nerve-racking on crutches. Someone has to be close to me in case I fall, as it is. But with the fatigue from radiation they could well become impossible. I'll really need it if I get any more tired than I already am, with a non-weight-bearing plaster cast to lug around. We might be eligible for a grant to pay for the rail.

We eat a rapid lunch and do my meds and head off again. Traffic. Nowhere to park. A long walk to the hospital. The 'ten years' dentist shows me how to use the fluoride trays she's made for my remaining teeth. She says my vermilion border is perfect and that this is a real achievement.

Vermilion border. I like the sound of it. Cosmetic and military at the same time.

The long, long drag of a walk back to the car.

When we get home there's a message on the answering machine about radiotherapy. Things are moving, at last.

I work on the *Dublin Review* piece, to calm myself down. It would be so good for me to finish it to draft standard before radiotherapy starts.

One of my schoolfriends, who is a writer too, brings our dinner – more food for the freezer. She's collected food from other people on her way.

We talk about writing, hers and mine. About the stories you can tell and those you can't. Stories that might not be ours to tell in the first place. Silences that can feel like collusion.

21 July 2006

I ring St Luke's and fix the verification appointment for next Tuesday. We have another long weekend to savour, free of hospitals.

Friends come over with food and plants and we spend the morning on the deck. It's a balmy day and I'm in my new clothes. One of them tells me that I look well, I just have a great new dimple. She says she's relieved.

It's a lovely way to spend the morning. Afterwards I go up and do some work on the piece, then we feast on trout pâté, hummus, egg-and-mustard salad.

The more work I do, the more I feel in touch with myself and with the world. And today I see my face almost restored

– or is it that I'm ready to accept this face as mine? I have a sense of being lucky and strong; I bask in it as much as in the summer air.

We spend as much time as we can outside now. The bees on the deck can't believe their luck. They gorge on the pollen – when they take off, they fall to the table, stunned, in literal overload. If you listen you can hear: a soft drone, the differentiated songs of birds, the world breathing. The sound of a door closing is a startling interruption.

Simon has anchored the glass vase in a large, two-tone cream and brown amphora. It looks stunning, purple and yellow star flowers wide open, yearning, nectar drops, pollen, laden with life. Peonies and primulae. It's just gorgeous. Spiderman poses among the herbs, where Ryan left him. I love the way plants exhale when you water them, as though in gratitude. In the same way that Lizzie, the cat, burbles when you let her in. Sometimes her burble is flat. That means *what took you so long?*

In a book that I've been given, there's a reference to Karl Menninger's *The Human Mind*, concluding that a free fish can't understand what is happening to one that's been hooked. That just about sums this whole situation up for me. Even the people who are closest to me, who see everything and have to deal with fall-out of every imaginable kind, every day, are not 'hooked' in the way that I am.

24 July 2006
Simon left on the 6.30 flight. A low tide of emotion in the night. We talk in whispers. And then he's gone. Sleep again. Up. Then work.

★

One of my schoolfriends drives me to the Dental Hospital, where I'm to see a new dentist. She braves the bus lane and a belligerent taxi-driver to drop me off at the door, impervious to horns and flashing lights. She'll park the car and go to the chemist to fill a prescription for me, while I go on inside.

The lift is not working. A man I've seen in here before appears at my elbow like the white rabbit from Alice, stabbing the buttons, agitated about the non-appearance of the lift.

'Come on,' he says, 'we'll find another one.'

He leads me to the back of the building, asking questions. He wants to know about the leg, the mouth, the various teams who've worked on me. I've no idea who he is, but I tell him anyway. I've had stranger conversations than this in other hospitals and he seems to know his way around. He walks fast, head bobbing sideways as he listens. He gives the impression of looking over his glasses all the time, talking fast.

'Who are you?' I ask when I can get a word in edgeways.

But I don't catch his name. The deaf ear slows me down in these situations. I ask if he's always on the lookout for stray women on crutches. His laugh could mean anything.

When we get out of the back lift, the second floor is deserted. That summer hiatus. A brief whiff of a thriller scenario crosses my mind: damaged woman, empty building.

But then a nurse emerges from a cupboard. The white rabbit asks where everyone is. 'Downstairs,' she says.

So we turn back, but now this lift won't come and we venture to the stairs.

'Can you do it?' he asks, looking from my crutches to the open-tread staircase.

We peer into the vertiginous well of the building. Vivienne Roche's evocative sculptures line the walls. This is an airy, cool vestibule, but it's still quite a drop.

I'm willing to try. I tell him that he'll have to carry the

crutches for me and hand them over. Just then a maintenance man comes out of the lift behind us and says it's working again.

I'm worn out but thoroughly entertained by the time we get to the right waiting area. I thank the white rabbit and say goodbye just as my friend arrives. In the same length of time as it's taken me to get from the front door up one floor in this building, she has parked her car *and* gone to a chemist's to fill a prescription for me.

On the way home we pass elephants in Booterstown. The circus is back in town. *Why not?* I think. *Why the hell not? Bring on the elephants.*

The Leah bean shows its splitting, wrinkled skin above the soil again. I put it in a bigger pot, add more soil, then water. Outside, Nessa is watering the garden, as Simon has asked her to do. I hope she has more luck with this than I do.

25 July 2006
I wake up with a sense of time opening out on the other side of all this, a return to normal.

My other leg is swelling and sore. It protests at always having to carry the weight. Imagine if it broke too?

We've arranged to meet the woman who had facial surgery like mine in the coffee shop after the verification session. We've spoken on the phone a few times by now. I don't need to describe myself to her. I'll be obvious enough.

In the waiting room, Sky News shows trouble in the Middle East. Underneath the TV an emotional family re-union is taking place. Other people are quiet, looking away. I'm called soon enough by a pleasant young man who talks me through the procedure and tells me that it'll last forty-five minutes or an hour.

I lie down on a narrow table. I have to take off my T-shirt. It's cold. They pull down my straps and drop my T-shirt onto my chest; when I say I'm cold they move it higher. There don't seem to be any blankets. They tell me to let them know when I need a break, that they can stop any time if I need to.

Then they fasten the mask over my face and neck, anchoring me to the table so that I can't move. They talk over me, numbers and angles and anatomical markers; a down-under voice and a cool metallic one. The pleasant young man seems to have gone. The machine moves with lots of clicking and whirring; the table shifts up and down. Light comes and goes on my closed eyelids, fastened shut by the mesh of the mask which holds me down. The table is cold and hard and after forty-five minutes I ask to sit up. A woman with a long face brings me a drink of water without once meeting my eye.

Lines come and go in my head. I wish I had a notebook to hand. In the control room there's a white-coated silence, faces intent on instrument panels, other workings and calculations. We're waiting for a doctor who won't answer his bleep. When he does, I lie down again. They clip the mask into its locks and it's dark again, spinning and clicking. Is it the table or the machine that moves? I can't tell any more. At last they let me up and I clump out, monster woman. And Nessa is there, waiting, with the wheelchair.

She pushes me around to the coffee shop to meet the woman who's had an operation like mine. She looks amazing, not at all conspicuous, like me. I wouldn't have been able to pick her out from the other people in the coffee shop except that she gets up and comes over to us, smiling, as soon as we come in. She's tall and stylish. Her scars are cleverly hidden in the contours of her face; those on her neck are invisible to me. After a while, we follow her yellow Mini to their house to meet her husband. We talk about cancer, diagnosis, surgery and afterwards; hints for radiotherapy. They are lovely, friendly people, upbeat and strong.

I hate meeting them like this, weak, bandaged and scarred, in a wheelchair. If I'm unrecognizable to myself, how can people who've never met me before ever find me, under all these layers of caricature? But if anyone understands this, they must.

When we get home we find the dog plastered into the corner of the hall, panting and shivering, legs splayed – not able to get up. We ring the vet – he's in surgery but will ring back. I can do nothing but sit in a chair close to him and try to encourage him to drink. He lies there, ears flattened, nose dry, panting and shivering. He doesn't look at us but wags his tail when we talk to him, as if he's glad we're here. His eyes are black and empty. He won't even take water from one of my syringes. Won't respond to a biscuit.

He's behaving as if he's been poisoned, but how could that have happened? He hasn't been out. Nessa flinches when I say this. 'Could slug pellets do it?'

It turns out that Simon asked her to use slug pellets around the base of the young trees in the back. She fetches the box and we read it. It says the pellets are safe to use around animals.

We ring the vet again and say we're on our way down. Emma comes home from work with Peter. Between the three of them they get him into the car, carrying him in a bedspread. I don't think I have ever felt so completely redundant in my life as I do when I watch them go. I can't even help to lift him. I feel a generation taking over and moving ahead of me.

This is what's supposed to happen, I tell myself.

But not like this.

The vet says Oz probably has heat-stroke. They'll keep him overnight.

I think I'm getting some hearing back in my right ear. Here's how I know: I've discovered that having one deaf ear is quite useful when you're on the phone in a house as loud as ours. With your hearing ear pressed to the receiver and your deaf ear open to the room, you're oblivious to what's going on around you. Now, I have to ask people to lower their voices. I gloat about this on the phone to Simon, who is in Tunisia.

26 July 2006

Jackie comes to sit with me while the girls go out. I fret about the bean, which shows no signs of growth. I ask her what she thinks. Her answer is to move it off the kitchen table. She hides it behind the radio when she thinks I'm not looking. When she's gone I put it back on the table again. Just under the surface of the soil, its casing seems to grow, but no shoots appear.

28 July 2006

I relax into doing some work, send off a draft of the piece to the *Dublin Review*. I'm giddy and euphoric – I've done it!

Outside, the bottlebrush tree is speeding up. Its vivid blossoms are lopsided, scarlet blurs. It looks scrawny, woody, untidy. A bit like me.

Two friends from my writing group come for dinner. We sit outside and eat Indian takeaway in the fragrant air. I've been told that radiotherapy will probably damage my sense of taste. My taste buds might as well have a party while they can. Cumin, coriander, cardamom. Savour them separately.

29 July 2006

It's a lovely Saturday, misty and damp and cool. Downstairs I bend to pick up a leaf from the kitchen floor and it turns into a moth and flies away. Later, in bed again, flapping triangles of dark alert me to the moth in this room, a low hum outside, my own beating heart. A dog barking.

30 July 2006

What I'd like to do on this Sunday is to go for a drive. It's a beautiful day. The blue is back in the sky after yesterday's mists. The birds purr in their trees, low warbles of contentment. Everyone in the house is asleep. I wish Simon was here.

A writer friend comes out and brings a picnic with her. She's going away to Connemara tomorrow. We eat on the deck, admiring the flowers. Then we drive to Sandycove and sit looking at the sea and natter about books, written and not. A blue van comes along and unleashes a gorgeous, sturdy toddler, who dances on the wall, life surging through his limbs, eager for the water. Couples evaluate the rocks, stare off at the horizon.

This place is in my DNA. The thing is, I need to be here to write it the way I feel it. All those years when we were away, absence was a hole in my heart.

The narrow street is jammed with cars. Men read their papers behind their steering wheels and ignore us. We talk about Connemara. One of the writing groups I belong to, the novelshop, will hold a week-long workshop down there in August. I have to miss it. Radiotherapy should have started by then.

'Why don't you come with me now?' she says.

For a mad second the possibility hovers, then vanishes. I have appointments this week, and what if I get the call to start treatment? How would I manage the train? I remember David's story. He got a seat, but only just. Stand on one leg the whole way across the country? I can't do it.

But I won't forget that she asked.

Those Sunday afternoon men – what are they hiding from? They sit in their cars on a glorious day, slumped, behind their newspapers while the sea shows off right in front of them.

One of my schoolfriends has come home from her holidays. She's brown and summery in a wide floral skirt and fun buckled shoes – she looks fabulous. I'm so glad she's back. The tides of summer – people are still leaving, but with her the return begins.

I'm sensitive to smells these days. I already think the iron I take turns my skin sour, but now I'm acutely aware of the slightly acrid smell of the PEG site, which is inflamed. It's oozy and crusty, the granulation is pinkish, translucent and veined. It's like a worm, coiled above my navel.

I have a shower with Nessa's help, plastered leg swathed in a plastic bag – we're getting good at this – and figure out that the patches were supposed to be changed yesterday but we – I – forgot. No wonder I got ratty last night and this morning. I need to print out a new routine – even the mouth exercises fall behind when people visit and stay a long time. I either can't do them or I forget to do them.

Here's a good thing – the swelling is still going down. I see my face in the mirror and don't wince right away. Is it possible that it's heading towards normal? I can feel the part above the dimple – does that mean I might get some expression back? Work it, work it.

My teeth feel smooth and clean after using the fluoride trays – the gel is like cold, minty glue. But they are stained, now, as if I were the heaviest of smokers. I don't know yet what my new jawline will look like.

The tight vertical scar down my neck threatens to split sometimes. It feels so taut that I could cut my finger on it.

That evil bean gleams through the surface of the soil again. Its skin is crinkled and splitting, like mine.

1 August 2006

My oncologist friend is home from Canada. She's in Kerry for a family reunion. She flies up to see me for the day. Nessa drives me to meet her off the airport bus and we have a couple of hours together. It's mostly chat and catching up and not much about cancer at all, you'd never know how often I've bent her ear on the phone in the last few weeks. But she does comment on what a brilliant job they've done with the surgery, how well the infection is healing. I feel enormously heartened by this, because she knows what she's talking about.

At last, the application form from the Irish Wheelchair Association arrives in the post. It says that there is a twenty-day minimum application period. We have to send a letter from our GP and some recent photos of me.

We go down to the photo booth at the local supermarket. It's the last thing in the world I want to do. I remember not to smile – my image is less frightening when I don't. I avoid looking at the photos before we put them in the envelope and drop it in the post. We wrote away for this form ten weeks or more ago, and we're only applying for a temporary permit! At this rate, I won't need it any more by the time I get it.

2 August 2006

We wake up to Oz in crisis.

There is saliva everywhere, the kitchen floor is wet with it, the window fogged. His legs are splayed unnaturally. He's panting hard. We get him onto the bedspread and the girls manage to get him out, into the car and off.

He's either had a stroke or he's been poisoned. I go on the net to check the slug pellets and discover that they can, in fact, have this effect on dogs. It's a bit too coincidental that this has happened both times that we've used them. If it's poison, he has more of a chance than if he's had a stroke. Apparently the symptoms and treatment are the same.

Poor, poor puppy. I wish I'd checked the net the last time. Nessa is beside herself. But she couldn't have known. We're waiting to hear from Mark, who is due home from China this morning. His plane is delayed – turns out there was a fire on board, they were diverted back to Paris.

Emma is working from home. She's not getting much of a start at her new job, what with me and the dog and our collective crises.

It's a beautiful morning though: bright and breezy. Lizzie is playing in the bamboo out on the deck as if nothing is unusual. She pushes between the stems so that they stroke her sides, reaches up to sniff them like a kitten. She eyes the span of the wall in front of her as if she was still young and lithe enough to jump it.

★

We ring up about Oz. He's stable, on a drip. Our vet says that if he's been poisoned, he could pull out of it after twenty-four hours. If not, it's in his central nervous system and we're in trouble.

Is everyone afraid? Am I more afraid than most people, or is it the same?

3 August 2006

The vet rings early in the morning to say that Oz is doing better, he's trying to stand.

Nessa spots a distortion on my right clavicle, wonders if it's a new lump? I check in the mirror – it's just that the alignment of that shoulder is changing. A new sharp hump rises from my scapula when I brush my teeth. I don't know where these changes will end, but my face is getting better.

I ring St Luke's to see what's happening about radiotherapy. They ring back to say that they hope to call me tomorrow with an appointment.

Now I panic. How will I get over there every day? Will I be able to drive by the time Nessa goes back to college? We make a list of people who've offered to help.

We ring the vet's and they say that Oz has managed to stand but he can't walk yet. If he can take even a few steps on his own tonight, they'll let him come home because he'll do better in his own environment.

More vigils to keep.

I keep thinking that it's later than it is in terms of days – today is Friday in my head and I'm worried about the *Dublin Review* piece, about co-ordinating the editing with my treatment and what happens if I'm so zonked by it that I can't think properly?

Because I think it's Friday, a deep part of me believes Simon will come home tonight. When I look up from my laptop to the actual space of the kitchen, the hum of the oven, sounds of the girls' TV show from the other room, I realize that he won't.

Basking is such an expansive, lazy word. I'm sitting beside a window in the sun. The glass accelerates the heat for me and for the busy fly who drones against the window. I have that slightly delirious sense of things happening, movement in my brain, the joy of a life of stories, and the luck of having it.

I'm aware of a tremulous, happy feeling. I'm happy to be alive.

We get updates about Oz, poor idiot, each one slightly better than the last. He can't come home yet. He's standing, badly, not walking. The vet says we shouldn't go down to see him because it would only distress him.

We spend most of the evening talking tough decisions, here and on the phone. Everyone agrees that if he is no better tomorrow, we'll let him go. It's not fair to him to prolong all this. I'll tell the vet when he rings in the morning.

On the phone from London, Simon says that Oz has been our lion. This undoes each one of us completely. I fall like rain.

Looking back at the fear of those early nights, all that hand-holding in the dark and how far we've come from there, reminds me of those families we knew in the States who used to sleep in one room, fully clothed, guns ready. I think my psyche right now is not so different from theirs.

4 August 2006

We're waiting for two phone calls this morning: the first from our vet, the second from St Luke's. And Simon will board his flight soon to come home.

The vet rings first. Oz has started walking! We can go down and collect him, he'll recover best at home from here on.

I can't wait. I ring the hospital. They have one last calculation to check. I'll start radiotherapy on Tuesday – four days from now.

A friend of mine has been diagnosed with cancer too. It feels as though an epidemic is breaking out around us. I ring to see how she is and she tells me she's waiting for the results of her scan, to find out if it has spread and how far. Her consultant has promised to phone her today, before the bank holiday.

In the evening she rings me, her voice in splinters. 'He didn't ring,' she says. 'I don't know anything.'

I feel such rage. I can just imagine how her day has been – watching the clock, jumping every time the phone rang, not letting herself talk to anyone for any length of time. Not daring to go out. And now she has this worry for the whole, long weekend.

The poor dog comes home. He skids around on the wooden floors like Bambi on ice. His back legs don't work too well. We put down rugs, the girls coax him along. They lift him up and down the back step to the garden. Nessa insists on sleeping on the couch so she can be near him, in case he needs anything.

6 *August 2006*

A visitor asks me to repeat every single thing I say. Am I that incoherent?

After a while I'm reluctant to say anything, insecure about my speech. I know I lisp sometimes, my voice thickens. When the visitors leave we go upstairs and I have a shower, my leg encased in a black rubbish bag, my hair falling out in clumps. It's getting so thin. Then I change the morphine patches, late again. That sharp hand claws at the side of my face and I'm jumpy.

We go to visit the little family. I haven't been to their house for months. I want to see the newly painted walls, the new floors, Ryan's *Incredibles* duvet and matching pillowcase.

The roadworks are still in progress on the way there. The acrid smell of tar. On the way we pass a field of Jacob sheep with their weird horns and goaty look.

7 *August 2006*

Now that we have a definite starting date, we know when we'll finish *this* phase. Twenty-eight sessions over five and a half weeks amount to something finite, something we can measure. We may not know what's beyond it, other than life, but life is a good start.

I can scratch my face above the dimple now and feel it. The lower quadrant is like a roll of iron. I'm baking under glass, the warmed sun melts through the window to reach me here on the sofa. Euphoric? Yes, I'm dazed with it. It's a beautiful evening. High blue sky. Mark and Nessa are outside cleaning the car and a light breeze flows through the house, cool, promising air.

I'm greedy for light. I hate the way dark takes me by surprise when it comes.

Chapter 7

8 August 2006

Today I step back onto the moving staircase of treatment. I'll hand myself over to someone else's schedule, someone else's idea of who I am.

We make a chart for the weeks to come and stick it to the door of a kitchen cupboard. I'm to have twenty-eight sessions of radiotherapy, given daily, Monday to Friday. That adds up to five and a half weeks. I can't drive myself to St Luke's because of the broken leg, but also because of all the medication I'm on. I still wear transdermal fentanyl patches, take large doses of paracetamol, difene and a stomach remedy to counteract the effects of that, pregabalin for nerve pain, amitriptyline for night-time pain. That's in addition to the supplements, which include a prescription form of iron which I find hard to tolerate. Because of the iron, I'm on two types of laxative.

Nessa is going to be my main driver. One of my school-friends, who works a four-day week, will drive one day a week and Jackie will take another. Other people have offered to fill in when they can, every second week, say, or on occasional days. We add their names to the chart and number all the sessions, then add the other appointments I'll have to keep. We'll cross off each one when it's finished. We stick the chart to the door of a kitchen cupboard, in plain view. It's our plan of action.

★

I wonder if the TV in the waiting area is there to stop us talking to each other, a weird plot for social control dreamed up by the Health Services Executive. Two fat, stoned-looking fish lurk in the murky water of the columnar fish tank.

A radiation therapist goes through pages of instructions with me. I've to rinse my mouth several times a day with baking soda and warm water to counteract the onset of mucositis, an inflammation of the mucous membranes which is likely to happen in my mouth in the weeks to come. I should avoid fizzy drinks and sweets which will aggravate my mouth and increase the risk of dental caries. I'm to stay out of the sun. Perfumed moisturizers will irritate my skin as it gets inflamed. I'm not to use lip gloss because of its petroleum base, which would burn my lips.

She gives me a copy of this list to bring home with me, then wheels me off into a small room. Two other young women in white uniforms come with us. A big, cream-coloured machine looms over the X-ray table. Shelves full of yellow masks, the imprints of faces I will come to know over the next few weeks, line the opposite wall. One of the radiation therapists lifts mine down from the shelf and holds it while we talk. I recognize the exaggerated hollow at the cheek. I tell them how much I hated the verification session and ask them to talk me through what happens. They are friendly and patient and say they will. Then we get down to business.

The X-ray table is narrow, with a thin mattress and a curved, U-shaped plastic block for my head. The Varian machine, with its curved, mobile arm, arches over it. There's a window into the control room so that they can monitor me when they leave. I take off my shirt and lie down on the table, fitting my head to the block, a guillotine. I look up into the black mechanical face of my treatment – round, metal, all shutters and switches and coils. Then they cover my face with the mask, and fasten it to the table with clips, so that I won't move. They take the time to make sure I'm okay with the mask before they continue, and I do get used to it very quickly.

Then the narrow table is raised, closer to the gantry. It feels sacrificial: some things must die so that I can live. They move the table from side to side, murmuring directions to each other as they position me so that radiation will be delivered to the precise area of my treatment field. They remember to talk to me too. They tell me what they're doing. A beam of light picks out the target drawn on the surface of the mask. It's a bizarre mix of the technical and the primitive: the machine, my mesh-mask, lines made by hand in permanent marker on strips of tape.

I understand what's happening with this alignment, so it doesn't freak me out, and neither do the noises – whirring, wheezing, clicking, stops. A drone. The radiation therapists leave the room, tell me they'll be back soon. A high warning beep accompanies their receding footsteps, like a lorry reversing. There's a pause, then the deeper, fiercer warning of the exposure button. They come back in to set me up for the next dose, given at a different angle and from a different direction. I don't feel anything – it's like having an ordinary X-ray. The actual irradiation only takes seconds for each field, and for me there are four fields, four exposures. Each time they reposition the machine they tell me what they're doing, and when they are about to leave.

I'm out of there in ten minutes, wondering what all the fuss was about.

At home, the phone keeps ringing and after a while it's all I can do not to snarl at people. There's a smell of rot downstairs and we're not sure where it's coming from. The girls go through the fridge and the kitchen cupboard, throw out mouldy oranges and sprouting potatoes, but it makes no difference. The smell is sulphurous, sticky. It reminds me of something, but I'm not sure what.

10 August 2006

A friend comes up from Wicklow to drive me to radiotherapy. We have to wait nearly two hours, but it's okay. We haven't seen each other for a while and have a lot to talk about. Then, while I'm on the table, the computer crashes. The radiation therapists remember to talk to me so I don't feel abandoned when I'm in there.

While I'm enclosed in the shell, I listen to the sounds of the equipment as it moves around me. I can track the buzz I hear back to the switch and on to the control panel, sending the radiation into action. I hear a high-pitched whine and imagine lethal darts unleashed on a search-and-destroy mission, amid a swarm of metallic killer bees. A friend sent a good luck message this morning that said to imagine blue sky when I'm enclosed by the machines, but I prefer my deadly golden bees.

The silent shells watch from their shelves, each waiting their turn to be taken down and used. Their strongly shaped shoulders and open nostrils give them a yearning look. They are negatives of everyone who comes in here, impressions of damage and disfigurement. I imagine they come down at night and play among the monitors and leads, mimic the warning beeps, dance until dawn.

I ask what happens to them when treatment is finished. Usually they're thrown away, but some people keep theirs. Straight away I say that I'll want mine. I don't know what I'll do with her, but I'll take her home with me and find out.

I feel invigorated and purposeful, my lethal darts in a quiver at my back.

12 August 2006

Today I woke late and sluggish. My dry mouth kept waking me during the night, I was desperate for water. My skin is red already. I know it's likely to burn but so what, it's all in a good cause.

We go for a drive – high tide, boats rocking in Bulloch. Simon points out that most of them have Yamaha engines. It seems like a good opening for a story. Imagine waking up on water, that slapping sound the water makes, the click of halyards. A lowered sky. No, sea-mist. No way of getting to shore. No way of knowing where 'shore' might be. And then an engine, gunning.

When we get home again, we sit down and work out Simon's travel dates and flights for the rest of the year, try to figure out taxes and money. We book the flights. It seems optimistic, to set up those dates as if nothing will change, nothing will go wrong. But we have to do it. Back into debt we go.

The stench of rot seems to come from the vent in the sitting room. Simon says something must have died there, mentions a rat that he saw in the garden last week. We're burning scented candles all over the house tonight.

13 August 2006

My brother is here from England. He has trouble looking at me.

I shake my crutches at him, flaunt my blue nail varnish. 'Aren't you going to tell me I deserve a break?'

Bad puns in worse taste are his speciality. But he doesn't rise to the bait.

'Have I put my foot in my mouth again?'

No joy. I forget that we've all had time to get used to the way I look.

We experiment with health drinks from different sources, enthusiastic while we combine ingredients. Brewer's yeast and manuka honey, blackstrap molasses . . . It all adds to the hag impression: *eye of newt and toe of frog, wool of bat and tongue of dog* . . . Powerful trouble, indeed. I overdo it and throw up, violently.

It's been a lovely day. There could be a conflagration coming, over and above what's happening in my body. The whole world could explode any minute and cancer would be the last thing on anyone's mind. But we have now, this minute.

Time whispers ghost stories in my ear, a high-pitched sound.

14 *August 2006*

In a dream, midges crystallize out of the air and become pointy-nosed bees in shaped swarms that emerge under the doors, through the windows. We try to run away.

When I wake up I remember that the bees are on my side.

Mind you, the dream could also be about the persistent smell of rot. We're sure by now that something has died under the house. Whatever it is, we can't find it so there's not much we can do. The process of decay will have to run its course.

★

The drive to St Luke's takes a long time today – but then I'm seen instantly. The secret necklace that I wear, a heavy metal chain, shivers at my neck but they don't see it. They lower the mask anyway. Fasten me to the table.

A voice comes into my head: *Ah, wouldya relax.*

The occupational therapist comes to assess our need for a handrail by the steps down to the house. It turns out that grants are meant for bigger jobs than this. We'll have to pay for the rail ourselves.

I'm very tired tonight. The lining of my mouth is inflamed and sore. Already I can see the white blisters of mucositis on my tongue. It seethes and stings. In the end I give in and go back to taking OxyNorm to supplement the transdermal patches.

Lizzie, kittenish and soft, comes to sit on my lap: she has an instinct for knowing who is sick, who needs her. She's fluid and warm and soft, claws sheathed. She brings me gifts of dried beetle shells.

I wake often in the night, my mouth like the inside of a brick. And I thought it was dry before this!

15 August 2006

Today the waiting area is crowded with wheelchairs and Nessa has to park mine over by the potted plant near a man with many dressings around a tracheostomy tube. He avoids my eye.

I remember that feeling.

There's a woman on a trolley. Someone wipes her face while a nurse sets up oxygen for her. I'm beginning to recognize the regulars, two women with identical faces and bodies, full expressive mouths, differentiated only by years and the clothes they wear. There are men who are told to drink water at set times from the cooler under the television.

I'm the only one with a wrecked face.

Inside, someone comments on my name. There are several stories I could tell them in response. I tell the one about Leah, the squinty-eyed sister in the Bible.

When Jacob wanted Rachel, her father made him work for seven years to earn the right to marry her. At last the wedding day arrived, but when the ceremony was over and Jacob lifted the veil from the face of his bride, he discovered that he'd been tricked: it was Leah he had married.

Nothing daunted, he turned around and went back to work for another seven years and this time he was rewarded with the bride he wanted.

We laugh. It's a good story. I'm quick to point out that the Leah of the story spells her name differently to mine. I don't say that Leah means 'weary', or that Rachel means 'beautiful', or even that Jacob was their first cousin.

I don't mention the stunted bean on the kitchen table at home either.

I lie down. They cover my face with my mask, anchor me to the table. I wonder if anyone ever asked those two sisters what they wanted. I wonder how they felt. The Bible isn't big on emotion, I find, although there's no shortage of drama, plenty of cases of mistaken identity and disguise along with plagues, pestilence and war.

There seems to be an issue with the settings today – they have trouble lining everything up. I'm concerned. The post-operative swelling is going down. Could there be a disjunction between their marks on the shell and the changing contours of my face and neck? They say not to worry about it, it's all under control.

I'm brought into a consulting room to see the doctors. The nurse puts silver nitrate on the oozing granulation at the PEG site to cauterize it and gives me a new dressing. It stings. 'Don't overclean it,' she says. If she could only see the gunk that comes out of it, sometimes . . .

At home, the bean reproaches me. They all think I should throw it away by now. They move it around, but I go looking for it. I feel compelled to track its progress, which is precisely zero. No tender shoots appear, just this drying shoulder of bean that shrugs above the soil, no matter how much I cover it.

Tonight I'm delighted with my life. Last night I was sore and miserable and afraid that my reaction to radiotherapy had already started and would get worse. But I've had a good day and feel well and strong and optimistic – we're *moving*, everything is moving and life beckons, a life beyond treatment.

Why do I feel so good? Because it was a productive day. I did some work and caught up with emails. The little family have come to stay for a few days and help out. Zita's speciality is giant pots of pasta with extra-cheesy sauce. Easy for me to eat. Big enough to feed anyone who might turn up.

And I'm reading a good novel. It's a lovely, normal way to end the day, to work and then write to friends and then come to bed and read. The river in my ear sings to me and my mind opens to possibilities, the light of a new book. Hope is yellow tonight, it takes me back years, to our beginning.

16 August 2006

There are voices in my head, carrying on a dialogue without me. I look up and Emma's face is at the door, smiling, her eyebrows up. 'Coffee?'

The sense of well-being from yesterday persists through a slow, lazy morning. Jackie brings me for radiotherapy and home again. When we get back we play snakes and ladders and chat while the dogs bite each other in their idle way, chewing the warm air.

My head is like a broken colander. Ideas fall straight through it. I ask questions I know the answers to and each time I hear them they are a fresh surprise, like what day and time Zita and Eoin are leaving for New York, when they are coming back. Ryan is coming to stay with us while they are away. We planned all this before I got sick.

I catch myself, the odd time, saying things like, 'Don't wake the fish,' but nobody bats an eye. Only Ryan says quietly, 'What fish?' but he drops it when I don't answer. I don't know what I mean. Maybe I was dreaming of the St Luke's fish in their dark water. Sleeping with the fishes.

The novelshoppers ring from Galway. They're planning a workshop in Spain, at the end of January. They check dates with me. They want to go ahead and book the tickets. I hesitate, then tell them to count me in. What the hell, it's ages away. I should be able to go by then. I might even have work to bring. I take out the draft of the novel I abandoned in April and look at it, try to see a way back in. The characters stay on the page, where I left them. I put it away again. Maybe later. Everyone says, give it time.

17 *August 2006*

People want courage in and from each other. And from books. Not politeness, not safety.

It's another day, beginning. Stirrings of awareness: *I am so lucky*. Hair falls from my head, curls around my fingers, dangles from my clothes. I'm moulting, worse than the dog, but there is life in my heart and in my veins. I sit here and stare across the bay while different people spin prayer spells on my behalf and across town a nuclear machine is programmed and ready. Different forms of magic.

Today the mask is tighter. That's what I get for complaining. They tell me that the swellings can change at different times of day.

I think: *Mind the gap*.

Some people come for treatment on their own. I can't do that because of my leg. But when you bring a friend, you bring a piece of your own world with you. That person knows who you are, even if you forget and no one else can see it.

I feel rotten tonight. My mouth is dry as sand. I wonder if I'm holding my tongue the right way during the exposures? Is it being over-exposed to radiation, or not enough?

18 *August 2006*

My disabled parking permit has arrived in the post.

Today's tiredness is a shock. My voice is small, my mouth unbearably dry. I hope it doesn't get much worse – last night I kept waking, frantic for water. And I have the runs. I feel as if a big grey hand is pressing me flat. Is this the tiredness they warn you about? But I'm only in my second week, about a third of the way through treatment. They'll have to bring me over there in a wheelbarrow at this rate.

I feel better in the afternoon. Out in the garden, there are pigeons bouncing on our neighbour's cedar tree. They gorge on the fruit, swing on the branches. Then they fly up suddenly, seven or eight of them, and fly away. The beat of their wings is loud through the glass. They're fun to watch.

There are moments when I realize that I am happy. Just now, the past and the future, everything I want or regret, are all held back as by a sea wall.

19 August 2006

Rain drummed on the roof last night, sheeting down. Today is slightly warmer and wet. I can see crystal drops dangling from the ends of flowers and leaves on the deck.

We go to the National Gallery to see the exhibition of Beckett's favourite paintings. This is important to me because I missed everything else in the centenary festival, around the time of the operation. It's the first time we've used the disabled parking permit and I feel guilty even though I'm in a wheelchair.

The exhibition notes are hard to read from a chair. I think fewer people stare, because the chair gives them enough time to avert their gaze? Don't be daft, stupid – it's because they have better things to look at. Get over yourself!

I see some work that I love, but in general the exhibition is disappointing. I'm heartened when I hear a lively young voice behind me say that a woman in a painting looks like Judi Dench. It brings us back down to earth.

My sense of civic ownership of this building is hampered by being in the chair. I want to kick forward and move at will, follow my eye, but I'm thwarted by Simon's pace. He has to keep asking me to repeat myself when I talk, but I don't much want to pitch my leaden, boxed-off voice any higher.

I wonder if I'll ever smile again. They have warned me that I won't, and that sensation and movement are two entirely different things. Smile, they say, to show people that I can't.

I think I feel a twitching at the corner of my mouth. But when I look, my face still has that frozen droop.

20 August 2006

The weird moves of being on crutches. I dip to one side, limp, swoop and glide – like a bat, a bird, a booby. I circle and dip again, stagger; bat things across the floor as if I'm playing hockey; sway with the weight of the carrier bag from my shoulder. You could choreograph this.

Dream a future: start now.

In the early evening we drive Simon to the airport through bands of falling rain. In my mind black wrought-iron gates, cathedral-shaped, swing open to infinity. In my mouth, hot fizz and seasalt; burning acid saliva. The crab was nothing compared to this. I dream of writing and writing desks, long driveways, high ceilings. Rooms falling silent for a reading.

The hills darken and rain falls and still we drive – home again. Back to grief. Food turns to sawdust in my mouth, congeals, impossible to swallow. A dusty, salty mouth. Blisters too. Tongue like a brick with sawdust at the back of my throat. They keep asking me if swallowing is a problem yet and I've said no, so carelessly. Now, suddenly, it is, and I'm only two weeks in to my treatment and Simon has gone. The

hot hand rests at my chin and wind sings high in my ears —
can I do this?

The skin at the fold with my neck loosens. It feels watery
beside the taut swollen mass of my cheek. Will it settle? Or
will it burst open, raging infection? It feels as if it could.

I worry about tomorrow. It's a big day for appointments
— St Luke's for radiotherapy in the morning, St James's
to get the cast off and an X-ray in the afternoon. I'm nervous.
What if my leg is destroyed beyond repair? Worse, what
if it goes again? Who do I blame, if my own bones won't
knit?

Lightning shivers down the bone, it finds me out.

21 August 2006

There's a shortage of spaces in the car park at St Luke's. Cars
circle like sharks, looking for signs of movement. Everyone
ignores the disabled parking signs, as usual.

I look daggers at a woman who's parked badly, across a
line. She's only left room for a bicycle in the second space.

Nessa is embarrassed. 'There's no need to be so pointed.'

I know she's right but I'm furious. I can't walk, can't drive,
and now we can't even park.

Waiting for radiotherapy, I see a woman whose swollen,
bumpy face flares a vivid red, like a burn or a strawberry
birthmark. She hides behind a newspaper, not inviting chat.
I wonder how old she is. Not much older than me. I wonder
who her surgeon is. If she'd put down her paper, I'd ask. She
has swollen flaming red pads of flesh on her neck and her
nose. I hope she's nearly finished her treatment. I'd hate for
anyone to have burns worse than hers. She's called in ahead
of me and I've lost my chance to speak to her.

The PEG site is very sore. It's thoroughly cleaned and

dressed by the nurses, who swab for infection. My mouth burns, inside and out, tastes of seawater.

We get into lunchtime traffic, head for St James's. A nagging black fly of worry is trapped in the car with us. Will they find something wrong and admit me again? My dread of institutions resurfaces: once they get you, they can keep you. It's a hangover from boarding school.

For lunch I decide to be healthy and buy a smoothie from the juice bar at St James's: cucumber and pear. It's frothy, brownish green, unappetizing. I can only drink half of it. The rest soon separates into foam and sludge, recalling previous eye-of-newt disasters. I may be restricted to soft foods, but this is extreme. All the bins are full, so in the end I leave it on a window ledge beside one.

There are long queues at the desk in the orthopaedic clinic. Everyone is tense but polite; we all know we're in for a long afternoon. We sit under signs which state that violent behaviour won't be tolerated.

The afternoon wears on. In the plaster room, the nurse removes the cast from my leg. The vibrations of the saw are ticklish, intense, excruciating. She cracks the plaster open and a smell of dead skin rises. Long hair, it's like a rainforest! The leg looks strange – scarred and scabbed – and feels worse, numb and tingly and useless. It's scrawny and heavy. Horrible. I'm glad I wore trousers.

The waiting area in the X-ray department is like an airport lounge, except for the oxygen tanks. The floor polisher curves across the floor, its long, snake-like flex threatening further injury to people who have plenty to be going on with already, thanks very much.

I make myself look at the leg again, pick a black fragment of staple from my ankle. The scabs have dried, at least. A cartoon baby on the wall pleads, 'Please, Mum, tell them I'm here.' I look at this and wonder why a character in my interrupted novel drinks. I want to give her a compelling reason.

A crooked man with a gnarled stick, his clothes too big, goes in to be X-rayed. I go in after him, crutch, swing, crutch, my own crooked mile. I can see the mark of his shoe on the paper that covers the X-ray table. On the way over to the pain clinic we pass the abandoned smoothie, looking if anything more separated, less appetizing than before.

In the loo, there is a beautiful woman, bald and thin, wearing gorgeous expensive clothes – champagne-coloured ruffled jacket, heavy linen multi-panelled designer skirt, brightly coloured bag. Our eyes meet in the mirror. I smile but she freezes me out. I'd meant to signal recognition and encouragement, but her look insists that there is no connection between us.

In the pain clinic we meet a patient from the ward. We wish each other luck. After she's called in, a black and white cat limps, leg rigid, in front of the window.

A big, blondey nurse comes barrelling down the corridor and stops in front of me:

'Are you for transport?'

'No.'

'Someone is.' She glares. 'There's an ambulance waiting.'

For a mad minute I wonder if she'll put me into it because *someone* has to go. She disappears off on her search.

Now a porter comes along. He's also looking for the missing transport person. They all think it's me, because of the wheelchair.

'I'm with her.' I point to Nessa, more glad than ever that she's here.

The summer afternoon is old now and I feel rank. My

dressings are seeping and my heavy head sinks towards my right shoulder. People are openly curious when they look at my lobster-red face, my straw-like hair. Let them look. I'm too tired to care. The hospital is emptying out, mine is the last appointment. On the way out to the car park, the sad brown smoothie reproaches me one last time. Is there a singular of dregs? A dreg.

We drive home under the lovely green hills, a pillar of fire on one of them.

23 August 2006

Jackie drives me in to the max-fax clinic. Everyone says 'Hello!' and 'How are you?' Wide smiles all around. Jackie says, 'It's like a party.'

I ask again if I can see the tumour. I assume it's doing time in a jar somewhere, languishing in the depths of the lab.

They say they'll look into it, but they're not sure it's possible. The tumour no longer exists in its original form. It has been sliced and diced, stained and thoroughly punished. But they'll try to follow this up for me, for the next time I come in.

Sinéad says that if any of it still exists she might try to get it out of the lab and bring it to me. I imagine her carrying it through the halls in a bucket, leaving me alone in a room with it. What on earth would I do?

We cross town to St Luke's for radiotherapy. There's heavy traffic, but we make it. The treatment is fine: quick and efficient. Then I have my first session of physiotherapy.

My newly cast-free leg is swollen and disfigured. The skin is marbled and dry, and flakes off. I can feel the screws they used to anchor the plate to the bone, under my skin. Scars and patches crumple the surface. The soft-voiced physiotherapist tells me that the swelling will go down with movement and exercise. I have to work at this, and at stretching the shoulder and the jaw.

The ankle feels nasty – numb and tingly at the same time. The shark bite shrinks from my touch and the area over the plate is bruised. I'd hate for anyone else to touch it even more.

But the physio puts her hand on the shark bite and leaves it there. She tells me that I should make myself touch it, or else it will get stuck in the habit of recoiling the way it does now. My leg and I have to overcome our mutual dislike and distrust.

The morning was bright, but it's a dark afternoon, floods of rain. The garden looms, wet and ominous with growth. A cousin is on the phone with hilarious grandchildren stories to cheer me up.

Lizzie brings dead spiders and pieces of web onto our bed. Downstairs the house reeks with the stench of decay. Autumn. Now I remember what the smell reminds me of.

When we were in Kenya, we drove across the Mara river, where hundreds of wildebeest had been killed by crocodiles during their crossing the day before. Bloated bodies swayed in the water; vultures roosted on them. The stench was overpowering.

People stopped on the bridge to take photographs.

Where does night come from? Does it rise or fall? Does it come from inside ourselves, do we spin it from our imagination or is it cast over us, a net thrown by a dark and jealous god? Does it come in the clearings, or reach the edge of the forest at the end of the story?

Flann O'Brien's De Selby thinks that it's an effusion of black light. Right now, that seems like as reasonable a theory as any.

24 *August 2006*

Every sick person needs a cat. Lizzie curls up, purring, in whatever curves she can find, with her *good* cat smell – of fur, and wind, and peat smoke.

It's a gorgeous morning, full of light and well-being. The girls look in to say hi. I feel deliciously spoiled, staying on in bed with no pressure to be anywhere or do anything. I'll read, drink the coffee they have brought me, luxuriate. I have radiotherapy this afternoon, but the whole morning is free and indolent.

The gift of writing is that everything I do or think is work, or an investment in future work. The doctors say to get out and exercise, but what feels right for me is this luxurious rest, rest with purpose.

You have to imagine your way through to a future sometimes, as if you pick your way across rocks at high tide, beyond that deep and narrow gorge to the open shore ahead. As if there's nothing in the darkness that might cause you to stumble, no accident or malice or bad luck; no other destiny than this.

My life is my life *as I have lived it*. 'What if?'s are meaningless.

How could I have been so foolishly arrogant as to speculate about the length of that woman's treatment or the stage she was at? I am now as scalded-looking as she was, and I'm still short of the halfway mark.

I do what the physio suggested and apply moisturizer to my leg. But I have a liar's touch, forced and insincere.

The scars know it and react. My skin recoils from my hand.

The skin of my chin loosens as if it might come undone and flap open: the hem of my face is dipping. My mouth stiffens and my sense of taste turns wooden. If despair has a taste, this could be it. I am bored by the food my daughters urge me to eat: yogurt and porridge, scrambled egg and mashed potato. I try to make noxious drinks with things like Brewer's Yeast and molasses added, but they make me throw up. Vegetable juice and smoothies are the best. The liquid supplements are toxic, but the petite dietician turns stern when I show signs of skipping them. 'You need them, Lia,' she says, wrinkling her young forehead. So I hold my nose and glug them down.

My digestive system is completely screwed between the iron and the drugs and then the laxatives to counteract the iron and the drugs.

How am I going to move forward into my life beyond this? When the treatment and the summer end and the girls go back to their lives – how will I do it?

Tonight I don't have to worry, they're all still here. Emma brings home a slip-n-slide for Ryan and begins to assemble it, then sees his excitement and realizes what she's let herself in for: she'll have to go through with it, the whole thing, despite the cold. And she does, full marks to her, and Eoin joins in. The rest of us watch and laugh at them, skidding along on the cold, muddy grass.

I put the dubious bean into one of Simon's pots, add some

potting soil and slip it outside onto the deck. Let's see how it fares out there in the elements, where it belongs. All the other plants are thriving out there, maybe it will too.

25 August 2006

Simon and Emma are already back at work. Soon Ryan will go back to school and that will be the end of the midweek visits. Nessa will start her final year in college. I'll have to start going to appointments on my own and how will *that* feel? Will I be brave enough to go out alone with this face? How will it be with a scorched tongue, a damaged leg and an unreliable memory?

One thing at a time, I remind myself.

The pigeons are bouncing and gorging out there, on a showery evening. The wind is out there too, juggling other sounds in the dark, voices. It could be poetry or violence or the insistent lines of a song. It sings motorbike songs and trees, conjures chimneys and dogs and drums.

26 August 2006

We all sit around the kitchen table, talking. I play games of magic and disappearance with Ryan, with coins and Russian dolls. Then Zita and Eoin take him home. Next time they come, they will bring him for his 'holiday', while they go to New York.

The things people tell you when they want to be helpful or reassuring! Someone mentions a woman who had fifty doses of radiotherapy, in tones that suggest that my twenty-eight are child's play. But *where*? I want to ask. What part of her body, what dose and how intense and at what risk of breakdown? I don't want to hear about people who are worse off than me. I already see them, every day.

We're all watching my skin and the incision site where the infection was, to see if it breaks down.

I've finally got the courage today to start reading John Diamond's book about his cancer. He is blunt and honest. I can relate to every single thing he says. He had a squamous cell carcinoma too, although he calls his 'indolent', i.e. slow moving. His, too, seems to have become cancerous from an early benign condition, a branchial cyst in his case. So far, so worryingly the same.

27 August 2006

A bad night. Sprinting for the loo, or what passes for sprinting when you're on crutches.

Simon wakes up and sympathizes. I lie down and hold his hand. When the light fades from our eyes we see the plough, framed in the window. He sees a shooting star but I miss it.

The Leah bean lurks somewhere on the deck and in the back of my mind. It reminds me of the voodoo giraffe I was given in Kenya last September. There was malevolence in the face of the woman who gave it to me. She was angry because I went to her sister's stall and not to hers, and in the end I bought a cheap necklace from her, one I didn't want. Victorious, she pressed the small wooden giraffe on me as if it was a gift, but I saw her eyes. I felt the sour blast of that look.

I gave the necklace away at once. Why would anyone take something from an enemy and wear it around their neck?

But I forgot about the giraffe and carried it home. Look at the luck it's brought. I'll have to think of a plan to get rid of it.

A heavy sorrow like a hand at my face presses me into sleep, but I'm up a trillion times in the night.

'What if it gets worse?' I ask.

Simon says, 'We'll stop.'

That's not an option, as far as I'm concerned. I'm determined to stick it out, even if what's left of my face falls off. And I have my wall-chart, to help me survive.

28 August 2006

Last night the black blanket of *No, I can't do it* settled around me like a cloak. But it's gone again this morning. A cousin has warned me how a friend of hers suffered depression during and after radiotherapy. Another one says that someone she knows was nauseated and threw up sometimes, like me. Yet these things are not on any list of side-effects that I've seen.

I wonder if I'll ever give workshops or seminars again, or public readings. Not just because of my appearance, but because of my leg and the limitations of my speech. They let me down at unpredictable times. If I'm out at night, I see how people respond to a slurred word or if my leg is unsteady – they assume I am the worse for wear.

God be with the days, is all I can say to that.

The light level outside has dropped and leaves flutter and wave in panic – rain coming. It's dark. Here's the lightning! I love it, being inside and watching.

30 August 2006

Today Zita and Eoin took off for New York and we have Ryan. Simon has taken some time off to be here too.

As I'm leaving the radiation treatment room in St Luke's, the radiation therapists tell me that my number of treatments is going to be increased. They don't know why.

I'm floored by this. First of all, I'm disappointed – I thought I was more than halfway through and I'm not. Second, I'm afraid: will I make it all the way? Third, I'm thinking: *Serves you right for thinking you were flying through it*; fourth, I'm grateful for the chance of extra treatment; fifth, I'm furious. If there is a change to the treatment plan, shouldn't they discuss it with me? Most of all I feel distrustful and that infects every single other thing I think.

The evening passes in a daze. The cold sickly knowledge that this may be the end, or the beginning of the end, sits on my shoulder, like a ghost. I look at Ryan and think I may never know his older self; I stand back and watch my daughters move beyond me, do things I can't do – and wonder if I'll ever get back to myself.

The doctors all tell me to get on with my normal life. Don't they know that I'm outside it, that I can't find my way back in? My life has been taken away from me. I have to learn to accept that I can't do things myself and they won't happen to my timetable. And I live on an impossible regimen of diet and exercises and flushes and mouthwash and fluoride trays and meds and appointments. It's a full-time job, this.

31 August 2006

I wake up feeling beaten. I had trouble breathing during the night, kept sitting up to fight for air, a flap closing on my throat. Last night I carried this despair to bed – that whenever I start to feel strong in recovery, something comes along to knock me back.

I wish my leg hadn't broken. I wish I'd found my way to the max-fax clinic sooner. When the tumour was smaller and the surgery wouldn't have to have been so radical. Before it got into the lymph nodes.

In the radiotherapy clinic, Professor Hollywood explains it all again. They want to give me the maximum effective dose of radiation without posing a threat to the graft in my mouth and to the incision wound in my neck. The extra doses the radiation therapists mentioned have always been a possibility and still depend on my condition as I approach the twenty-eighth treatment. I'm doing so well, they want to keep going a little longer. He takes his time, makes eye contact, pitches his voice low and slow.

I calm down.

Simon takes Ryan off to look at the fish. They find rocks painted as ladybirds on different windowsills around the hospital and bring me round to look at them when I'm finished.

Added to my palette of background noise now, I hear the pitch and whine of my Roentgen hornets. I visualize them as in a comic, like the *Victor*, say. Deadly and always victorious in the end.

And I'm learning to touch my leg. My friends have given

me an astonishing range of moisturizers and lotions and I apply them diligently to the shark bite and the area where the plate is. It doesn't recoil as much as it did. I feel sorry for it.

3 September 2006

Simon has gone. At the airport and on the motorway a sense of summer ending, traffic build-up on the roads.

Ryan is so beautiful and pixie-like in his sleep. Imagine, the click of crutches and an awkward kiss might be all he remembers of me, no matter how much I love him.

4 September 2006

We wake up when Zita and Eoin come in from their travels and sit around listening to New York stories over breakfast. There's a whole world out there. They say I should go. I say I will.

I wonder.

Physiotherapy is good for me. It's nice to have this warm-skinned, soft-spoken young woman coax your muscles and tell you everything is going to be okay. A bit of massage, stretching out, checking strains; then exercise demonstration, reassurance, encouragement. I can do all of it, but I'm tentative. She says the ankle's most likely fine, and not to worry. The mouth opening might increase again, if I work at it.

Heartened, we go round to wait a long time for treatment. One of the rooms is being serviced, and a busload of patients have come in from somewhere, so there's a backlog. I'm the most monstrous-looking person I've seen, I tell Nessa on the way over. She denies it, but she's wrong.

'Why am I the reddest person here?' I ask the radiation therapists.

They laugh. 'Other people's treatment areas might be covered by their clothes,' they say. 'Did you ever think of that?'

It's getting harder to swallow. I have a cramp in my tongue. I listen to the wind in my ear as the tone of the world shifts, attentive to the fabric and structure of veins.

Oz has started to eat his front leg, where he had the needle for the drip. He has to wear one of those buster collars to stop him worrying it. He looks pathetic, barging through the hedge with his cone head; sitting in the kitchen like the *His Master's Voice* label. What is it with our animals, the sympathy illnesses and limps and disfigurements?

7 September 2006
There's a grey-faced woman in a wheelchair in the waiting area today. Nessa says that after I was called in this woman bragged about all the different places her cancer has been found. I've come across this weird phenomenon too: even in this, people can be competitive.

One of our cousins comes to cheer me up but I'm as sick as a dog this evening and won't be cheered.

8 September 2006
A rotten night. A bitter morning. I've to drag myself around, can barely lift my head, do no exercises. A friend drives me in to St Luke's for treatment.

In the radiotherapy clinic they prescribe an antibiotic and order an X-ray to check my leg because I'm worried. The radiographers ask me if I think the ankle has gone again, but how do I know? Look what happened last time.

The X-ray shows no fracture.

Back to the nurses for dressing and neck check (it's better today). It's late when we finish.

In the car, when my friend mentions cancer I contradict her.

'I think I don't have it any more. They've taken it out – now we're just blasting the site, to be sure.'

Then I'm afraid that I've jinxed myself by saying that I think it's gone.

Home to an empty house. Here's a first: I have keys and let myself in. Three fat bluebottles drill the glass of the kitchen window. I let them out and get back to the novel I'm reading, *Gilead*, by Marilynne Robinson, which I'm loving, with a kind of awe.

When Ryan complains about the homework he has to do, on the phone, I tell him about mine. I've to practise standing on one leg, for physiotherapy.

'Try it,' I say. 'It's harder than you'd think.' I hop around, try to keep my balance, while I talk to him.

He does. He says he doesn't wobble at all, it's easy.

9 September 2006

A friend collects me to go for a walk with another friend along the promenade in Bray. We arrange to meet in the car park. When we get there I remember that I'm not supposed to be in the sun. Luckily I'm wearing one of my new big scarves. We swathe my face and neck in purples and greens and yellows before we set off.

When we get back to the car there's a piper piping beside it, right there in the middle of the tarmac. Heavily cabled white socks, blue tartan kilt, black jacket, his colours are as loud as mine. He's not busking, he's just singing to the autumn sun. People stroll past as if this is the most normal thing in the world.

In the car, we talk about what you learn when mortality tugs at you. The weight of your past and how your concept of the future changes; what love becomes.

But when I really face the wall, the idea that I might die, I baulk and turn away. I wish I could write something meaningful and unforgettable about that – and in the light of that. I worry that I've let my mind soften and run, like butter. I worry that it could turn rancid. I can't concentrate on anything, have trouble finishing my own sentences. I read no newspapers or journals, I know nothing that's going on now, at home or abroad. I've forgotten any intellectual argument I ever engaged in. All those years of study and excitement and passionate research, gone.

Anything that makes you feel most passionately alive, no matter what it is or why, is the thing you should spend your time doing.

10 September 2006

The house is full of fat, slow bluebottles. One of my schoolfriends, who has brought breakfast again, puts four of them out of the house, through the kitchen door. One remains, out of reach.

Today I'm fretting about the tongue. What if the crab has

spies up there in the very place that I'm guarding from radiation? My friend is calm and sensible. She points out that the treatment fields suggest that the tongue is not a target.

I ring a friend who does deep-tissue massage. She helped me a lot when I had trouble with my back years ago.

I tell her that when I finish radiotherapy I want to put myself in her hands. The words crack something open that I didn't even know was locked. It's such a relief to talk to her – like opening a door, or finding a direction, at last.

I tell her that it is an extraordinary thing to have been in that place where I had no voice and lost the use of my leg and then to have come back from there. I feel as if I have been given a second chance. The attempt to articulate this veers off into cliché. You could spend your whole life trying to find living words to express it. The hooked fish set free.

Every single thing is a metaphor. A few days ago a daddy-long-legs freaked me out in the bedroom – it was one of my rough nights. Emma lured him out. Tonight he is suspended near the corner of the ceiling, as if in flight. He must be caught in a web. He hangs there like a warning to the flies.

11 September 2006
When I wake up I put my hand to my face and it feels more like *face*, even *my* face. The jutting ledge of my chin is closer to having what you might call a line. Right now it's more of a disturbance.

That daddy-long-legs is pressed to the glass of the window looking out. He wasn't caught after all. I open the window for him. Cool draughts of air flow in. It's misty outside.

★

At the radiotherapy clinic, we discuss balancing aggression with caution in the decision about the number of treatments I should have. They talk calmly and evenly about terrible things like infections in the metal in my mouth that could lead to its removal. This could develop weeks or even months after radiotherapy finishes, so the decision is not a simple one. I push for aggression and they push back with warnings. The risk of infection already exists, but it's low. However, it increases significantly after the twenty-eighth treatment.

On the phone from Tunisia, Simon reminds me that I simply don't know enough to make an informed decision about this. I have to trust their expertise.

I wonder, do I have a creative thought in my head? Just the rushing of time through my dead ear.

The texture of water has changed, for me. It sits like paint on my tongue.

12 September 2006

It's a wet morning, the first heavy rain in ages. Emma's car skids into a high kerb. She's okay but the car is damaged and of course I'm useless to her. Peter goes to help her out instead.

Tonight a friend has a play opening in Project. I wish I could go, but I feel too leaden.

I talk to the chemist about changing the way I take iron. I can't tolerate the syrup any longer, it makes my stomach heave. We'll try a different kind. In the meantime, I have to put up with the antibiotic and the laxative.

I'm on my way out to the recycling bin stoking up a rage about all of this when a pencil line of sunlight touches my face and I shake myself: I have *today*. Four months ago, or even less, I was so broken that being on my own sofa made little difference to me, no matter how much I wanted it to.

I can see myself getting to a stage where I would hide from the world. That is just plain stupid. I've been given another chance. Am I going to hide behind my door and sulk, or am I going to step outside and take it?

I need to work or I'll explode.

Eoin comes in the afternoon and puts up a steel handrail at the steps. It's smooth and bright and solid. Just knowing it's there makes me feel safer.

I make a fly-trap. I tape a blue plastic bag over the vent in the living room where the smell seems strongest. Let's see what emerges from the stinking underbelly of the house. When I close the door to the kitchen an evil rustle makes the hair stand up on the back of my neck – but then I realize that it's caused by the change in air pressure in the bag. Here's something to scarify the girls with later.

16 September 2006

We're babysitting Ryan tonight – all three girls are going out. They look startlingly beautiful. Each one of them shocks me, as if I've never seen them before, the artistry of how they put themselves together for whatever an occasion demands.

We give Zita a lift into town and on the way out again we stop for petrol. Simon goes in to pay. Ryan and I are playing in the car, laughing our heads off, when I catch my reflection in the mirror. My face looks dead. It's empty of expression, twisted and gnarled like an old tree branch, fallen. Medusa, I turn to stone.

The disfigurement is one thing, but what I really hate is the complete lack of expression. It's as if I'm not there. The lights are on, but nobody's home. I sink further into that cave of being, underground, out of reach, and think about the people I will meet from now on. They will never know me as I was. Their perception of me will begin with this uneven, immobile face.

Well, you'll just have to live with that.

17 September 2006

We go to see *Little Miss Sunshine*. Hilarious dysfunctional-family fare. There we are, spread out along the front row with food and drinks, my one remaining crutch on the ledge in front of us, my bad leg up. We laugh so hard that we're snorting and hooting and crying. Dysfunctional, us? When we come out Simon checks his ticket and discovers he's booked on an earlier flight than we thought. There's a mad dash for the airport, but he makes it on time.

18 September 2006

My neck is bleeding. That image of the head falling off comes back to haunt me.

My friend in Canada warns me that the symptoms of radiotherapy peak ten to fourteen days after the treatment stops. Take stock: my skin is raw and bleeding and looks ulcerated. My tongue is one raw nerve, my gums and teeth are sore. I have mucositis blisters on my tongue, and clumps of fibrosed tissue stiffening my mouth. My voice is erratic and my swallow goes the wrong way; my hair is so thin and dry it's like an anorexic haystack. On top of all that, I'm fighting nausea, after the gum-soaking routine.

Oh, and I have the runs. That's so normal by now I almost forgot to mention it.

20 September 2006

It's the last day of my treatment.

In the waiting area Sky News is on, as always. The background music of this experience has been football and weather. Today it's the Ryder Cup and weather – disruption by rain and consequent traffic.

Old hand, I open my eyes under the mask. The table moves. Voices that are familiar to me now murmur positioning before they leave the room. Then the beep, and the exposure, the high-pitched whine of the hornets unleashed to find any lurking microscopic particles of crab, wherever they are hiding. I cheer them on, for the last time.

I like these young women. They are friendly. Out in the nurses's area, too, people smile and say hello. I've been coming here for six weeks. Each of the nurses has had a view of my pierced and flabby stomach with its green and red 'exudate'. The word has the ring of fire and brimstone. Effluvium, Joyce might call it.

After physio, and a trip to the clinic, we take a break in the coffee shop with our max-fax friend. She and I have taken to meeting in hospital waiting rooms and coffee shops. It is the right side of my face that is altered, her left. We sit good ear to good ear and compare notes on our experience. I'm lucky to have her to talk to.

Then I go to meet the pain nurse, who advises me to use OxyNorm again when the skin hurts and at night, so I can sleep and have a better chance of healing. I don't want to increase my medication, but what she says makes sense.

My tongue feels as if there are thorns spiked into it. Thorns or hot iron nails. I see barbed wire anchored to soft, red, pulsing flesh, a torn tongue.

We drive home in the rain under a black, black cloud, the remnants of Hurricane Gordon which is disrupting the Ryder Cup. How could they not have expected rain, in Ireland?

I've brought my shell home in a plastic bag. She looks bizarre, straining against the cellophane, as if she's straining for breath, suffocating.

David Bowie's 'Free' is the soundtrack in my head. Melo-dramatic, rolled and loud.

I dance on my one crutch in the kitchen and think about the books I want to write. There's no reason to think I won't. We have just pulverized whatever traces of the cancer were left behind after surgery. The greatest risk of recurrence is in the first two years. Once I get to five years I'll be laughing.

Nessa and I have a mock sleepover to celebrate. We watch a bad film on TV and eat cake and ice cream in our pyjamas. In my case, it's crumbs of cake dissolved in melted ice cream. I can't taste it, but I relish the fact of it.

It's after midnight and I should go to sleep, my eyes have begun to falter. But I can't go without registering the fact that I feel so very lucky, blessed with luck, to be alive, to be through the next hurdle, to be out of the trap and on my way forward, gathering momentum towards recovery.

And here's a news flash: I could swear I feel the hint of a smile.

Chapter 8

21 September 2006

I thought for sure I'd get some work done once radiotherapy was over, but I'm flattened. You'd have to peel me off the couch. We went shopping and it wiped me out – I underestimated the energy it would take to negotiate shopping trolleys and the curious eyes of children in a crowded place.

There's a big storm outside, half the street is being blown into the house. I'm sorting through laundry and dreaming about the millions of ways that it's possible to live a life. It seems meaningless and flat when I write it, but the thought gives me a jolt of delight. There's so much out there and I'm still here to do it.

The wind beats the house and Oz is a furry blond pillow on his new bed on the floor beside me. Here I am, crocked. Metalmouth. I register different levels of pain and the loss of taste, hearing, sensation in parts of my face, scalp and neck and at the same time there's a soft, silky cushion in my cheek and a faint, sweet taste, a flood of saliva that is distinctive in this arid time. To have any saliva at all is a miracle.

I ring my max-fax friend, ask what she is doing. She's having coffee and eating a KitKat.

'A KitKat,' I say, jealous. I wonder when (if ever) I'll get back to the simple joys of a bar of chocolate. 'Large or small?'

'Small,' she says. 'I don't do "large" any more. It's like Toblerone.'

We sigh, for Toblerone. I sing the jingle.

'Never mind,' she says. 'We can always gnaw on it.'

This sheer pulsing pleasure I feel is a delight in being alive, in having a house to be alive in, a family to be alive with and meaningful work to do – it's a slow but certain glow that liquefies and spreads. I remember when Clair's mother-in-law was dying a slow and quiet death, she woke up each morning and said: 'Oh, it's lovely to see another day.'

That's how I feel now, every single morning.

22 September 2006

The diarrhoea is bad this morning and I call to cancel some appointments. It's too tricky to organize someone to drive me when I'm like this.

One friend has sent me loads of rescue cream for my skin and another brought an aloe vera plant that sits on the kitchen windowsill, ready to go into action. I'm rinsing out my mouth with baking soda every chance I get. With luck, we'll stave off the worst of the after-effects. If only the diarrhoea would stop.

I get a call from Luke's to say that the swab they took from the PEG site shows an infection and so does the neck wound. I'm to be very careful. I have to watch out for signs of worse. The infection at the neck could spread inwards, to the metal or bone in my mouth.

The nurse on the phone suggests that the PEG tube may need to come out, but I'm more worried about that unpredictable metal. I want to get through all this without them having to remove the graft from my mouth.

★

I have a complete freak-attack when something slips from my hands and the syringes, bowl and OxyNorm bottle skitter away on the wet counter surface, the precious OxyNorm going down the sink.

I shriek and Nessa comes running to see what's happened. I'm trying to control the various spillages – from PEG tube, bowl, bottle. She helps me to clean it all up.

'Don't worry, we'll get more,' she says.

'I've no prescription!'

'We'll get you another one.'

'When? When?' I'm like a harpy. 'You're going back to college . . .' and then I stop short. What the hell am I doing? I may be scared, but it's not her fault.

Turn it around and get excited instead. And *write*.

There's a thorn in my tongue and my rough-edged tooth comes to nestle in the sorest spot of mucositis, worrying away at it. Even water burns it. When I cough, a taste of metal surges to the back of my throat. And there's a scary feeling of not being able to swallow, which comes and goes. The pump at my ear washes past, telling me how my heart is working.

Strangely, I think about meat. Even though my feelings about the ethics of the meat industry haven't changed, I have a minor craving – must be a deficiency. Eat beans. I'll have to liquidize them.

I'm nervous about this weekend. What if the PEG infection gets worse, where do I go? I'm between hospitals, not sure who to call.

Ideas rise and fall around me, inside and out, visible and not, felt, imagined. The dark woman who opens my heart. The dancer. The silent house. Moonlight falling across broad wooden boards. A square chest under the window. A quest,

strange creatures – unicorns. Footsteps. The sea. A cove.
Green light. A caravan, a crowded church, a pulpit. A man is
speaking, eyes seek me out. People stir, rustle leaves, a tree
standing, a tree fallen – what's the difference? I can raise it or
destroy it.

While I write, I'm aware of the open door at my back, the
light leading to the flight of stairs up to the dark of the attic.
I half wait for Nessa to come down and berate me: why am
I still up? But back on the page we are in Brittas Bay, that's
my mother on the beach, saving a man so he can die again,
at another time and in another place.

I put out my hand to catch electricity. I thought it was a
piece of paper. Rain just woke me. Rooms are like stage sets.
All you have to do is think: *what can happen here?*

24 September 2006

During the night my PEG leaked copiously onto the sheet.
I wake up in a mess.

One of my schoolfriends brings scones for breakfast and
olive oil from the Sierra Nevada. Another brings raspberries
from her garden. When they leave I ring St Luke's to ask
about my leaky PEG site. They say these leaks can happen
with infection, not to worry unless I get pain in my abdomen
and if I do, to go to the gastrointestinal review clinic in
St James's.

Relieved, I ring Simon. Then I cry when I hear his voice.

I'm almost afraid to go to sleep – in what way will my body
let me down tonight? I don't think these are the pains they
meant when they said to go in if . . . I do *not* want to go back
in to hospital.

Each half hour drags heavy feet towards morning. Every

sound a wasting. No wonder some people can't bear to be alone.

25 September 2006

Big Monday: today Zita goes back to work, Nessa goes back to college and I go back to my own resources.

I get up just after ten, relieved that none of my systems leaked during the night. Maybe the antibiotic is working. The morning goes just emptying the dishwasher and getting ready for a friend to bring me to Luke's. I'm chewing Imodium at this stage before I can go anywhere. I get my dressing checked, fall asleep in the waiting area, wake to the pain nurse. Discuss all the various symptoms and remedies. The diarrhoea is probably due to all the meds I'm taking. One of them is notorious for causing digestive problems. I've had a problem with taking iron all along but I need it.

I take more Imodium for the journey home. At home I keep falling asleep. Well, they warned me that I'd get tired. I'll get through it.

Even getting a pint of water for myself seems like a huge, insurmountable task. I'm on the verge of panic, or breaking down. But only briefly. I'll be all right. I just feel vulnerable. And lonely. Also, like a failure. I'm not sure where that's coming from, but it's how I feel. And the drag of nausea, along with self-pity, as I face into another night and wonder what humiliations are waiting for me now. My aching, useless ankle still looks distorted. But I've the orthopaedic clinic next Monday. I'll make it that far anyway.

26 September 2006

Nessa is in college for the whole day. A friend has given me a manuscript to proofread. Work! Yay! I feel *useful*, for the first time in ages. I'm making a contribution to something and someone that matters to me. The long, empty day flies in quickly. I'm never alone when I have work to do.

Emma is going to the Orkneys to see how her Ph.D. research on tidal power functions in the field. Before she goes she has to do sea/survival training. Among other things, she has had to launch herself off a six-foot ladder into deep water. She says she just managed to avoid knocking herself out on a girder.

Even in the whole of my health, I could never have done that.

I'm so tired my eyes slide off the lines and I can see writing underneath, outlines of words in a faint reddish brownish ink, tracks heavily written, jumping to the surface like fish – take us! Catch us! They may as well be crying. And I write on, putting my overlay on what I can't see underneath – notes towards what? My interrupted novel has sunk underground.

At night, I hear the *krrrk!* of insects and sleeping grass, all seems well when I wake up and uncoil my foreign body, come upright, a deep, deep cough giving me satisfaction, as if something old and wise is at work. On the loo I sway and dream.

27 September 2006

I have a black lack of energy, and pain at the PEG site, so that I grunt with pain when I move. I feel drained. My clothes get looser. I take small handfuls of Imodium and go to St James's.

There are the familiar crowded corridors with various members of the team flying up and down but smiling and saying hello, the usual components in the crowd – someone agitated about having been kept waiting so long; an elderly couple with resignation stamped all over them, shoulders sloping down into their wrists, clothes in faded shades of beige and blue.

We enter the sanctum. Professor Stassen opens a laptop and shows me photos: of the tumour pegged out on corkboard in an approximation of its original shape; of me on the operating table with the tracheostomy and my face opened up; of the bulk of my lower jaw with teeth still attached; of the fatty-looking inside of my cheek. Great vessels exposed.

After the initial seconds of adjustment, the thing that shocks me is not seeing myself in that condition, but how big the tumour looks, about the size of my fat purple bracelet.

They ask me how I am, how I feel when I look at all of this. I tell them I'm fine, and it's true. None of it really seems like *me*. The face on the screen is different, from another time.

They tighten and clean the PEG, mutter a little at the state of it. They say they'll take it out the next time I come if I still don't need it. They can't be sure that I won't, until two full weeks have passed after radiotherapy.

28 September 2006
I'm still chewing Imodium, take double quantities any time I have to leave the house.

Jackie comes to bring me to St Luke's. I've no energy but I get myself out and into her car, gut clenching. She gives me worried looks, asks if I want to go back. I say no. I'm struggling, but I don't want to miss physiotherapy – and maybe there's a part of me that wants someone to see how sick I am.

We're stopped at a traffic light when I can't hold on any longer. I have to say, 'Oh, please stop – pull up on the grass, pull up on the grass!' and I spill out of her car and use the door as a non-shield between me and the traffic while my bowels open, right there on the grass verge. I'm helpless and shaking.

Lucky for me that Jackie travels with seven different types of wipe and an airplane sick-bag, not to mention the towels I've brought (just in case), so we clean up as best we can and go on. I'm faint. Now I appreciate what that word really means.

When we get to St Luke's I throw up in the loo. My lovely physio takes one look at me and says, 'Oh, I don't think so.'

Within seconds she has me in a wheelchair and round we go to the nurses' station. Next thing I'm on oxygen, wheeled off to the clinic then back, round to X-ray where I can barely talk to the radiographers, back to the nurses's station. All the time I'm afraid that I smell, and I try to remember how many days it has been like this. About three weeks.

They want to admit me, keep me in for observation over the weekend. I start to cry, tell them that Simon is coming in this afternoon, I haven't seen him for two weeks, he'll only be here for two days . . .

They relent in the end. I'm to stop taking the antibiotic, take plenty of Imodium and ring them tomorrow to check in. If I'm not okay, I'm to go in then. We all hope that this is my rock-bottom, that I can kick up from here.

Home and on the couch again, I drift in and out of sleep – hot water bottle and the gorgeous soft blue blanket a friend sent from Boston. Getting comfy.

I'm amazed by how low I can go and still be okay. I'm glad it was Jackie, though.

29 September 2006

A slow start, blissful. Lizzie brings the garden in, tugs twigs out of her fur with her tongue, her weight moulded into mine. Then Simon brings me to my friend down the road, for a session of deep-tissue massage.

I'd forgotten the joy of walking into that glowing, fire-lit room, forgotten the smell of hot ash and strong branches, the background sounds of a fire like rough music – spark, snap and crash, whisper.

There's an undernote of flame in the silences, where she feels her way around the new geographies of my body, making the PEG site grumble and spit like a sulky kitten. We laugh, and it doesn't seem so threatening any more. Whatever she does to my shoulders and head is effective. I'm sleepy afterwards and *hungry*.

I eat a slice of spinach quiche and we go for a drive in brilliant sunlight: hot glass, blue sea and boats – a bizarre black and orange container-vessel at anchor in the bay – the Vico Road and its Southern hills; then home again to apple crumble and custard and another snooze, distant sounds of phones ringing and the piano. Then I'm awake – the cat is kneading the blankets and purring.

2 October 2006

Simon has gone, Emma is at work, Nessa is in college. I begin to feel myself detach from everyone around me – buried even, in a tunnel of loneliness and weakness. I see faces I love at a distance I think I'll never be able to cross.

Jackie comes and we've a quiet drive in to the orthopaedic clinic at St James's. Queue, X-ray, queue; back, queue. The young doctor with the dimple is happy with how the leg looks, says the average recovery time for a fracture of the tibia is five months. That makes me feel better. Only four months have passed, there's still time for improvement. He says it's okay to walk, and I can drive whenever the physiotherapist tells me that the leg is strong enough.

Round to the pain clinic. We share a waiting room with another crowd, and they're in for a long wait as well. Their secretary makes an announcement to say that their consultant has been delayed because he's talking to a person who has been bereaved.

Why do they say this? Is it because it's an unanswerable reason to keep everyone waiting? Or is it a reminder? *Listen, buddy, one day you're going to be in the shit too, so just be quiet and wait your turn.*

A florid woman behind us mutters that a man was seen ahead of them because he complained. Her father is eighty. They drove up from the midlands this morning. His meds are due soon but she left them in the car. She thought they'd be back on the road by now.

Sweetheart, you are singing my song.

Her father is getting nervous. He's also turning grey. Traffic builds up in all our minds, listening to her and thinking about the time, as rush-hour approaches.

At last we are called in to see the pain team. We discuss the impact of various medications on my bowels. This must be so much fun for Jackie – but I don't think she minds too much; she shows signs of growing fond of this mellow-voiced pain man.

It turns out that the antibiotic I've been taking stimulates peristalsis, it's even given to ICU patients to keep their bowels active. No wonder I've been so ill. At least I've stopped taking it now. We go on to the idea of reducing my medication to a level where I'll be able to drive again.

A few days of sickness have made me lazy about stretching my mouth, so now my jaw is seizing up. Each tiny step, whether it's opening my mouth or flexing my ankle or learning to touch the skin on my leg without flinching, will build up into a path that leads back to my life. I may not get back to exactly where I was, but the path back to wherever I'll rejoin myself starts here and I'm the only one who can cross it – not the sympathetic health workers, not my friends, not even my family. It's me, I have to do it.

When I bring that thought back to its beginning, I can see that I'm already on that path. I don't have to 'get there', I'm already there.

At times today I wondered about other people in the hospital, what stage of their journey they may be on – and would it help them if they came across someone like me and I said, 'Look, six months down the line, here I am, recovering: alive, conscious; thinking about a future'? Would it help, as meeting someone else has helped me? Or would they run a mile?

I wonder. I begin to look as if I might be in trouble. My clothes hang loose from my crooked, shrinking frame.

4 October 2006

Thought for the day: the time they give you is not your own. If you think in terms of so many years or months or whatever, it doesn't take into account the time you have to spend in hospitals, in surgery and recovery, time spent ill or in physio, time spent sitting in hospital corridors waiting for tests or appointments, or in traffic jams on your way to and from procedures, waiting in corridors – not to mention what they do to you, what you have to recover from and how you feel.

This is my first day of cutting down the level of morphine I'm taking. I'm wearing a smaller patch. A little grumpy, maybe, but doing okay.

5 October 2006

I take out my interrupted novel and look over unfinished scenes. The time flies.

Then Nessa takes me to get my hair done. The disabled parking spots are blocked. Of course they are. We drive round the back and all of a sudden I see that it won't be possible to park, I just have to get out of the car and go in by myself. It's like when you know the water is cold and you have to jump in suddenly to get it over with – that's pretty much how I get out of the car. Nessa is startled but I wave her off. 'I'll be okay.'

The salon is busy, young people flying around, women telling stories in loud voices, lots of hand gestures. I read *Suite Française*. Professor Stassen recommended it. People come over to chat. At the sink, I ask the girl who washes my hair to be careful along the damaged side and she's angelic, gets it exactly right, as if she can see where the pins-and-needly bits are. I drift off to sleep under the hot towel.

6 October 2006

A call from St Luke's – I have to go in to the clinic this afternoon. They want to send me for endoscopy to investigate my stomach and tumultuous bowel. I don't want to go. They want to discuss it.

While I wait I dive into the lovely refuge of *Suite Française*.

Think of all the books that have pulled me through difficult days like this one. Outside, the sad flames of our neighbour's tree grow dull, as if they know this will be their last summer. She's decided to cut it down next year.

A friend comes to drive me to St Luke's. When we get there, all the handicapped spaces are used or blocked, so we park out on the street. On the way in I have to detour and throw up in the loo, more diarrhoea. The physio is reluctant to work, arranges for me to be seen by a doctor instead.

There is huge debate as to what's going on. One theory is that the last antibiotic could have caused this latest bout of diarrhoea, but it might equally be an infection, or some bug I've picked up because my resistance is down. In the end they give me a prescription for an anti-emetic, a new antibiotic and a new painkiller – it all seems like so much guesswork to me, not that different from the eye-of-newt approach.

I'm alone in the house. The autumnal darkness outside seems significant. I am casting a net over my life and dragging it around to face the sun. Once it's infused with light it will breathe and move freely again.

8 October 2006

I check my email every few minutes. I'm waiting for Brendan's response to the piece I sent him. It's like being a teenager, waiting for a boy to call.

I have an image of a ladder, an old wooden ladder. When I feel really sunken and low I want to climb out through my eyes, across to the person I look at – do they ever see that need?

Then there's the ladder of recovery. Bit by bit, I climb it, rung by rung. I can't go faster. My tendency is to jump the hurdle hard, and to clear it – but then I land in the muck on the other side. Well, here's the crash now, this bout of diarrhoea that won't go away, this infection. Whatever it is.

9 October 2006

Last night was weird – Emma went to bed early because she had to leave at the crack of dawn to go to the Orkneys. I got all weepy when she said goodbye, rambled on about what a gorgeous baby she used to be. She laughed at me for being so ridiculous, going on as if she's never coming back.

Now here we are, Monday. A brand-new week. Emma has arrived safely in the Orkneys and Simon is in Paris. It's time to get to work. I have a short story in my mind.

That I can feel hunger. That it can be satisfied. These things are extraordinary to me. I could have been dead by now. And I'm not, my birthday coming.

11 October 2006

This turns out to be a red-letter day at the clinic in St James's. Sinéad asks how I am and I'm evasive because, hey, there are a lot of people here with nothing to do but listen. Then the crowd eases, so I tell her about the diarrhoea.

I get a call from St Luke's to say there's *E. coli* in the PEG, it needs to come out. The infection in the neck is different and less worrying. I'll see them tomorrow anyway.

I go in to see the dietician, who weighs me, and then lectures me – in the sweetest possible way – about challenging myself to eat better and maintain my weight.

So then I go in to the clinic and we have a bit of chitchat and then suddenly Professor Stassen is pulling out the PEG,

me going *Ow ow ow, it hurts!* and with a series of hefty tugs –
me hanging onto his hand, trying to hold it back – it's out.

Nessa's face wrinkles but she doesn't look traumatized. The
nurse with green eyes puts a dressing on it. Then they tell me
that my treatment has finished. From now on, I just have to
be checked once a month or so, either here or in St Luke's.

I had no idea it was going to be such a significant day when
I got up feeling so rotten, dragged the husk of myself around,
wincing from the soreness of the infection. Last night the
PEG acted like a geyser, small hot eruptions of bubbles,
gurgling like a storm drain, most peculiar. Today the hole
where it used to be is doing the same.

They tell me it'll close over very quickly. The dietician
says they can shock you, they close so fast – if a tube falls out,
you have to get in there with something to keep it open, fast.

12 October 2006

I do all right at physiotherapy in St Luke's today, even on
the evil bike. This is a stationary machine that measures the
relative strength of each leg. At first I got exhausted after
three minutes. Now I'm up to ten. Then I have to try to
stand on a wobble board, a wooden platform about eighteen
inches square mounted on two semicircles. It's a disaster. My
sense of balance has deserted me. The soft-voiced physio tells
me that my ankle doesn't know where it is.

Meanwhile, I keep seeping and seeping. We use wads of
hand towels to pad out the dressing, but still it seeps through.

At the radiotherapy clinic the nurse asks if a doctor has
spoken to me and I say no. She asks me to wait. When she
comes back she has a doctor in tow and I know something's
up. They've found an infection in my faecal sample. And
blood. And my haemoglobin has gone down to 8.4 – a 20

per cent drop in two weeks. They say it's no wonder I'm so tired and washed out. They chat about the infection and how they've asked for more cultures, and I'm yakking on about how it's good to know there's something there and now we can deal with it, etc., when they tell me bluntly that this means that I must have the endoscopy, to find out where I'm bleeding from. They will arrange it for me, at St James's.

I stop hearing what they're saying then. All I want is to get out of there.

The nurse is sympathetic and changes the sodden PEG dressing. She uses one of those super-absorbent seaweed plugs and then a big pink pad – I look set for the Flood. But of course it only lasts about half an hour – do the makers of these dressings ever test them in field conditions?

At home, my gut starts to twist and cramp and I have to sprint for the loo and then the long clean-up process, the babywipe stage and the disinfectant stage. I creep out, wrapped in a towel, and get the washing machine started. Then I go for a shower. Then I clean the room again, exhausted.

I have to wonder what I've done to deserve this. At last, the 'why me?' Why anyone?

14 October 2006

A second bellybutton has appeared where the PEG tube was, above and slightly to the left of my navel. What they don't tell you is that you will be leaking for days. How water runs straight through, from your mouth through the tube to your skin, your clothes. If I didn't feel so sick I'd think this was funny.

★

I get the promised response about the piece and it's terrific.

Elated, I reduce the morphine to a single 75 mcg/hr patch. This is a definite milestone – it's the level at which they suggested I might be able to start driving, when my leg is strong enough.

We laze around for a bit and then Simon and I go for our ritual drive through Wicklow. Today on the road above Enniskerry we had sunshine on our right and mist billowing up towards us on our left.

Our house is on a fault-line, for weather. We're used to seeing rain through one window, sunlight through another. Sometimes that's how I feel, like the fault-line between a world of illness and one of health. I'm the crack through which unpredictable events will erupt, any minute.

Here's another milestone – I keep forgetting to use my crutch. I put it in a corner and then I can't find it or don't need it and off I go. Almost the whole day, this time.

15 October 2006

I can't believe the depth of sorrow I feel when Simon leaves. I cling, bury my ruined face in the expanse of his grey jumper. How the hell did this happen? How did I come to this? Dependent, needy, dull. And I'm constantly insecure, asking, 'Am I shouting?', or, 'Do I smell?' It could be part of one of those 'declines' that people analyse in retrospect. If it is, there's damn all I can do about it because at certain times I feel weak enough not to care. That's what frightens me.

The dog is restless tonight. Flat-eared, slack-eyed. I rub his back with my crutch, a thing he's come to enjoy. He settles at last.

16 October 2006

An unbelievably horrible start to the day. After my shower they could hang me from the walls, no paste. I fret about the journey to the Dental Hospital. Nessa says, 'Cancel.' She does it for me. I spread myself on the couch.

I'm getting paranoid about travelling in someone else's car, being in traffic or in a public building. I have to pack a change of clothes, a spare towel, just to travel a few miles down the road.

Is it a test? Each time I have to find a place to hook my finger under the collar and hoist myself up to face this thing again and get on top of it.

I ask Nessa to look for disposable adult nappies in the supermarket, and she does, God bless her. And brings them home.

17 October 2006

My forty-ninth birthday is coming. When I reach it, I'll have outlived my father, I won't be in the danger year any more. This was the first major target I set myself when I was diagnosed, just over six months ago. Zita has come up with a plan, to have a pyjama party here at the weekend. We'll all wear pyjamas and watch videos.

I've agreed to go for the endoscopy. I talk to my friend the oncologist, in Canada, for a long time. I wish she was here now.

18 October 2006

The tree next door leans so far over it may as well just lie down on our wall and flare one last time. This is where courage fails. A person could just give up.

But the birds make a wooden sound with their wings. Around here, wood pigeons and magpies favour different trees, like gangs and neighbourhood bars. The magpies also like to strut around on our flat roof, driving Lizzie crazy. I'm with the wood pigeons, myself. If you ask me, magpies are the war criminals of the avian world.

In Anne Tyler's *Digging to America*, there's a scene where a character thinks about his wife's dying, as opposed to her death. He wonders which was the day when *she* died, the person she was. Before she turned into the invalid.

I have to start fasting now and to drink a vile substance called Kleenprep, to empty out my system before the endoscopy tomorrow. I fight nausea with every mouthful. It's like drinking salty paint.

The cat keeps vigil with me. I'm tired but restless. Don't have time for sleep.

Everyone I talk to seems shocked that I'm going ahead with this test when it just came out of nowhere. Do I really need it? they ask. And why, exactly, did I let the doctors talk me into it?

I don't want to have it, but in the end I couldn't find arguments strong enough to oppose them. I just rolled over and said okay. Every single thing about this illness came out of nowhere, if you ask me. Here comes the speeding car, the corner. And here's me, the wreck.

★

I take out the *Dublin Review* piece and make corrections and I'm working across the border of midnight and into my birthday. This is the only piece of work I've managed to finish in the six months since all this started, but right now it's enough. I am triumphant. Exultant, even. I feel a huge weight lifting, as if I don't have to be afraid now.

I send the corrections off without letting them sit over-night. I would never normally do this, but I don't know what's ahead of me tomorrow. What if I got this far and then couldn't see it through?

19 October 2006

My forty-ninth birthday, the one I wondered if I'd ever see. A day for an endoscopy. Great.

Nessa gets up before me. When I come downstairs, still calm, reminding myself *it's not here, it's not now*, the hall is full of coloured balloons, like globes of light for me to wade through. Then a stash of cards and stuff; lovely flowers from the girls, a CD of poetry and one of music written by the son of a friend. Books. Notebooks.

Then Jackie arrives to drive me to the hospital. When I open the door she says, 'Well, Li, this is going to be the most interesting birthday yet.'

I have to laugh. I'm as weak as a puddle but we get out to the car, me in my nappy, and head off into the traffic.

The endoscopy suite in St James's is down an unobtrusive corridor and in to the right. It's like entering a new circle of hell – it turns and turns into a vast area, which must be one of the biggest departments in the hospital. The workers are colour-coded – blue for nurses, green for cleaning staff, blue and white for clerical. The doctors stroll around in scrubs. They are in green too but you'd know they aren't cleaners.

We wait in the bright, clean reception area with the usual leaflets in containers on the walls. Then I'm called in. The nurses back here are a familiar mix of Filipina, Indian and Irish. Sinéad drops in to keep me company until I'm wheeled off.

They are all a bit breezy and dismissive as I recite my warnings, about the graft and about mouth opening and about the PEG and about infection. They seem to take scant notice of the drugs I'm on and what I'm allergic to. A tall, suave doctor comes in rubbing his hands, jovial and friendly.

The needle goes in, and we begin – the mouthpiece is too big and I yank at my mouth, trying to open it wider, while they hunt for something smaller. The doctor bends down and says don't force it, and I like him better. I lecture him about sedation. I don't just want to forget about this, I tell him. I don't want to feel it in the first place.

The next thing I know I wake up and my position is reversed in respect of the screen and him, and I'm looking at the eerily beautiful interplanetary world of my own colon, labyrinthine coils and chambers with an artificial orange glow. It's a bit like the lava lamp at home, with discrete particles floating through it in places and angry red areas. I'm entranced. They say that, provisionally, they think I have ulcerative colitis or Crohn's disease. They'll take a few samples from the ulcerated areas for testing.

I say how lovely it all is. I'd like photos.

Then I'm in recovery. Sleepy but fine. The consultant comes in and shows me a letter, my provisional report. Colour printer, colour pix. I remind him that I want copies and drift off to sleep again. When I wake up, Jackie is out in the waiting room. I get dressed and go out to join her. They bring me tea and digestive biscuits, but there's none for her. I leave with a prescription for three new drugs on top of the ones I'm already taking.

The rest of the day is a blur. At home, the phone keeps ringing but I can't talk to anyone. Our GP rings, because she got a letter to say that I was being sent for the endoscopy and then Jackie dropped my new prescription in, so she put two and two together.

20 October 2006

I wake slowly and alone. I have nowhere to go. I think about yesterday's provisional diagnosis. It doesn't make sense to me. Crohn's disease and ulcerative colitis are both chronic inflammatory bowel diseases. It seems a little coincidental that a chronic bowel disease should surface now.

I ring our GP because I haven't a clue what I'm taking. She explains each of the three new drugs to me. She tells me that everyone who has a test like this has a sample taken, even if they are sixteen years old and it looks perfectly normal. It certainly makes sense for them to sample the ulcers they found in me, it's nothing to worry about.

One of my schoolfriends comes to mind me for the day. We go over everything. I feel well and optimistic while we talk. At least *that's* over with.

I think I have aged about twenty years in the last few months. It's as if there's a cliff somewhere and someone is randomly shoving people off it. We all have to walk past and it's a matter of luck who falls.

Simon asks, from London, what kind of day it is and I say it's trying to be bright, trying to shine, like the rest of us. He says that people at work have asked him why he's not here. I say supportive things, but part of me wonders the same thing. Then I say – but if I said that I needed you here, you'd come. And he would.

★

I can hear: foghorns, church bells, a seed dropped by a bird or an insect hitting the window; water running and something chirping in the walls of the house. Pain sings into my ear, hypnotic. The stench of death has gone. Whatever that was, it's over.

Oz sleeps beside me, golden, in the sun. His deep breathing. The cone off, he's given back to us.

Chapter 9

21 October 2006

I wake suddenly and throw up. Relentless waves of vomiting and diarrhoea follow. I can barely stand up without support. The girls call our GP. She comes when her morning clinic has finished.

Our GP says I need to go in to St James's. She rings for an ambulance. It takes for ever to get here. While we wait, the girls pack a bag for me. I tell them which one I want, the lilac backpack I brought to Kenya. I don't have to tell them what I need: notebook, pyjamas, toothbrush, tongue depressors, meds.

The ambulance men carry me out on a sort of folding chair. It's a bit dodgy on the stairs but I don't care if they drop me. I don't care where I'm going. I'm completely numb. Outside, the street is quiet. There's no one around.

Nessa comes with me in the ambulance. Emma takes her own car. There's no siren, we're much too grim for that.

One of the ambulance men sits in the back to keep an eye on me. He tells bad jokes to distract us.

'I love wimmin,' he says. 'My favourite is the breast stroke. Oh no, wait, that's swimmin'.'

That's the kind of thing. My brother would love him.

I'm aware that my infected neck wound is pressed against the uncovered surface of the gurney. I wonder who else has lain on it in the last few hours and why. There's not much I can do about it.

I get a cubicle in A & E straight away. Zita is there ahead

of us, waiting with one of my schoolfriends. All I can do is lie there and ache. I'm tormented by thirst, but by the luck of God the bouts of diarrhoea have stopped.

My friend tells us stories she's heard in the waiting room. There are rumours that a man who's broken bail has been spotted in the hospital. Security are on to it.

People peer through the gap in my curtains, looking for relatives or just plain curious.

A doctor is trying to find a vein in my arm when a man with a scarred face and blood on his clothes wanders in to the cubicle to ask if we know the way out. The doctor is exasperated. 'Could you ask someone who isn't actually taking blood at the minute?'

My friend keeps us posted about what else is going on. A Polish plasterer who's been working in the hospital has crashed his motorbike and broken his wrist. The staff are sympathetic but his girlfriend's fury is vocal. The man who has broken bail is caught, handcuffed and led away by two gardaí.

The doctor finds a vein and sets up a drip. Then IV antibiotics. I'm wheeled off to X-ray. The plasterer is there too, mourning his useless arm. Back in A & E, another passer-by puts his head through the curtains and morphs into Simon, computer bag on his shoulder.

'We have to stop meeting like this,' I tell him.

'What did you say your name was, again?' he asks.

He's home for the week.

The little voodoo giraffe is in the hidden pocket of the lilac backpack. I ask Nessa to take it out and put it in the yellow Medical Waste bin, for incineration along with the rest of the hospital waste. I have to explain what it is and why I want to get rid of it this way. I know they think I'm crazy, but it's the best thing I can think to do with it.

★

After a few hours, I'm moved to an observation ward, one of the mixed rooms I dread. I'm barely there when I start to throw up again and they move me to an isolation room opposite the nurses' station that has just become available. It's the luckiest break I've had in a long time: in the side room I have the luxury of a bathroom to myself. I don't know how I could have borne sprinting for the loo in a bathroom shared by six men and women.

There are warning signs at my door, people have to wear plastic aprons when they come in to see me. I'm not allowed out. But I can barely leave the bed, let alone the room.

23 October 2006

Emma leaves on an early morning flight for Germany. She's going to a conference, for work. She thought she'd have to cancel it when this latest drama started. I'm glad she's able to go. Simon comes to sit with me for the day. He reads to me from the papers.

I ask the ward sister to let my many teams know that I'm here, and I text Sinéad myself, to tell her what's happened. She drops in to see if I'm okay. At this stage, every time she sees me we laugh, over some new disaster.

Various doctors come around with different suggestions as to what might be wrong with me.

My haemoglobin is low so they give me a blood transfusion. I'm not too thrilled with the idea, but I don't have the energy to argue. It's October and I'm a vampire. First they took blood from me, now they're putting it back.

While I'm here I'm to be evaluated by the gastrointestinal people – another new team.

★

The lovely recovery nurse from months back, when I had the PEG tube put in, comes down to say hello. Her friend saw my name on the bags of blood in the fridge and told her that I'm back. I wish I had more energy to talk to her.

24 October 2006

Nessa tells me that she has to rub Oz's back with my crutch to comfort him while I'm gone.

There are stains on the walls and ceiling of this room that I don't want to know about. I am pasted to the sheets, I can hardly move.

Sometimes a place can feel like the past, locked in.

A few days of neglect and my jaw is clamping shut. Simon comes to sit with me. He thinks I'm reacting to the extra three prescriptions thrown in on top of everything else I'm taking, that my system went into overload.

I don't have visitors, apart from immediate family, because of being in isolation, but I'm happy enough to spend long hours watching autumn sunlight play on the wall, black and white images of moving leaves, an oriental effect.

A line in a book I read recently comes to mind, about people whose lives are smaller than they have to be. It's something to think about.

They give me two more units of blood. Change the line in my arm when the vein gets infected. I still have IV fluids, antibiotics, steroids.

Outside my window the shouting starts. *No!* and *why did you?* and *just friends!* accompanied by bangers, fireworks, sirens, tears. Hallowe'en music.

25 October 2006

This morning I wake up feeling optimistic for the first time in ages. It was the second lot of blood that did it. I'm hungry. I haven't eaten for five days and maybe that's a good thing. My poor old system has had a break. But as soon as a tray of hospital food is carried in through the door my stomach slams shut. Whatever chance I have of getting strong in here, I'll need outside sources of food to do it.

I ask Simon to bring in salads. I find my Ziploc bag of tongue depressors and start stretching my mouth open again. Pace the length of the room, give my weak ankle as good a workout as it can get. I have been five whole days in one room and I'm only now beginning to pay attention to what's outside it.

My room is half underground. When I look out the window I see the rich loam of autumn: earth and leaves and occasional litter from the hospital bins. I wonder briefly where the incinerator is, but I don't really want to know. Leaves that have already fallen pile up and blow against the bins and the bases of trees. Looking for a way home? Confused, maybe, as to what comes next? Or calling the others to come on down.

There's a woman on the ward who's waiting for a CT scan. She sends delegations of her visitors up to the desk to find out when it will happen. The nurses are patient, but they always say the same thing. They've sent down the request, they've no control over when it happens. I hear this several times a day.

On this ward it's the nurses who take blood. My veins are a challenge. Like submarines, they sense the needle and swim deep to avoid it. But as my arms bruise and puncture, the rest of me is getting stronger. I've been off the more troublesome medications for a week and I've been on intravenous steroids and antibiotics as long as I've been in here. Then there's the fact that my system had a complete break from food until today. I've had no iron – and before that we had switched to a milder form. Whatever the reason, the vomiting and diarrhoea have stopped. I'm beginning to feel normal again.

As I get better the isolation rules relax. I talk to the nurses about their circumstances – children and parents left behind, living in rented houses with people they barely know and don't always like. One of the ward assistants is a student in Russia. She does a year of college, comes here for a year to earn the money she needs to live on when she goes back to do another year of college and so on. The lives people lead, the choices we make. I remember coming back here with three kids, one suitcase each and a wooden crate in the post.

26 October 2006

I am stronger every hour. Simon brings in the corrections for the *Dublin Review* piece. I text Brendan about changes. He offers an editorial meeting in the hospital. I like the idea, it sounds glamorous. But I'm still in isolation. We talk about possible extensions to the article, a part two, then a part three. I ask if he thinks there's a book in it and he says yes.

Exhilarated, I edit the piece and exercise the ankle, shoulder, jaw. I start to walk, pacing the dimensions of this room. There's new jewellery swinging from my veins when I move, a double cannula. I wonder what's happened to the voodoo giraffe. It must have been incinerated by now. But it wouldn't do to get too cocky.

A new doctor appears and leaves a fresh antibiotic. Apparently the neck wound is infected with *Staph. aureus*. I'm lucky that it's not the MRSA strain, which is resistant to antibiotics.

I put off taking the new antibiotic because I've just swallowed a handful, literally, of other tablets – painkillers and steroids. Next thing the doctor comes flying back in.

'Are you allergic to penicillin?'

'Yes.'

'What happens when you take it?'

'The mucous membranes in my face swell.'

The new antibiotic is whipped away.

The pathology results from the endoscopy suggest that my inflamed and ulcerated bowel is caused not by some chronic bowel disease but by medication, most likely the non-steroidal anti-inflammatory drugs (NSAIDS). No one is surprised. It's very good news.

The staph infection at my neck is a more worrying development. They order a bone scan to determine whether the infection has spread to the bone inside my mouth.

I can't go home before I have the scan, like the woman with the demanding relatives. They want to see what's happening with the graft in my mouth. There's no guarantee that I'll get the scan before the weekend.

Now the other woman's impatience makes sense to me.

The skin of my face is much more puckered and worn than it was. I can't purse or smack my lips any more, or whistle.

Oh well, put on a brave face and go walking.

Yes, actually, this face *is* brave, it's been through a lot. Last night I looked at it in the mirror above the sink and thought, *this is my face now*.

Outside it's another washed blue day. The leaves confer, susurrate, blow. There is gold in the light, and the steel of winter. We are having a spectacular autumn. There is loam at my window, washed by yesterday's rain. When I close my eyes at night I think: sediment. I'm down here with the roots.

And I can read again. I'm tucked up in bed with Forster, listening to him talk about aspects of the novel. I've heard all this before, but I'm never bored by it. In here it's more vital than ever. He reminds me of who I am.

27 October 2006

I go down for the scan, to a room where the clock has stopped at 9.10. A bored woman with a heavy voice says that I can see the scan but changes her mind when I spot what's going on. There are bright areas in the image that show the grafted bone reacting. It looks as if there is infection there.

Outside an elderly man in a wheelchair is, quite literally, kicking up a fuss. He spins his chair, one leg raised. He has an aquiline, angry face. A radiographer tries to calm him down, dodging the raised leg.

'My bum is sore in this chair.' His eyes bulge. 'I've been sitting here too long!'

I take my new worry past them all, the angry man and the radiographer and the quiet grey-haired woman who was there when I first went in.

The max-fax team come to see me, a cavalry, striding down the corridors. They are dashing in their surgical blues. I imagine that other patients watch their progress with jealous dread. Who could want such disfigurements as mine? But who could fail to want those smiles, those hands, marshalled in their defence?

It turns out that the microbiologists think the graft should come out of my mouth because the bone is infected. My team want to know what I think.

'No!' I say.

We all look at each other. I think, not about my face, oddly enough, but about my leg. If the bone graft is removed, all of that will have been for nothing.

'Is this life-threatening? I mean, right now?'

'No.'

All the gold and the steel I've been soaking up through the window in this week underground rises in me like sap. The way I see it is that one of three things can happen. Things can stay the same, which is not ideal but it's manageable. They can get better, which would be great. Or they can get worse, in which case we can discuss it further.

'They can't have it,' I say. 'I don't have another leg to give them.'

I'm very clear about who 'us' and 'them' are in this equation.

Professor Stassen smiles. 'We'll keep an eye on it,' he says. 'And see how we go.'

I smile too. 'Look,' I say, pointing to the lopsided lift of my mouth.

There's joy in his face when he sees it.

'That's brilliant!' he says. 'That never happens! Any surgeon will tell you – it's not possible. I cut those nerves.'

We beam at each other, gleeful. We've got away with something.

Anything is possible.

It's Hallowe'en weekend and they let me out. The traffic on the M50 is brutal and I love every diesel-laden inch of it. All over the city there are fireworks going off. Anywhere you care to look, there are explosions of coloured light in a brooding sky.

It's cold. Throughout the weekend we get the winds the

emergency services hoped to avoid. Pre-pubescent girls in bright mini-skirts masquerade as fairies on the streets, their glittering faces set against winter, against the deeper dark that comes when the hour turns back, against the very idea of fire.

The neighbourhood kids come round to scare us with their costumes and their masks and I scare them right back with my face.

It's great to be home.

Postscript

Here's a thing I've learned: time can work for you as well as against you.

At first I thought I would never get used to the sensation of the skin on my neck being too tight for me. But I did. And then it eased.

Today, the pain in my face comes and goes. It's tiring, but it's more or less manageable. The infection in the bone graft has settled. I still feel that hand at my chin but it's not always unfriendly, and at least I'm here to feel it. My sense of taste came back, and although I'm a slow and messy eater, I enjoy food again. My digestive system is back to normal. A hundred times in the day or night my mouth feels like the inside of a brick and then a hasty glass of water spills down my chin by mistake, but, hey, worse things can happen.

Sensation has returned to parts of my face in unpredictable ways. When I drink something, I feel hot or cold liquid spill along my cheek and fill up the external shell of my ear. There's a spot at my right temple that exudes sweat when I eat, or even when I think about food. I've always been a fiend for chocolate, but now I literally break into a sweat at the thought of it. And if I get pins and needles while the facial nerves try to reconnect, as far as I'm concerned they can keep trying. They might get it right one day.

I wake in the mornings with a sulky, stumpy leg that has to be coaxed to the stairs and wheedled the whole way down – but I can walk, and it doesn't usually hurt. Thanks to my physiotherapist, I can touch it without flinching. It's getting stronger. I can drive.

The car is a great place for doing facial exercises, I've discovered. You can scowl and snarl at passing motorists all you like, squint, try to touch your ear with your tethered tongue – no one pays any attention. Belting out songs to the radio is part of this unofficial exercise programme – those high notes are great for stretching out the mouth. I can't whistle yet but I can *pssht!* for the cat and even purse my lips, so we live in hope.

My second navel is getting smaller. I suspect I'll miss it if it goes altogether. I have developed a fondness for my eccentricities: one damaged wing, an unstable leg, a tendency to drool when I eat and honk when I laugh, the ear that sings a constant, high-pitched song to me but can't hear what other people say.

When I began to go out and about on my own, I felt a mixture of nervousness and defiance. Both turned out to be unnecessary. Sometimes people look at me twice – of course they do. I would myself. But the looks I get don't feel hostile, more like someone checking – *did I really see that?* For the most part, people are far too busy with their own concerns to notice. Most people don't recognize the new me the first time they see me, but I'm used to this now. I tell them who I am in the same breath as I say hello. It doesn't bother me at all – I know that their hesitation is not just because of my face. My hair is longer than it used to be. I am thinner than I've been for years. Don't we all go around in disguise, of one form or another, all the time? Well, this is mine.

Soon after I came home from my stint as a vampire in hospital at Hallowe'en, my daughters took me out to buy some new clothes.

They shook their heads at my choices, steered me towards

newer, brighter items in smaller sizes than I was used to. In the end Nessa got exasperated.

'You act as though clothes are just something to put on!' she said. 'As if you want to cover up.'

I could see that she was right. I didn't have to cover up – in fact, there's not much point in trying. So I took the bundle of hangers from Emma's outstretched hands and went in to a dressing room. I hung up the clothes, took off my own badly fitting ones and stood in front of a full-length mirror for the first time in months. I barely recognized myself. I was thin. In profile, I had no bum. My skin was loose – they don't warn you about that in diet books.

My daughters were waiting. So I tried on the clothes they had selected for me, discovered that I liked them, and put them on the credit card before I could change my mind. I went home a new woman, complete with a decent pair of jeans, bright T-shirts, a strongly patterned skirt and close-fitting, colourful jumpers. It wasn't long before I was able to put on boots, so that now when I go out, no one would guess that there's anything wrong with my leg.

Nine months after the operation, a friend helped me to set up an appointment to go in to the pathology laboratory to see the slides that were made from my tumour.

I woke up early that morning, when the light was on a blue-grey cusp, the trees still black. Wood pigeons warbled and murmured as if they had never heard of night, or magpies. The lights of the city pulsed, orange, across the bay. Two ships were at anchor, intense fields of blazing white light on the smooth, stretched canvas of the sea.

I was nervous. My scars were acting up. But the journey across town to St James's was as familiar and easy to me by then as any I have ever made.

The pathologist was warm and patient as she showed me how to use the microscope. When she opened the folder with my name on it and I saw the slides, I was taken aback because they were stained the colour of damsons, matching the jumper and scarf I was wearing. Strong colours, my armour for the day.

Through the microscope, a patterned world emerged. It was weirdly beautiful, intricate and contoured – like a topographical map, in fetching shades of pink and purple. I saw nuclei and bubbly cell walls; tiny dark tadpole-shaped cells and ladder-like ones; a blurring where the tumour was.

She showed me how close the tumour got to the bone: right up to the edge. Looking at the slides, I felt curiosity and awe. I could see signs of inflammation where the bone reacted to the fact that the tumour was there. It had changed. It was getting ready to defend itself. Later, this would seem like the most important thing I saw. This reaction. It proved something to me.

When I left the lab I went to the coffee shop and wrote about what I'd seen. The hospital felt like a friendly place, unthreatening. My car waited in the underground car park, I had the keys in my pocket. On the corridors I met people I knew, exchanged greetings, told anyone who might be interested what had just happened. I went up to my old ward, where they teased me about my enthusiasm for my slides.

At home again, my sense of excitement grew as I let myself feel the full impact of what I had seen. Not only the slides themselves, but what they meant. I was on the right side of that microscope, looking at what was left of my tumour. And I was able to stand up and walk away, to leave it behind.

Dublin, May 2007

Acknowledgements

Parts of this book were first published as 'The Crab' in *The Dublin Review*, Issue 25, Winter 2006.

With a few exceptions, I haven't named the individual friends, relatives and medical personnel who appear in these pages. That doesn't lessen my sense of indebtedness to each and every one of them. You know who you are.

Among the skilled doctors, nurses and medical practitioners who took me in and looked after me, special thanks are due to Professor Leo Stassen, Professor Donal Hollywood, Dr Kate O'Leary. Thanks also to Dr Shanker Mohan, Dr Mohammad Issrar, Dr Motaz Kabadaya, Dr Harsha Jaya-sundara, Dr Khosa Allah Dad, Dr Jennifer Hogan, Dr Seamus Mc Menamin, Emma MacDonald, Orla Brady, Dr Greg Paton, Yvonne Lyden, Noreen O'Regan, Jo Johnson; to Dr Joe Fitzgerald, Dr Pat Scanlon, Mr Eamonn Beausang, Dr Denise McCarthy and Dr Osama Omer; to Joanne Barry, Iris Curtin, Adrian White, Dudu Mkwanzai, Helen McElhin-ney, Nelson, Dorcas, Alison, Maura, Siya, Emma, Catriona, Gavin, Ciara, Binelda, Girlie, Theja, Sincy, Jisha, Ann Marie, Sarah, Shannon, Aileen, Celia, Sujesh, Louise, Shareen, Gerry, Catherine, Mary, Magda and all the rest of you who nursed me through the major operation and afterwards; to the nurses of St Luke's Hospital (especially Marie, Olivia, Niamh, Mary Ellen, Helen, Conor, Fiona Gilbert), who kept an eye on my progress while ostensibly concentrating on changing my dressing over a period of weeks during and after radiotherapy; and to all the radiation therapists (Síle, Patricia,

Rachel, Ann Marie, Susan); to Sinéad Connors, the head-and-neck nurse at St James's Hospital, who was my rock and point of reference when I was uncertain where to turn; and to Niamh Moylan of the physiotherapy department at St Luke's, who steadied me more than once. Dr Kate Lochrin was a mainstay of long-distance information and support.

Thanks also to Dr David Borton, Professor J. Reynolds, Dr Nasir Mahmud, the plastic surgeons, the staff of ICU and A & E and the orthopaedic, gastrointestinal and microbiology teams who, between them, mopped me up and set me on my feet again at different times; to Bernie O'Sullivan, Marie O'Brien, Therese Stymes, Eimer Mithen, Wenda Thomas, Dr Mary Toner, Dr Davis Coakley; to the theatre nurses, especially Mary and Mary Paula; to Brigitte Walley for everything she does; and to the people who donated the blood I needed, both during surgery and afterwards, when I was at my lowest ebb.

Thanks to the Lios Aoibhinn Cancer Support Centre, especially Anne Hayes, Cecilia Keenan, Wendy Marlatt; to the staff of the Dalkey Pharmacy: Blaithin, Tom, Ciara, Louise; to the staff of the Beechlawn Medical Centre in Monkstown; and to everyone at Peter Mark's in Killiney, especially Barbara.

And thanks to my wonderful, tough, generous and funny friends for their time, their love, their stubborn belief in me: for all the scarves and moisturizers and perfumes and exotic pyjamas; for the books and music and inspiration; for taking me out for walks and drives; for lifts to and from hospital clinics and for entertaining me with outrageous gossip and jokes while we waited around; for pretending not to mind about rush hour on the M50 or the Rock Road; for all the dinners and the ice cream; for the emails and text messages and the presents that sometimes appear on these pages, especially:

Ruthie Ashenhurst, Sheena Barrett, Sheila Barrett, Carmel Benson, Elma Carey, Evelyn Conlon, Susan Connolly, Colette Connor, Paul Cusack, Sandra Delamer, Susan Delaney, Eileen Dennan, Ciara Dwyer, Claire Eliet, Claudette George, Greta and the Italian class, Tony Hickey, Dermot and Maura Hourihane, Sinéad, Fiona and Mona Keane, Alison Kelly, Belinda Martin, Joan McDonnell, Eithne McGuinness, Marita Conlon McKenna, Liz McManus, Madeleine and Betty Moran, Margaret Moriarty, Hilary and Shane Murphy, Éilis Ní Dhuibhne, Brendan Nolan, Clairr O'Connor, Mary O'Donnell, Judith O'Keeffe, Aisling Prior, Denise Reddy, Jim Ryan, Bernie Sanger, Victoria Sargent, Bob Simpson, Clare Tempany, Mairide Woods. Bernie Mc Knight has been my companion-at-arms since the first phone call.

Thanks to the committee of Irish PEN and to the members of the Tall Storeys writing group and the Women Writers' Web, who not only kept a seat for me while I was gone but sent me bulletins from their travels across the country and around the world. The members of the novelshop (Ivy Bannister, Mary Rose Callaghan, Celia de Fréine and Catherine Dunne) urged me to write this book and offered as much critical insight, faith, support and hospitality as anyone could ask for while I wrote it.

Thanks, as ever, to my agent Shirley Stewart and to Patricia Deevy, Michael McLoughlin, Ann Cooke and everyone at Penguin Ireland – not only for help with this book but also for the flowers, the parcels of books, the messages (the deadlines!). The book would not have been written if not for Brendan Barrington, who first published the article ('The Crab') from which it grew and then stuck with it through the sometimes rocky months that followed.

I can't say enough about my oldest friends, from school and thereabouts, who stepped forward immediately to form a protective ring around us and did all of the above and a lot more to help not only me but all of us: Ann Marie Hourihane, Felicity Hogan, Sheila McGilligan, Zita Reihill. Thank you.

Thanks to my family, especially: David Collins, Sam Collins, Clair and Sean Callan, Trudi Mills, Joe Mills; Adam, Chara, Zoe and Kevi Chishios; Anne Browne, Mary Fitzgerald, Antonia Hart, Hilary and Shane Murphy, Prue Rudd, Susan Towers, Frank and Pam Robinson.

Most of all, thanks, love and apologies if I've said too much or too little, to my sister Jackie; to my daughters Zita, Emma and Vanessa Robinson; to Eoin O'Byrne, Peter Stringer, Mark Nelson; to my husband Simon; and to Ryan, who dreamed up the shark.